PRAISE FOR
THE LAST SECRETS OF ANNE FRANK

"Part biography and part whodunit, this book is, above all, a bereaved son's cri de coeur, simultaneously mourning and celebrating the mother he lost even before she died."

—*The Wall Street Journal*

"An important contribution to the literature on Anne Frank."

—*Kirkus Reviews*

"[A] superbly well-written, intimate, engrossing, and heartrending reckoning with the endless damage done by genocide."

—*Booklist* (starred review)

"The unspeakable tragedy of Anne Frank will never lose its haunting power over successive generations. This gripping account adds a missing human dimension to the story of the young girl hidden in an attic during the Nazi occupation of Holland—and those who helped and those who betrayed her. I read it in one gulp—as will you."

—Kati Marton, author of *The Chancellor*

"This book, as much a work of painful family therapy as painstaking historical analysis, throws unexpected light on the people who protected Anne Frank and perhaps on the one who betrayed her. A riveting read."

—Peter Hayes, author of *Why?: Explaining the Holocaust*

"It took a network of courageous helpers to allow Anne Frank and her family to hide for as long as they did from the Nazis. It only took one person to betray them. This is a book that not only offers tantalizing new clues about their betrayer; it also sheds new light on the least known helper in a saga that encapsulates the tragedy of the Holocaust."

—Andrew Nagorski, author of *Saving Freud: The Rescuers Who Brought Him to Freedom*

"This powerful story brings to life Bep's heroism and illuminates generations of a Dutch family, its secrets, and the trauma the Nazi occupation bequeathed to the future."

—Pamela S. Nadell, author of *America's Jewish Women: A History from Colonial Times to Today*

"For long, the story of Bep Voskuijl, one of Anne Frank's courageous helpers, has been mostly kept in the dark. This captivating book tells her moving and tragic story, her wartime assistance in the Secret Annex, and the long shadows of the war on her life and her family's. The book distinguishes clearly between facts and possible interpretations."

—Dr. Bart Wallet, professor of early modern and modern Jewish history at the University of Amsterdam

THE LAST SECRETS *OF* ANNE FRANK

....

THE
UNTOLD STORY
OF HER
SILENT PROTECTOR

....

JOOP VAN WIJK-VOSKUIJL
AND JEROEN DE BRUYN

SIMON & SCHUSTER PAPERBACKS
NEW YORK LONDON TORONTO SYDNEY NEW DELHI

For Bep Voskuijl's (great-)grandchildren
Robin, Elly, Jochem, Hester, Casper, Rebecca, Kay-Lee, and Ryan:
the new generations, the inheritors of this story

THE LAST SECRETS OF
ANNE FRANK

CONTENTS

PROLOGUE

A Letter from Belgium

This project did not begin as an investigation into the darkest corners of the Secret Annex. It began with a letter sent to me in 2009 by a fifteen-year-old boy in Antwerp named Jeroen De Bruyn. Like millions of other children, Jeroen had been touched by Anne Frank's diary, which his mother first read to him when he was just six years old.

By any measure, Jeroen had been a curious and unusually mature child. As soon as he was able to understand that the world had once been at war, he asked his mother for details. She told him the stories that she had heard growing up—about neighbors forced to wear yellow stars and V2 rockets exploding on the streets of Antwerp. The next question was something that children always ask and adults often forget to: *Why?*

His mother had no real answer, so she turned to one of the most famous documents from that time, *Het Achterhuis* (The Annex), known in English as *The Diary of a Young Girl*. Some people will probably think that Jeroen was too young to be exposed to such a difficult text, but I believe we tend to underestimate what children are capable of understanding or expressing—as Anne's diary demonstrates so powerfully. Besides, Jeroen's mother didn't read him the whole diary, just excerpts, carefully avoiding the most upsetting passages.

Jeroen was fascinated. He spent hours staring at the black-and-white pictures of the swinging bookcase and the tiny, cramped confines of the Secret Annex. He could not wrap his little mind around why whole families, even young children, needed to hide like mice to avoid being killed. He started asking his mother more questions about the war, and in time she brought him other children's books on the subject. When Jeroen got a little older, he began checking out books on the Holocaust from the library himself. His parents thought his budding interest was a bit strange, yet they were open-minded liberal Europeans, more inclined to explain the harsh reality of the world than to hide it from view.

In time, the children's books and animated movies were replaced with thick histories and grainy documentaries. The stories and pictures became more explicit, more terrible. By age twelve, Jeroen had seen every available film about the Holocaust—Claude Lanzmann's nine-hour documentary *Shoah* made the greatest impression on him—and he had read every book he could find about Anne Frank. The more Jeroen learned, the less he understood. How could it have happened on the same placid, tree-lined streets that he walked down every day? How was it that his grandmother, the same woman who sent him silly text messages, could have seen it all with her own eyes? Neighbors rounded up. Swastikas on the streets. The city in flames.

Jeroen's grandmother was also named Anne. She was born the same year as Anne Frank—1929—and during World War II lived for a time with her grandparents only half a mile from the Frank family apartment in Amsterdam South. In the early days of the Occupation, she fell in love with a Jewish boy named Louis. Though he managed to slip out of the Nazis' grasp by hiding in the Dutch countryside, most of his family was murdered at the Sobibor death camp in eastern Poland, where a staggering thirty-four thousand Dutch Jews were killed in approximately five months between March and July 1943. Was it that grandmother, Anne—the same age, same city, same name—who kindled Jeroen's obsession with Anne Frank? Because that was what it turned into: an obsession, a need to know everything that had happened inside the Secret Annex.

Jeroen printed out hundreds of articles, made scrapbooks, spent his school vacations in Amsterdam at the Anne Frank House. He bought a scholarly edition of the diary and pored over the footnotes. His teacher thought his "research," the expanding set of files he created on every aspect of the case, was just the idle hobby of a schoolboy with too much time on his hands; it wouldn't amount to anything. Yet Jeroen was enterprising, even as a teenager, and he could read between the lines. He was interested not only in what was known about the case but also what was unknown or misunderstood. He began to focus on the people who had guarded the Secret Annex, those who had risked their lives to keep Anne and her family safe for 761 days—until, not long before the Liberation, they were all mysteriously betrayed.

From his reading, Jeroen realized that three of the "helpers," as they are known in Dutch, had already been studied extensively: they had given copious interviews, written their own memoirs, or had been the subjects of books and documentaries. Yet there was another helper, who happened to be the youngest, about whom next to nothing was known. The usual explanation for why there was such scant information about this helper was that she was shy and self-effacing by nature and had played only a minor role in the drama of the Secret Annex. But Jeroen could see, based on the evidence, that none of that was true.

In fact, he was beginning to suspect that the youngest helper may have been the most important to Anne. She was her best friend and closest confidante. In the face of great danger, she had acted heroically. Yet for some reason that Jeroen could not figure out, she had spent her entire life after the war hiding from what she had done.

That person was my mother, Bep Voskuijl.

From the moment the Secret Annex was raided by the Gestapo on August 4, 1944, until her death on May 6, 1983, my mother actively avoided the subject of Anne Frank. She declined public recognition for her involvement in the case and refrained from talking about the role she had played with her closest family, even though she privately grieved the loss of her young friend, and would name her only daughter, Anne, in her memory. The reason for her avoidance had nothing to do with Bep's unassuming nature, as had earlier been thought. Rather, Bep had been traumatized by what she had lived through, and she avoided attention because she had secrets she wanted to keep, secrets she intended to take with her to the grave.

Jeroen knew he had a story. The only problem: he was just fourteen. He could get only so far on a biography without the participation of Bep's surviving family, the people who knew her and had access to whatever documents she had left behind. Yet he feared, correctly, that we would dismiss him because of his age and inexperience.

In 2008, Jeroen turned fifteen, the same age that Anne was when she died of typhus in the Bergen-Belsen concentration camp. Shortly after his birthday, he finally decided to approach my family. He couldn't find a way to get in touch with us directly, so he wrote to Miep Gies, then the only surviving helper from the Secret Annex. Her son, Paul, fielded the request and sent it along to two of my siblings. They said they were not interested in talking about our mother and that, anyway, they had little to share about her. In his note, Jeroen had not mentioned his age and background, but after his first attempt failed, he decided to write us a longer letter, straight from the heart.

In five pages, he described his intentions, the documents he had found, and new facts he had put together, and then he asked for permission to interview us. He still could not bring himself to disclose his actual age, so he tacked on a few months and made himself sixteen. Then he mailed the letter to the Anne Frank House in Amsterdam, which forwarded it to me.

· · · · · · · · · ·

"I am a 16-year-old boy from Antwerp," Jeroen's letter began. "For a long time, I've been very interested in the story of Anne Frank." Jeroen told of his fascination with the Secret Annex, how by degrees his focus had shifted from Anne to the helpers and then to my mother. He was amazed that "so little was known" about her. He said that he had "assembled a file" in which he was trying to "put the pieces of the puzzle together." Each new fact he uncovered on a dusty reel-to-reel tape or in a newspaper archive made him feel "euphoric." He felt that Anne had had a kind of double in my mother, a young guardian on the other side of the bookcase who had been a close friend, who had also fallen in love during the war, who had had her own fights with parents and siblings, who had spent the Occupation living in fear of being found out. Bep was still just a sketchy outline, but "bit by bit," he said, "I am getting to know her better."

I was skeptical of Jeroen's youth, but I was immediately struck by his sincere desire to understand my mother. In a sense, I had spent my whole life wanting the same thing. Before I received that letter, no one had ever asked me about her role in the Anne Frank story. The outside world wasn't aware of her past, and within the family we had an unspoken rule never to discuss what happened during the war.

Yet over the years my mother told me things that she kept from everyone else, even my father and my siblings. For a time, I was to my mother a bit like what she had been to Anne: a confidant and protector. But the twists of life had complicated our relationship; as close as I got to her, I never understood why, exactly, her experience tortured and haunted her the way it did.

I wrote Jeroen back and said that we should meet and that I would be happy to visit him at home in Antwerp to learn what he had discovered and discuss his proposed project. I traveled with my wife, Ingrid, from our home in the eastern Netherlands. Jeroen struck me as earnest, sweet, and intensely focused. He had covered his parents' kitchen table with books, all heavily annotated with yellow Post-it notes, and he created a detailed outline for our conversation. He had just found a rare recording of an interview Bep had given on a visit to Canada in the late 1970s. He played the tape for me, and it was the first time I had heard my mother's voice in more than three decades.

I couldn't escape the feeling that that meeting with Jeroen was almost preordained. I had carried around my mother's secrets for years, and only now did I realize that I was waiting for an opportunity to share them, to make sense of them, or—as Jeroen put it—to put the pieces of the puzzle together. We did not know that day that the process would take us more than a decade. I'm still not sure why I trusted that teenager with my family's secrets or why I told him things that had been buried long before. Perhaps there was something about his youth that disarmed me.

In any case, I told him that I would help him however I could. I didn't expect my other family members to follow suit, but when I contacted each of them, none was opposed to my participation. Of course they could not imagine then some of the uncomfortable conclusions the evidence would point us toward, the trail of betrayal we would uncover. Contrary to the illusions we had grown up with, the Voskuijls were not all that different from other families in wartime Amsterdam, in which resisters and collaborators often lived under the same roof.

In the beginning, I did not intend to be Jeroen's coauthor but simply his guide: to share what I knew and open whatever doors I could. Yet it became clear as the story changed, expanded, and cut closer to the bone that Jeroen could not write it alone. We eventually decided, despite the differences in our ages and backgrounds, to become partners in the project. For the sake of clarity, and to better convey my firsthand experience of growing up in the shadow of the Secret Annex, we would write the book in my voice. But it is just as much Jeroen's story as mine. Having watched him grow up from a precocious teenager into an accomplished journalist, I look back on our work together feeling a bit like a proud father. And this gets to the heart of what our book is ultimately about: though we talk about war and the Holocaust, about collaboration and betrayal, there is no other way of describing this book than as a family story. And as my mother knew well, there are two kinds of family bonds: one forged by birth, the other by circumstance.

Joop van Wijk-Voskuijl
Heemstede, the Netherlands
March 2023

PART I

ANNE

Never have they uttered a single word about the burden we must be, never have they complained that we're too much trouble.

—*Anne Frank about her helpers, January 28, 1944*

CHAPTER 1

The Bookcase Swings Open

In a typical year, around 1 million people walk along the tidy banks of Amsterdam's Prinsengracht Canal and make their way to the nondescript warehouse at number 263. Once inside, they climb a steep staircase, step into a narrow office corridor, and come face-to-face with a well-worn wooden bookcase that is also a portal into a secret world.

Swinging open on hinges, the bookcase reveals a doorway. The visitors step through into a tight maze of rooms, where they try to imagine what it was like to be Anne Frank: the unrelenting fear, the slivers of daylight, the chestnut tree outside the window, the boy upstairs, the stifled laughter, the boredom, the arguments, the dogged hope. And the decision to write it all down, to record that voice, at once ingenuous and mature and often very funny. A voice that still speaks to us today.

Most years, I make my own pilgrimage to the Anne Frank House. I become one of those million visitors to the Secret Annex. When I go, I think about Anne, of course, and her family and the four other Jews who hid there, as well as the twenty-eight thousand Jews who were in hiding at the same time elsewhere in the Netherlands. But I also think about Johan Voskuijl, my maternal grandfather, the man who built the revolving bookcase and installed it in the greatest secrecy in the summer of 1942. What, I wonder, made that perfectly ordinary Dutchman do something so extraordinarily dangerous? What made him risk his life to hide Jews when so many of his countrymen were reporting them to the Gestapo?

The numbers never get any easier to look at. Seventy-five percent of Dutch Jews were murdered in the Holocaust, giving the Netherlands the highest death rate among all Western European countries occupied by the Nazis. Only five thousand of the 107,000 Dutch Jews sent to the camps made it back alive. One of these "lucky" few was Anne's father, Otto Frank. He stood six feet tall—I remember him towering over me when I was a boy—but weighed less than 115 pounds when he left Auschwitz.

By the time he made it back to Amsterdam, Otto knew that his wife was already dead. "All my hope is the children," he wrote in 1945 to his mother, who lived in Switzerland. "I cling to the conviction that they are alive and that we will be together again." While he waited for news about Anne and his older daughter, Margot, he visited my grandfather's bedside. Johan was then sick with stomach cancer; he had just months to live.

My thoughts often return to that moment, the meeting of two fathers on the edge of an abyss. I think about the helplessness they must have felt and wonder what comfort, if any, they could have derived from each other. Did they shake hands? Did they embrace? What was said? Did they talk about who could have betrayed them? Did Otto tell Johan that he was worried about Bep and that he intended to do what he ended up doing: watching over my mother after Johan was gone, becoming a kind of surrogate father?

When I enter the Annex, such questions come flooding back. I have spent my whole life asking these questions only of myself, and now, at the age of seventy-three, I want the answers, I want to get as close to the truth as I can, even if it becomes . . . uncomfortable. Now I am finally ready to understand Anne Frank's story alongside my family's, ready to see the Secret Annex from both sides of the bookcase. My goal is to solve a mystery that has united us, a mystery that haunted my mother's life and tore a hole in our family that to this day has never been repaired.

A GHOST IN THE CANDY STORE

My mother had been a surprise—or, you might say, an accident.

When my grandmother Christina Sodenkamp discovered that she was pregnant in the winter of 1918, she felt too young, at nineteen, to have a child. She had been dating her boyfriend, twenty-six-year-old Johan Voskuijl, for only a few months. They had never broached the subject of marriage. They were not in love, and they had a combative relationship that would curdle with time. Yet what could be done about it? In those years, in polite society, you had no choice. So Johan and Christina became husband and wife, exchanging vows in their native city of Amsterdam in February 1919. My mother, Elisabeth Voskuijl, was born a few months later, on July 5.

A moonfaced, pudgy baby with cute crinkled lips, she was sometimes called "Bep" for short and sometimes "Elli." After a while, the name "Bep" won out, and it stuck for the rest of my mother's life. So when Anne, imagining a future published edition of her diary, gave my mother the pseudonym "Elli," it was almost as though she activated an alter ego that had been lying dormant from the beginning of Bep's life.

My mother's first few years were relatively idyllic, compared to what would follow. Though her father, Johan, had no formal education, he was an autodidact, good with numbers, and extraordinarily hardworking. He taught himself accounting through textbooks and correspondence courses. And around 1920, he landed a steady job as a bookkeeper that allowed him to raise his growing family in relative comfort. A second daughter, Annie, arrived in 1920, followed by three more girls: Willy in 1922, Nelly in 1923, and Corrie in 1924.

Despite all those mouths to feed, by 1926, when Bep was seven, the family was financially secure enough to leave their dreary working-class neighborhood and move into a spacious second-floor apartment in a corner house on Fraunhoferstraat in Watergraafsmeer, a leafy residential neighborhood in the east of Amsterdam.

For a few years, my mother had a storybook Dutch childhood: Nice clothes to wear to school. Wholesome food on the table. Church on Sunday. Summer vacations at the beach with friends. Yet life at the Voskuijls' was never exactly warm and cozy. Johan was a strict father. A product of the Dutch Reformed Church, he demanded that his children be silent during mealtimes, as food was seen as a gift from God. His acts of kindness came not in words but in deeds. A gifted woodworker, crafty and patient, he loved building intricate wooden airplanes and other toys for his children's birthdays. "What Papa's eyes saw," my aunt Willy used to say, "his hands could build."

My mother did well in school, particularly in math and Dutch. She had inherited Johan's photographic memory and his gift with numbers, skills that would come in handy much later. She studied hard, did her weekly chores, and loved to play outside with the children from the neighborhood.

Among those children was a boy named Jacob. He was around Bep's age, and he lived two floors below the Voskuijls in an apartment behind his family's drugstore and candy store, Nabarro, which occupied the ground floor of the building. Years after the war, my mother and I walked past her old home on Fraunhoferstraat. She told me that the window of the store—which was then occupied by a paint shop—had once been filled with trays of candy and she would play hide-and-seek beneath the trays. I still remember the strange, glassy look that flashed in her eyes when she told me that story.

After the Nazis invaded the Netherlands in 1940, the Amsterdam police compiled at their request a list of every Jewish-owned business in the city. They did not forget to include the Nabarro shop. First non-Jews were made to boycott the store. Then it was shut down. In 1942, Jacob, his younger sister, Selma, and both his parents were put on a train to the transit camp of Westerbork, and from there they were deported to Auschwitz, where all four of them were murdered. Jacob's immediate family was not the only branch on the tree to be cut down. His grandfather and two of his aunts were gassed in Sobibor; three of his uncles and another aunt died in Auschwitz. Thirteen of his cousins were also killed in the camps.

I am not sure whether my mother knew exactly what had happened to Jacob's family or whether she was thinking about them when she told me how she'd used to play under the trays of candy. But I mention this story because I want to say up front that if all you know about Dutch Holocaust history is Anne Frank, you might have a false idea of what happened here.

As one of the Dutch survivors of the Holocaust explained years after the war, Anne Frank's diary actually served as a tremendous "public relations exercise" for the Netherlands, giving people the mistaken impression that "the Jews were all in hiding here, and that the entire Dutch population was in the Resistance"—doing essentially what my mother did, risking their necks to save their Jewish neighbors under the noses of the Nazi persecutors, the *real* "bad guys." In fact, the truth, which had been hidden for so long behind our "clean facades and flowerpots," as the Dutch historian Geert Mak put it, is a lot messier.

The Germans orchestrated the Holocaust in the Netherlands, but it was the Dutch who carried it out—and carried it out "like clockwork," in the words of Adolf Eichmann. Historians have revealed the full scope of our collaboration, which involved by one estimate a half-million citizens. By contrast, there were never more than sixty German officers in Amsterdam at any time during the Occupation (although the large number of enlisted troops made the Germans a visible presence). That means that, by and large, it was the Dutch who rounded up the Jews, Dutch bureaucrats who created the maps and lists that pinpointed their locations, Dutch clerks who impounded their possessions and stamped *J*'s on identity papers. On nights when there were raids, the Municipal Transport Office in Amsterdam organized special trams to ferry Jews from the assembly points to the central station, and Dutch Railways ran night trains to Westerbork and the German border. If any civil servant or conductor refused to work those shifts, it was not mentioned in the official records.

Excepting a few heroic cases, Dutch law enforcement officials embraced their new jobs as Jew catchers with alacrity. "Concerning the Jewish Question," the Austrian-born Johann Rauter, the head of the SS in Amsterdam, told his boss, Heinrich Himmler, in 1942, "the Dutch police behave outstandingly and catch hundreds of Jews, day and night." Another SS officer, Willy Lages, a name that will become significant in our story, estimated after the war that "we would not have been able to arrest ten percent of the Jews" without assistance from the Dutch police.

HARD TIMES

And so I return to the question that Jeroen had as a little boy, the question of *why*. There may never be an entirely satisfactory answer, but to begin to cobble together one and to begin to understand what happened to the Franks, Jacob's family, and my own family, we must travel back to the years before the war, to the 1930s, when normal life began to tear at the seams.

Anne Frank was born on June 12, 1929. Four months later, the stock market in New York crashed, plunging the whole world into an economic crisis. By the early 1930s, nearly one in five people in Amsterdam was unemployed. Social services were cut, causing riots, brick throwing, strikes. Bep's family wasn't spared: Johan lost his steady job. With her father out of work, Bep had to quit school when she was just twelve to help care for her siblings. Her only brother, Joop, whom I am named for, had been born in 1928. And the last of her sisters, the twin girls Diny and Gerda, were born in July 1932.

Bep spent most of her teenage years looking after the children, and in her spare time she worked as a chambermaid, a waitress in a cafeteria, and the counter girl at a bakery—anything to contribute a few guilders to the family expenses. I grew up hearing stories about the grim poverty of those years, made all the worse by the memory of how things *used to be*. The family had to leave the charming apartment above the candy store and move to a four-room flat on Lumeijstraat, in a drab working-class quarter in Amsterdam West. The place would've been small for a family of five, but for a family of ten it was absurd.

Every week, Johan took his ride of shame to the Poor Relief, with the twins strapped to each end of his bicycle. There he would receive a box with bread, butter, sugar, and fruit sprinkles (*vruchtenhagel* in Dutch), commonly used as sandwich toppings so you weren't eating bread alone. As the depression wore on, government benefits were slashed. Inflation increased. The Voskuijls tried to tighten their belts further. Now there was no money for new clothes, towels, or dish-cloths. There was never enough soap in the house and only one rough sponge for washing. The twins slept together in a single bed; when it was very cold, they used their father's jacket as a blanket. To save on electricity, candles were used to light the house at night.

Whatever money the family had was spent on food. Christina scrimped and saved in the kitchen and made frugal dishes, such as potato stews flavored with bits of sausage. Johan got half the pot, and the rest was divided equally among his wife and children. Christina's daughters later remembered that even in the darkest days of the depression the meals she cooked were always tasty, even if there was never quite enough to go around. As the 1930s ground on, it seemed that all they had was less and less. And Johan had little to offer in the way of hope. He would just grit his teeth and tell his children, "We need to carry on."

· · · · · · · · · ·

It wasn't just in the Netherlands that people were being pushed to the edge. In early-1930s Germany, Otto Frank witnessed the dissolution of everything that had once meant home. His family, which owned a small bank, was deeply entrenched in the upper class of Frankfurt's Jewish community. Otto, a liberal, secularized Jew, had grown up without a religious education and felt like a German citizen first and foremost. He was proud of his service as an infantry officer in World War I, and he believed that he had earned his place in the country and his family had a future there.

He was not clannish by nature. Rather than raise his two girls in Frankfurt's privileged Jewish enclave, he and his wife, Edith, decided to move to the more rural, more thoroughly German middle-class neighborhood of Marbachweg, where very few Jews lived. They were happy there at first. Yet the family's fortunes declined precipitously in the early 1930s. After the stock market crash, the Frank family bank lost 90 percent of its revenues. Economic conditions worsened throughout Germany—there were tax hikes, unemployment, cuts in the social safety net. All of it made people angry, and Adolf Hitler exploited their anger. The National Socialists' share of the German vote grew from just 3 percent the year before the stock market crash to 37 percent by the summer of 1932.

Otto was unfailingly polite and didn't like to complain even when life in Germany got difficult. He would be the last one to attribute a dirty look or an unkind word to anti-Semitism. He maintained that in the early 1930s, his family had not been discriminated against by their neighbors in Marbachweg. Yet the Franks' landlord was a member of the Nazi Party, and their own friends in the neighborhood later recalled that the family had felt threatened there and that the girls had been spooked by storm troopers marching by, singing Nazi anthems. They fled the neighborhood in the early 1930s and eventually moved in with Otto's mother in the center of Frankfurt. But their problems did not stop.

In January 1933, Hitler became chancellor of Germany. Almost immediately, there were indications of what was to come. That spring, the first concentration camp opened in Dachau. The government instituted a nationwide boycott of Jewish businesses. Students in Berlin burned thousands of books by Jewish authors. Otto could see that in small ways, Hitler's anti-Jewish policies were already affecting his family. His older daughter, Margot, was segregated from the Aryan students in her school and told she had to sit in the corner of the classroom with her Jewish classmates. His younger girl, Anne, was about to start kindergarten. What kind of childhood could she expect in Nazi Germany?

It was time, Otto finally decided, to start over. A new life in a new city. The family had good reasons for choosing Amsterdam. Otto had spent part of the 1920s there working for his family's bank. His Dutch was serviceable, and he still had business contacts there. Was it safe? Well, the Netherlands did share a border with Germany, but to Europeans in that period the country seemed as politically neutral and above the fray as Switzerland. The Dutch had not fought in World War I and had managed to stay on the sidelines during every continental conflict in recent memory. On top of all that, Jews had always been a visible and accepted presence in Amsterdam, where they lived in relative peace.

Otto had other choices, in theory. He had family and connections in France, Great Britain, Switzerland, and the United States, but he would need a residency permit to immigrate to any of those countries. And for that, he would need a way of making money. In Amsterdam, he thought he had found one. Otto's brother-in-law, Erich Elias, had a relationship with a factory in Frankfurt that produced pectin, a food additive used to thicken jellies and jams, which it sold to consumers under the brand name Opekta. Elias had recently opened an Opekta branch in Switzerland, and he thought that Otto might be able to replicate his success in the Low Countries. That would require Otto to teach Dutch housewives, who had been making their own jam for generations, a new and improved way of doing things. Sure, it was a tough business, but it would be his. And the important thing was that it would get his family out of Germany.

LUNCH ON THE MERRY

By her sixteenth birthday, my mother already looked less like a little girl and more like the modest, sturdy young woman pictured in the exhibits at the Anne Frank House. She had a shy little smile, an owlish face, and lovely blue-green eyes that were partly obscured by her spectacles. She wore ribbons in her curled hair and rouged her cheeks. She may not have been a great beauty, but she had a good mind—and enough sense to know that it was being wasted changing diapers on Lumeijstraat. As she sat in the dark, windowless hallway, helping her young sisters study Dutch verb conjugations by candlelight, she couldn't help but feel that she could do so much more with her life.

She decided to follow her father's example and teach herself a trade. In 1937, she enrolled in the Instituut Schoevers, an evening school for girls and women who wanted to learn secretarial work. By the time she was eighteen, she had earned certificates in shorthand, bookkeeping, and German. There was no twist of fate that led to her job at Opekta; the vacancy was advertised in the newspaper. Sometime in the spring of 1937, she was called into Opekta's office on Singel Canal, where the company was located before it set up shop on Prinsengracht, for an interview. Otto liked her immediately and hired her as a shorthand typist, although her responsibilities would soon expand greatly.

Bep was happy just to have found a job, but Opekta quickly turned into something more. The office was made up of a tight-knit group of people bound together as much by affection as by their professional duties, a group she would soon call the Opekta Circle. She took her lunch every day with her coworker Miep Gies, a small

Austrian-born woman in her late twenties who managed the payroll and fielded product questions from customers. Miep and Bep talked about everything: the cute warehouse boy downstairs, Henk; Bep's exhausting sisters; her slim romantic prospects; and, of course, their boss.

Bep had never met anyone with Otto's mix of courtliness and kindness. His thick German accent and imperfect attempts at speaking Dutch only added to his charm. When Otto invited Bep to his family's apartment for lunch a few months after she started her job, she didn't quite know what to think. Miep, a regular lunch guest of the Franks, told her not to worry, that it wasn't some kind of test—it was just Mr. Frank's way of welcoming her into the fold.

The Frank family lived in a new housing development, the Merwedeplein, in the Rivers District of Amsterdam, where many families fleeing Germany had recently settled. About a third of the neighborhood's population was Jewish. The brown-brick apartments, with small balconies and white wooden shutters, were arrayed along a grassy triangular plaza where children played in nice weather.

Life on "the Merry," as Anne called it, was comfortable. Most of the apartments had been built in the past decade, and everything seemed new and clean, making it an ideal spot for uprooted people, a blank slate. Bep was dazzled by the Franks' apartment: the expensive furniture they had brought from Germany, the ancient grandfather clock, Otto's library with books in several languages. Yet none of it felt stuffy or overly grand, and there were dolls, crayons, and children's toys everywhere. Life at the Franks' seemed to revolve around the children: Margot, age twelve, and Anne, nine.

Otto's two girls couldn't have been more different. Margot had been a preternaturally quiet baby who had slept through the night almost from birth. Infant Anne, on the other hand, had been a handful—colicky, she often needed Otto to rub her belly for hours before she would fall back asleep. Margot had grown into a bookish and introspective girl, a bit of a perfectionist who weighed her words carefully and as a consequence didn't say much.

Anne, once she got over her initial shyness, never seemed to stop speaking. The nine-year-old was a jumble of contradictions: her eyes and smile expressed such vitality, yet she was actually a rather sickly child. Her mother called her *Zärtlein* (fragile one). She was too frail for gym class, and she suffered a string of ailments—from whooping cough to chicken pox to a touch of heart trouble—that left her bedridden for weeks at a time. Cautious around strangers, she also could be direct and feisty. When she was just four years old, she hopped onto a packed tram car with her grandmother and was offended that no one stood up. So she barked at the other passengers, "Won't someone offer a seat to this old lady?"

Anne had green eyes, long eyelashes, and an adorable bucktoothed grin. She held her dark hair back with a barrette. Her idiosyncratic (some would say difficult) nature explained why her parents decided to send her to a Montessori school in Amsterdam, where each pupil was allowed to express his or her individual personality and the curriculum was tailored to their interests.

Bep was amazed that an institution even existed where math could be taught as a game. Yet so much about life in the Frank family had the aspect of a game, of fun. The girls called their father "Pim" for some reason, and he wrote them funny poems for their birthdays and told them sweet made-up stories about invisible fairies—the Good Paula and the Bad Paula—whose hiding place you could discover if you stayed absolutely quiet and still.

Bep loved the atmosphere and freedom in the Frank family. She had been taught by Johan to be modest—the children in his house were "to be seen, not heard"—but at the Merwedeplein, she learned to join in the conversation. Plus, everything there was so *nice*. Mrs. Frank brought out tasty rolls with cream cheese and sprinkles. There was lemonade and milk that came out of a bottle instead of the rickety cans that Bep was used to at home. Each dish on the table seemed to her more luxurious than the next, and they were all served on a lazy Susan, so you could spin the platter and take whatever you wished.

Bep had rarely seen food of such quality. Nor had she encountered parents who actually *listened* to their daughters almost as if they were interested in what they had to say. "It was obvious," my mother admitted to me, "that we came from different worlds."

Anne always loved it when Bep visited. Maybe it was because Bep had grown up caring for so many younger sisters, but she knew just the right questions to ask to get the gears in Anne's mind going. Sometimes Anne would drop by Opekta's office and fool around on Bep's typewriter. One day, Anne said, she would make her living on one of those machines. She dreamed of becoming a journalist, but she said with great seriousness that she would not let her career ambitions stand in the way of having a family. She hoped she would marry "the man of my dreams" and have lots of children. I could imagine my mother's smile hearing such a statement from that precocious child, the openhearted expression on Bep's face that said *tell me more*.

A decade separated Anne and Bep in age, but their bond was instant, and soon it would become essential to each other's survival.

CHAPTER 2

Yellow Stars

In the early morning of May 10, 1940, Germany invaded France, Belgium, Luxembourg, and the Netherlands. After months of false alarms and empty threats, the Dutch were caught off guard. My mother said the Nazis had appeared like "a bolt out of the blue." They claimed that they had only good intentions, that they had come to protect us—their Aryan cousins and "close relatives." But really what they were doing by invading the Netherlands was blasting their way around France's Maginot Line and preventing the Allies from building a North Sea beachhead from which they could eventually attack the Reich. There was no way Hitler could win the Battle of Europe, he calculated, without taking the Low Countries.

On the day of the invasion, Queen Wilhelmina of the Netherlands—whom Anne Frank idolized and whose picture she would soon paste above her bed in the Secret Annex—went on the radio to urge calm and order. But who could be calm and orderly with the constant blaring of air raid sirens, with swarms of Stuka dive bombers and Heinkels raining hell from above? There were explosions at Schiphol Airport, reports of German paratroopers disguised as Dutch Army officers or common farmers landing in tulip fields and village squares. The Nazis seemed to be everywhere, all at once. Tanks and artillery moved swiftly across the border in a race to the sea. Soon the Luftwaffe would turn the old town of Rotterdam into a fiery ruin.

After just five days of Blitzkrieg, it was all over. Despite a few

valiant scenes of resistance, the Germans had broken the Dutch
Army's back by applying overwhelming force at high speed. The
surrender meant occupation. The Dutch people tried to deny the
victor some of the spoils. They set fire to the oil stockpiles around
the port of Amsterdam, creating a huge column of black smoke
that reached high into the sky. And they made sure to hide their
treasure: the best Rembrandts in the Rijksmuseum were evacuated,
the most precious stones in Amsterdam's diamond district were se-
creted away. Yet the 140,000 Jewish residents of the Netherlands
were left to their fate.

In announcing the surrender, the commander in chief of the
Dutch armed forces told his countrymen that he had no choice, that
accepting defeat would not merely "prevent further bloodshed" but
stave off "annihilation."

Yet what of the annihilation that such a decision would *facilitate*?

"All I can say," he added, "is, trust in the future."

The queen, at least, had the decency to tell her subjects to "think
of our Jewish compatriots" before fleeing the Netherlands on May 13
on a British destroyer. Thousands of Jews, hearing that there were
ships bound for England at the Port of IJmuiden, tried to follow the
queen's lead and escape. But the ships were all full, and the port had
been secured against rioters. There was nowhere else to go but home.

All around Amsterdam, in the balmy spring air, smoke billowed
out of chimneys as people hurriedly tossed their anti-fascist magazines and books by Jewish authors into the fireplace. Most Dutch
Jews had thought that this day would never come. Most of them
had actually believed that Hitler would respect Dutch neutrality,
and they had laughed off the local offshoot of the Nazi Party, the
NSB, which for all its loudmouthed provocations had received only
4 percent of the national vote in the most recent election. Right
up until the invasion, most Dutch Jews regarded those who chose
to flee the country as alarmist and, worse, unpatriotic. One Dutch

survivor of the Holocaust recalled that in 1938, when a Jewish lawyer in Amsterdam named Mr. Gans decided to immigrate with his family to the United States because of the political climate in Europe, his friends thought that the man was "both mad and a coward."

"We are Dutch," they said. "And we will stay in the Netherlands."

Now many of those same Jews bitterly regretted their decision to stay. For some, the sense of imminent doom proved too much to bear. An estimated 150 people in Amsterdam, most of them Jewish, died of suicide in the immediate aftermath of the surrender rather than waiting to see what the Nazis would bring. In a few cases, entire families poisoned themselves or shut their windows and turned on the gas. On May 15, at 10:00 a.m., Jacob van Gelderen, a Jewish economist and the vice chairman of the Dutch Social Democratic Party, was found in his home in The Hague, lying on his bed with his wife and two adult children. None of them was breathing.

Otto Frank would never have contemplated doing something so rash. He believed he would find a way out for his family, and he tried to conceal the most frightening possibilities of what could happen from his two little girls. Yet unlike many Jewish residents of the Netherlands, he knew full well what the Nazis were capable of. After all, that was why he had fled Germany in 1933 to come to neutral Holland. Now that his new home was occupied, he began to wonder whether he could pull off the same trick again. He tried to get visas for the United States and Cuba. But all the exits were blocked off. Even money and connections didn't seem to help this time. Otto's relatives in Great Britain had earlier begged him to send the girls to live with them. Yet now German bombs were wreaking havoc in London and other English cities on a nightly basis, and Otto couldn't bear the thought of scattering his family. He believed that, come what might, they would be safer if they all stuck together.

And at the beginning of the Occupation, he had reason to be

optimistic. As disquieting as it was to see the occasional SS officer lazing on the canals and Wehrmacht troops marching across Dam Square, most people in the Netherlands were pleasantly surprised by how "normal" everything felt during that first summer of 1940. Businesses reopened, life resumed, the Germans mostly behaved themselves. They even left the Jews alone at first, except for issuing new requirements for kosher butchers that affected only religious Jews. Some people began to suspect that the Occupation might be less of a catastrophe than had initially been feared.

But as the summer ended, so did the reprieve. In August, all German Jews who had arrived in Holland after 1933 had to submit their names to the Nazis. Otto Frank dutifully followed the order, which by January was extended to every Jew in the Netherlands.

Before the Jews were rounded up, they were restricted. They couldn't sit on park benches. They couldn't use public transportation. They couldn't teach in universities or hold public office. They couldn't keep more than a thousand guilders in cash. They couldn't go to cinemas, hotels, the beach, swimming pools. "We're not likely to get sunburned," Anne wrote, trying to look on the bright side. Before long, she would be forced to leave her Montessori school along with eighty-six other Jewish children—only twenty of whom would survive the coming storm.

The first large-scale arrests occurred on February 22 and 23, 1941, in the old Jewish quarter of Amsterdam. In the midst of a pogrom in which NSB thugs and Nazis pulled Jews off bicycles, ransacked Jewish-owned businesses, and savagely beat people, 389 Jewish men were taken into German custody. They would eventually be sent to Buchenwald and Mauthausen; only two would survive the war.

The Dutch didn't just sit idly by and watch that crime happen. They were outraged. The Communists called for a national strike to protest the treatment of Dutch Jews. And remarkably, on February 25, 300,000 Dutch people answered the call. They stopped working. Restaurants, shipyards, train stations—everything shut down. Life in Amsterdam ground to a halt. It remains the biggest strike in Dutch history. And though it was brutally suppressed by the Nazis a few days later, it seemed that for a moment the Dutch had followed through on their queen's request, that they had not forgotten their Jewish compatriots.

There were also smaller acts of courage. In the spring of 1942, one of the most infamous anti-Jewish decrees took effect: the requirement to wear the yellow Jewish star. A few Dutch non-Jews pinned the star on their clothes in protest and solidarity. They also used humor as a defense. The Dutch word for Jew, *Jood*, which was written in stylized Hebrew letters on the star, was turned into an acronym for the phrase *Joden overleven de ondergang van Duitsland*: "Jews survive the downfall of Germany."

And who could doubt that? After all, the joke went, "It was written in the stars."

THE HOME FRONT

Bep remembered feeling helpless in the early months of the Occupation, but she couldn't reveal the extent of her fear and anxiety without alarming her younger siblings. She was the eldest of eight children, their caretaker and role model. "Bep told us difficult times were ahead but that we would make it through," remembered my aunt Diny. "She didn't want to cause a panic."

Yet Bep's mother, Christina, *was* panicked. She had barely been able to support her family even before the Occupation, and she feared that the war would make their lives even harder. It didn't take long for her fears to come true. That same spring, Johan lost a poorly paying job he had found working at a furniture shop, plunging the family into more dire straits.

While Bep and the older girls struggled to feed the family, Johan stayed at home, tinkering with his wooden toys and impatiently following the progress of the war in the newspaper. He was desperate for something to do. After every air raid, he climbed up to the roof to pick up shell splinters and other debris that had landed on the building. The man was a scavenger, my grandmother told me, a person who could find a use for things that other people threw away.

Johan felt that whatever ability he had was being wasted. He wasn't working, he wasn't fighting, he was just watching—and worrying. He tried to stay positive. He told his family that they would make it through, that better days would come, but it was hard for him to say the same thing to his many Jewish friends. He hated seeing what the Jews of Amsterdam were going through, how they were made to wear those stupid yellow stars and stripped, bit by bit, of every little freedom and dignity that made life bearable.

Johan used to say he liked Jews because of their humor and wit, but I think he just saw his Jewish friends as ordinary people, and if he liked them, it was for who they were as individuals. Whenever he had a Jewish friend over for drinks or a game of chess, he insisted on walking him home afterward, explaining to his wife, "I need to help with something." That something was pointing out the best route to take to avoid Kraut patrols.

Of the half-dozen or so Jews whom Johan counted as good friends, he was closest to a man named Jonas Bed, a textile merchant around his own age. They loved watching the soccer games together at the home stadium of the Amsterdam soccer club, Ajax. After every game, they would go back to Lumeijstraat and talk and drink and laugh late into the night. In 1942, when German raids began to sweep through the city, Johan told Mr. Bed to stop going to the stadium. But Mr. Bed thought he was overreacting; soccer was one of the few outlets he had left. He continued to watch his beloved Ajax until one day he was arrested at the stadium. The Nazis sent him to Bergen-Belsen, where he died in early 1945, in roughly the same time and place as Anne and Margot Frank.

"I warned him *not* to do it!" Johan told his wife helplessly.

Johan did not have a bigoted bone in his body, yet as much as he thought that anti-Semitism was a scourge, he knew it was not some alien concept imported from Germany. It existed in the Netherlands, of course, even under his own roof. His wife, Christina, was not fond of the Jews. And his tempestuous teenage daughter Nelly, who was seventeen at the start of the Occupation, believed all the things the NSB said about them: that Jews were *Untermenschen*, subhuman creatures, who smuggled disruptive political ideas such as communism into the Netherlands and defiled its racial purity.

Unlike my mother, who was mild-mannered and respectful, who always got along with her strident father, Nelly and Johan fought constantly. They shared some traits: They both had analytical minds and strong wills. They were good at math and liked solving puzzles. They even looked alike, with the same hooded eyes and pursed lips frozen in a perpetual frown. But whereas Johan was modest, Nelly was ostentatious. She liked putting on makeup; she liked talking up her budding schoolyard romances. She was even something of an exhibitionist. When Johan wasn't around, she sometimes slunk around the house wearing nothing but a brassiere and panties—scandalous behavior in those days—until Christina told her to put something decent on.

During the Occupation, she was seduced by everything German, especially the language, which she practiced until she could speak it almost flawlessly. She added a combustible element to the crowded hovel of the Voskuijl home. She was bitterly dissatisfied with life there—the meager food, the biting cold, the perpetual lack of money and new clothes. And she made her dissatisfaction known and spread it among her younger sisters, always muttering under her breath, always picking fights. *Teenage nonsense*, my mother thought. *She'll grow out of it—sooner or later.*

But at times Nelly could make my mother feel more "under siege" sitting inside the crowded house on Lumeijstraat than if she were walking around occupied Amsterdam to a soundtrack of air raid sirens and anti-aircraft guns.

OFFICE POLITICS

Luckily, there was the office, which became a kind of sanctuary, a home away from home for my mother. Despite all the setbacks and complications of the Occupation, business at Opekta was good—so good, in fact, that Otto was expanding. He now traded not only in pectin but also in spices. And for the first time since arriving in the Netherlands in 1933, he had begun to turn a profit. The Occupation had, ironically, opened new markets. Otto may not have realized it at the time, but one of his clients was now the Wehrmacht, which bought pepper and nutmeg from him through an intermediary. By the end of 1940, his business had grown to such an extent that he needed a larger office.

He rented a narrow four-story brick building on the Prinsengracht dating from the eighteenth century that was just a stone's throw from the famous Westerkerk church. Included in the lease were a warehouse space on the ground floor, office space on the first floor, storage rooms on the second and third floors—and a warren of rooms in the *achterhuis*, the "house behind," that could be accessed through a narrow corridor. Anne loved visiting the new office. When she wasn't having girl talk with Bep or Miep, she was usually pulling little pranks, such as pouring glasses of water out the second-floor window, frightening passersby on the canal.

When Bep learned that the new, larger warehouse space needed to be staffed, she saw an opportunity for her father, who was restless at home. *Nothing ventured, nothing gained*, she thought before suggesting Johan for the job.

Otto Frank was enthusiastic about the idea, and he hired Johan in a temporary capacity, but my grandfather quickly proved himself indispensable and was given a full-time role. Before long, he was supervising the whole warehouse: grinding and mixing the spices, packing them into containers, overseeing the shipping process, and making sure the workers stayed in line. Bep was glad she had something to share with her father. She told me it added "another dimension" to their relationship, a closeness, a confidence, that was unique in the family.

With Johan's arrival, the cast of characters at Opekta was being rounded out. In addition to Miep, the small staff included Otto's second in command, Victor Kugler, a German-speaking man from Bohemia with a little mustache and nervous, darting eyes. He was a spiffy dresser, handsome in a reedy, emaciated way, like a figure in an Egon Schiele painting. My mother couldn't take her eyes off him, but she tried to look away when he spoke to her to keep from blushing.

Another employee was Johannes "Jo" Kleiman, a good friend of Otto whom he had met while working for his family's bank in Amsterdam in the 1920s. Kleiman joined Opekta in 1938 and looked after the books. He was pale, beak-nosed, with round glasses and a pleasant face. "He was a quiet person," Miep Gies once said, "whose personality immediately inspired feelings of trust."

Miep, Jo, Victor, Johan, Bep: those five people would in short time become the helpers of the Secret Annex. Yet their first act of conspiracy was bureaucratic in nature. In October 1940, five months after the Occupation began, the Germans decreed that "all industrial and commercial firms in the possession of Jews or with Jewish partners must be registered. Failure to do so will be penalized with a prison sentence of a maximum of five years and [payment of] one hundred thousand guilders." Otto and his employees had no illusions: they knew that once the Germans learned that Opekta was Jewish owned, the company would immediately be seized.

So the more senior members of the staff—Miep, Jo, and Victor—put their heads together and came up with a solution that cunningly circumvented the Nazis' intent. In November 1940, the ownership of Opekta would be transferred to Jo Kleiman. Meanwhile, Otto's side business trading in spices, called Pectacon, was liquidated and a new company, Gies & Co., was founded. Kugler was appointed the managing director, and Miep's husband, Jan Gies, whom the business was named after, became the chairman. That created the illusion that both firms were in "Aryan" hands. Otto would remain in charge—just not on paper.

The plan was risky. Jews were already being denounced, and Otto was the subject of at least one blackmail attempt during that period.* Bep played along without asking many questions; she immediately understood the stakes. Johan knew that his eldest daughter could be trusted, yet what about the rest of his family? It was not exactly a secret on Lumeijstraat that Otto was Jewish.

"I don't want any more talk of our boss," Johan warned his children one night. "That could not only be dangerous to him, but to us as well."

Otto's business was safe, at least for the moment. But his family was very much in danger. On July 5, 1942, Edith Frank received a summons from the Central Office for Jewish Emigration. She thought the nightmare of a letter was meant for Otto. Then she looked again

---

* In April 1941, Otto Frank paid the Dutch Nazi Tonny Ahlers a certain amount of money in return for a letter Ahlers had intercepted. In the letter, written by Frank's former employee Joseph Jansen and addressed to the NSB, Jansen described a conversation he had had with Frank in which Frank had questioned Germany's eventual victory.

at the envelope to discover that it was addressed to her sixteen-year-old daughter, Margot. "You are hereby ordered to participate in the police-supervised expansion of work in Germany."

The Franks understood what that message really meant, and they were ready for it.

CHAPTER 3

Full Secrecy

Miep Gies was a small woman, just under five feet tall, but formidable. It was her job at Opekta to field customer questions and complaints, to deal with the outsiders. The last time I saw her was in 1999 during a visit to her home in the harbor town of Hoorn, north of Amsterdam. She was about ninety then, and I hadn't laid eyes on her since I was a boy.

My mother had known she could always count on Miep, even if she felt privately that her more senior colleague could be short-tempered and emotionally distant. Long after both women retired from the company to raise their families, they made sure to keep in touch. And now Miep welcomed me and my two older brothers, Cok and Ton, into her home with open arms, as if we were extended members of the family. We each gave her a kiss on the cheek. Her doting son, Paul, served us tea and pastries. Miep's husband, Jan, who had done his own part to protect the Frank family during the Occupation, had died six years earlier. So every August 4, Miep marked the anniversary of the raid on the Secret Annex all by herself, holding a silent vigil.

There was a somber quality to our visit—no one said as much, but it was meant to be a kind of goodbye. I will never forget how Miep began the conversation: "Now, while you still can, ask me what you want to know."

Miep was born Hermine Santruschitz in Vienna in 1909. She grew up in the terrible poverty that followed Austria's defeat in the First

World War. Her family could barely afford to feed her, and by age eleven, she had grown weak from malnutrition. As part of a relief program, her parents sent her to live with a Dutch family in the university town of Leiden. Her host parents gave her the nickname Miep and, with the blessing of her biological family, eventually adopted her.

Miep was one of the first people whom Otto Frank hired to work in the office after he moved to Amsterdam in 1933, and at the end of the war she gave him a place to live and a shoulder to cry on when he came back from Auschwitz with nothing—his home destroyed, his family murdered. She was "the famous helper," the one who was named in the film and stage adaptations of Anne Frank's story, while my mother stood somewhere in the background, hidden from view, usually by her own choice.

Though she became a minor celebrity in her later years, Miep had never sought glory or recognition. Until the late 1980s, she lived a quiet life in Amsterdam as a homemaker. She wrote her best-selling 1987 memoir, *Anne Frank Remembered*, only at the urging of an American writer, Alison Leslie Gold, and in her book she came off as unsentimental and even self-effacing about her role in the drama. "I am not a hero," she wrote. "I stand at the end of the long, long line of good Dutch people who did what I did and more—much more."

Miep first made an impression on me in the early 1960s. I must have been around thirteen years old at the time, and I had grown a little wary of her visits, because her mere presence seemed to bring back painful memories that would disturb the always uneasy peace in our household. I knew by then that if my mother started even *thinking* about the Secret Annex, she would get a migraine, slip into a depression, and spend much of the next day in bed. So when I saw the gloomy look that came over my mother's face as she and Miep talked quietly in the kitchen, I burst into the room and interrupted what was no doubt a private conversation. "Are you talking about the war *again*?"

I hoped that Miep wouldn't make much out of my intrusion, that she would interpret it as just the outburst of an annoyed adolescent, but she picked up on the genuine fury behind it. She froze, while my mother started sobbing. Realizing my blunder, I tried to put my arm around my mother to comfort her, but she regained her composure just in time for Miep to put me in my place. Yes, she told me sternly, they *were* talking about the war. "But, Joop, you shouldn't get so worked up about it."

Then, looking at my mother, she said with a little smirk that they had had some experience with difficult subjects and that "Bep and I surely wouldn't have managed without each other." She then gave my mother a hug, and I left them alone to continue their conversation.

As a young boy, I found it amazing how living through roughly the same experiences during the war had had such different consequences on Bep and Miep's personalities. If anything, the ordeal had only toughened Miep. She had become impassive about most things, including her rising fame. Over the years, she received a series of human rights awards and was knighted by Queen Beatrix of the Netherlands, and an asteroid was even named in her honor. Whereas my mother . . . but now I am getting ahead of myself.

While you still can, ask me what you want to know.

After we exchanged a few more courtesies, I told Miep that there *was* something I never quite understood: Why had my mother been the last person on the Opekta staff to be told about the Secret Annex? Had Otto not entirely trusted her, even though she had been working for him for five years at that point, even though she had become a friend of the family who had spent time at his house and gotten to know his children?

"Joop, it wasn't a matter of trust," Miep told me flatly. Otto and the others hadn't wanted to involve my mother because she was "still a young girl with her whole life in front of her." In the spring of 1942, Bep was just twenty-two years old. Victor and Jo were in their forties. Miep was thirty-three. Her husband, Jan, was thirty-seven and a social worker inclined toward activism, who had many contacts in the Resistance. The older members of the Circle knew the risks. They understood that if the Nazis found out they were hiding Jews, they could be thrown into jail or sent to a concentration camp. They were not sure whether Bep would be able to fully comprehend the danger involved. Miep explained to me that the reason they had ultimately brought her in on the plan was that they had felt they had no other choice. For one thing, there was no practical way she could continue working with them in that small office on Prinsengracht without knowing what was happening on the other side of the wall.

And, more important, they needed her help.

• • • • • • • • • •

It was Otto who first came up with the brilliant idea to turn the *achterhuis* into a safe house, to disappear into the belly of his own business, a hiding place so obvious yet unassuming that no one would ever think to come looking for him there. The idea may have been in the back of his mind as early as 1940, when he rented the office space on Prinsengracht knowing that there were extra rooms in the core of the building whose existence one could not discern from street level.*

When Otto took over the space, however, the annex was accessible only via an entrance on the ground floor located *outside* the office. Sometime during the early days of the Occupation, he decided to have a stairway leading to the entrance of the Annex quietly built in the little hallway in front of his private office. That stairway turned out to be extremely useful; the helpers could visit the Annex without being noticed by the warehouse staff or a nosy neighbor.

---

* During a 1981 interview with the Dutch State Institute for War Documentation (RIOD), Bep claimed that Otto Frank had been searching for a hiding place as early as December 1940. We don't know whether Otto himself was the original source of that information.

Late in the spring of 1942, Bep started noticing that her colleagues were acting strangely, whispering to one another. She saw furniture being moved into the *achterhuis* and heard many more footsteps than usual on the little stairwell outside Otto's office. *What is going on?*

She would search the faces of her colleagues as they left Otto's office, looking for a knowing glance that would lead to the long-awaited explanation or to her being let in on the secret. But week after week it did not come. Bep did not understand why she was being kept in the dark. She felt she was already in Otto's circle of trust. She knew about the maneuvers to Aryanize the company, and she knew that Otto was still the one in charge—information that could get them all into deep trouble. Hadn't she already proven her loyalty?

Then, one day in June 1942, Otto finally called Bep into his office. The way he asked her was strange, less a request than a test: "Bep, do you agree that my family will go into hiding in the Annex?"

She was shocked, but she answered simply, "Yes."

She gave the same answer when Otto asked if she, along with Miep, could look after the Frank family and another Jewish family who would take shelter there: bring them food, run errands, keep them safe. After the war, my mother downplayed that moment, saying that her response had been "natural" and "human." She had considered it a matter of "duty," if not to some country or creed, then to her friends. Otto had always been kind and generous to her and to the Voskuijl family. Now he needed help. That was it—a simple "yes" that would endlessly complicate her life.

A GUIDED TOUR

At the end of June 1942, Otto took Bep on a tour of the rooms that would soon become the Secret Annex. She was the last of the four office workers to step inside. They took the little staircase from his office—soon to be known as the *helperstrap* (helpers' stairway)—and entered through a still unmasked gray door. Right after the entrance came another, steeper stairway, with a tiny passage on the left. The passage led to what would soon be Otto and Edith's bedroom. Otto showed Bep another little room next door where his daughters would sleep. Then they went up the stairs into a large, light-filled space that would serve as a kitchen and dining room as well as a bedroom for Otto's business colleague Hermann van Pels and his wife, Auguste. Their fifteen-year-old son, Peter, would sleep in a tiny adjacent room.

Though the layout—the succession of stairs and walls and nooks—made one feel like a mouse lost in a maze, it wasn't exactly a small space compared to some of the other hiding places around town, although Bep could not imagine how two families could be confined in those 450 square feet for months, possibly even for years, without ever stepping outside.

My mother was already somewhat familiar with the rooms, since they had previously been used to store old office files. For a time, Victor had also used the space as a laboratory for mixing new food products. Yet now the Annex looked less like a storage space than a secondhand shop after an earthquake. There was rubbish everywhere. Over the past few months, furniture, rugs, and other sundry household items had been secretly transported there from the Frank family home. It had to be done that way since Jews were forbidden to move furniture in the street. An item would be picked up, usually by Jo Kleiman's brother, who ran a pest control service (and so was often seen visiting apartments), and quietly deposited at Kleiman's house before it was surreptitiously dumped into the Annex on a weekend evening when no one was around.

As the weeks passed, cardboard boxes, clothes, sheets, and blankets accumulated on the floorboards and beds. Planks of wood lay here and there. Bep could see that much work had already been done: a new bathroom sink had been installed, and a broken toilet had been repaired. The laboratory's small kitchenette had also been replaced with a much larger, modern eat-in kitchen. But there was still much more to be done.

Otto explained that he planned to spend the next few weeks getting the space ready. He had set his family's move-in date for late summer but then pushed it up to July 16. He knew that it was only a matter of time before the Germans would be knocking on their door. A rumor was going around that the Nazis were planning to deport *all* the Jews in Holland—who knew where, or to what end. But he thought that maybe they had a bit more time. He understood that once they went into hiding, there would be no going back until the war was over. Otto didn't dare tell Anne and Margot the plan—he didn't want to frighten them or burden them—but one day that summer he gave Anne a hint of what was in store. "We'll leave of our own accord," he said, "and not wait to be hauled away." There was no need for her to worry. The important thing was to cherish her freedom, or what was left of it: play outside, eat ice cream, lie in the sun, at least on her apartment building's rooftop if she wasn't allowed onto the beach or into the swimming pool. "Just enjoy your carefree life while you can," he said.

MOVING DAY

Sunday, July 5, 1942, was exactly the kind of beautiful summer day that Otto wished his daughters would soak up. It also happened to be Bep's twenty-third birthday. Sometime that afternoon, she received a message from her boss. She may have thought he was calling to wish her a happy birthday. Instead she got the startling news about Margot: the Nazis had sent a Dutch policeman to deliver the letter on a Sunday, when the post office was closed. Bep knew that meant the plan would have to be accelerated. But she was astonished when she found out that the Franks planned to move into the Annex the next day, July 6. Ten-year-old Diny had no idea what was happening, but she saw that her sister's mood abruptly changed from festive to frightened—and resolved.

"We have to do something," Bep muttered under her breath before throwing a few things into her bag and rushing out of the house. My mother took off on her bicycle, but it's not clear where she went— perhaps to meet up with Miep and the other members of the Circle.

The next morning, as soon as she got to work, Bep was called into Otto's office by Jo Kleiman. From now on, Jo said, "full secrecy" would be the order of the day. She couldn't mention the Annex to anyone, not her boyfriend, not her sisters, not her mother, and initially not even her father in the warehouse downstairs. The important thing was that the Franks had arrived safely, although they were exhausted from their journey to the office.

Otto had made it look as though his family had fled to Switzerland, abandoning their apartment in Amsterdam South in great haste, sending decoy letters to his far-flung relatives to keep the Nazis off their track. He even scribbled a bogus Basel address on a notepad left in the apartment. Anne packed her own bag. The first thing she put into it was a red-checkered diary that she had been given as a gift for her thirteenth birthday a month earlier. "I hope you will be a great source of comfort and support," she wrote on the first page.

Her initial entries were a fairly typical record of adolescent life under the Occupation: notes on her family, friendships, and assorted frustrations or, as she put it, the "musings" of a thirteen-year-old "chatterbox." Yet her diary would soon become something else entirely: a window into the Secret Annex.

Because Jews weren't allowed to take public transportation, Anne, Otto, and Edith had to walk the 2.5 miles from the Merwedeplein to the Prinsengracht. They couldn't take suitcases with them into the Annex, as they would attract attention. So they put on layer after layer of clothing, hoping to avoid German soldiers along the way. Luckily, the pouring rain kept patrols off the streets. Miep had come a bit earlier to pick up Margot. The two ladies took their bikes to Prinsengracht. Jews were forbidden to own, much less ride, bicycles, so Margot was taking a big risk by being on a bike (and not wearing her yellow star), but the idea was to make her look like an ordinary young Dutch woman riding with her friend to work.

For Edith and Margot, the stress of the journey proved to be too much. As soon as they reached the Annex, they collapsed onto unmade beds. So it was left to Anne and Otto to move in as Miep and Bep stocked the kitchen with fresh food.

My mother caught a glimpse of the hiders as soon as they arrived. She could see with her own eyes the uncertainty and fear in their faces. Otto seemed grimly determined and very quiet, but at a certain point he gathered his family and spoke to them. He explained that they would be living there in close quarters for an unforeseeable amount of time and that they must try to live as harmoniously as possible. Their situation was precarious but not hopeless; they were better off than many others: they had a place to hide, they had friends they could trust, and, most important, they had each other.

As Margot and Edith rested, Otto and Anne unpacked boxes, filled the cupboards, made makeshift curtains by stitching together strips of old fabric, and tidied up until "we fell exhausted into our clean beds." The next day there was still more work to do: scrubbing the kitchen floor and fixing the lights. It wasn't until Wednesday, July 10, that Anne was able to record "the enormous change in my life" in her diary.

Anne compared the Annex to "some strange pension." It was damp, and the whole space leaned slightly to one side, a typical feature of old Amsterdam buildings. Yet it seemed to her to be "an ideal place to hide in." On July 13, about a week after the Franks moved in, the van Pels family arrived ahead of schedule. There were more and more reports of Jews being rounded up, and, as Anne put it, "safer to leave a day too early than a day too late." By the end of July, six thousand Dutch Jews had been transported to the death camps, a number that would grow precipitously in the coming months.

Tens of thousands of Jews were now hiding all across Holland. The Franks knew that there were bounties on their heads—initially 2.5 guilders for every Jew found, but the Nazis kept raising the price as their hunt intensified until it reached 40 guilders.

Anne was always nervous that a neighbor might notice them. In the daytime, she could manage her fear; she was too busy, and everything was so new and even a bit exciting. Yet at night in her room she could sometimes not bear the silence, and there was one person in particular whose company she missed. "I wish like anything that I could keep Bep back at night when she is the last to leave," she wrote.

My mother would soon understand just how much Anne and the others relied on her, and wherever she found herself over the next two years—in the office fussing over invoices or in the drafty bedroom she shared with her sisters—her thoughts would never be far away from the Secret Annex.

CHAPTER 4

Mouths to Feed

My mother spent the war searching for food. Shortages and rationing made it difficult to feed a typical family in Amsterdam, much less eight Jews in hiding who had no legal way of obtaining ration coupons. Certain food products, such as sugar, had been rationed even before the invasion. But once the Occupation began, the food situation rapidly deteriorated. All imports from outside the Reich dried up. The Nazis confiscated nearly 10 percent of domestic food production, which was sent to Germany to feed the war effort. Cheese was rationed. Meat and eggs became scarce. You could find only ersatz versions of coffee, tea, and tobacco. Every shop had a long line outside and fewer and fewer products on the shelves.

The quality of produce, a point of pride for Dutch farmers before the war, became abysmal. Anne recorded the unappetizing menu in the Secret Annex: breakfasts of dry bread and fake coffee, dinners of rotten potatoes, the kitchen always reeking of spoiled plums and brine. Cookbooks were published with recipes for lean times. They had tips on replacing meat with chopped beans or mussels and conserving cooking fuel by blanching vegetables or eating them raw. Because of the shortage of meat, people started to catch birds in the street and even stray cats, a fact that Anne—who had had to give up her beloved cat, Moortje, before moving into the Annex—recorded with horror.

It helped that the Secret Annex was attached to a food additive business. Otto had taken care to lay down a large supply of canned vegetables, fruit, fish, and condensed milk, as well as several kilos of wheat starch, before going into hiding. They also could skim from Opekta's regular deliveries of sugar. But that was still not nearly enough food for eight people to survive on. Getting more would prove to be a major problem that often fell to Miep and my mother to solve.

Miep did as much of the food shopping as she could. Sometimes she returned to the Annex from her rounds so overloaded with bags that Anne said she looked like "a pack mule." Yet she could not spend too much of the workday out of the office, because she had to be at her desk to field calls from customers. My mother's job as a typist, on the other hand, could be done in the small hours, freeing her to spend as much of the day scavenging as necessary.

It was dangerous work, often done under the noses of German troops and Dutch spies. Jan Gies would supply her with forged or stolen ration tickets (obtained through his Resistance contacts), which she would then take to friendly merchants. There were two green-grocers where she liked to buy vegetables and a butcher friend of Hermann van Pels who was often able to give her a bit of extra meat. Jo Kleiman also had a friend who worked for a baker and would deliver a large quantity of bread each week—far more than was needed for four office workers—without asking any questions.

If you couldn't find what you needed in a regular store, there was always the option to go underground. "Everyone's trading on the black market; every errand boy has something to offer," Anne wrote in her diary. "The milkman can get hold of ration books, an undertaker delivers cheese." The most important thing was your contacts. *Who do you know? Can they be trusted?*

"We constantly lived in fear of being watched," my mother once said of her daily trips to supply the Secret Annex. "But the fact that we were doing the right thing made us feel protected."

Getting food in wartime involved charm and guile as much as

courage. Bep always made sure to bat her eyelashes for a certain milkman who lived in Halfweg, a town outside Amsterdam. And she never forgot to mention the fact that she had seven hungry younger siblings waiting at home.

"Here, take this," he'd whisper. "Some extra milk for all those mouths you have to feed."

This milkman was not exactly attractive—he was around fifty years old—yet my mother flirted with him shamelessly. Years later, she remembered such interactions with a roguish smile. "My boy, we did *a lot* to get food in those days."

As the war ground on, my mother got cozy enough with the milkman that he even turned up as a character in Anne's diary. On one occasion, he confided in Bep that three of his sons were hiding out in the countryside to avoid being pressed into forced labor by the Germans. On another, he told her that he had just lit the cigarette of a Canadian airman who had parachuted from his burning plane during a dogfight. Even if Bep was running late or did not feel like listening to the milkman drone on, she tried to smile, to seem as though she cared, to protect her source. Years after the war, Miep once explained that shopping for the Secret Annex had required "certain theatrical qualities." You could not directly ask a shopkeeper for more than your ration. You couldn't dare inquire about buying something "under the table" unless you knew that the person on the other side of the counter could be trusted. Compassion, deception, humor, sincerity— all were fair tactics.

When my mother could not find enough fresh food to supply the Annex in the shops of Amsterdam, she rode her bike to farms on the edge of the city in the Watergraafsmeer neighborhood. She knew the area well; it was not far from the leafy street where the Voskuijl family had lived until 1933. She would travel from farm to farm, knocking on the door, quietly, politely asking if anything was for sale. *Some extra milk? A scrap of meat? Some old potatoes?*

Although the Nazis forbade farmers to sell directly to consumers, many of the rural families took pity on the people who showed up at their farms out of desperation. Or they wanted to make money off them, knowing they could charge more for their produce than food factories would pay. Some farmers also hid Jews and other people on the run from the Germans. My mother probably visited Anna's Hoeve, a farm in Watergraafsmeer operated by the Oostenrijk family, to ask for food during the war. Little did she know that in a basement, hidden beneath the hay, was another Secret Annex sheltering two people.

One day in 1944, my mother had a lucky streak in Watergraafsmeer: each farm she visited had something to offer. She stuffed the potatoes, leeks, and cabbages into a wicker horn that hung from her bicycle, and when that was filled up she began using jute bags. It was far more food than was safe to carry without being detected, yet it was too good an opportunity to pass up.

The distance between Watergraafsmeer and Prinsengracht was about three miles. Breathing hard from the strain of carrying that much food, my mother had already reached Westermarkt, a stone's throw from the Annex, when she heard something that made her heart stop. "*Wo gehen Sie hin?*" The question was in German. "Where are you going?"

My mother might have hoped that the question was directed at someone else, anyone else, but when she lifted her gaze, she met the blue eyes of a young soldier on a bicycle wearing the black uniform of the Waffen-SS, the international paramilitary group made up of particularly fanatical Jew haters and headed by none other than Heinrich Himmler. It had some twenty-five thousand members in the Netherlands.

Most Dutch people could understand German—many words in both languages have common origins, and elementary German was a required subject in Dutch schools. My mother had also obtained a certificate in German from night school. Her aptitude with the language might have been one reason Otto had hired her, and now it was coming in handy once again. Trying to appear innocent, she carefully explained that this food was for her family, that the reason it looked like so much was because she had seven siblings—*all those mouths to feed*.

The young Nazi was smiling, and he seemed to buy my mother's story—or want her to think as much. She noticed that his much older comrade was watching the scene at a distance. As the younger one began to search her bags, she tried to conceal the horrified look on her face. *Will I be arrested? Will they find out about the Annex?* But to her great surprise, after confiscating about half the vegetables for himself, he told Bep she could go on her way.

As she climbed back onto her bike, my mother couldn't help but feel that she had gotten off too easily. She slowed when she reached Prinsengracht, but something inside told her *keep going*. In a split second, she decided to ride past Opekta and head home to Lumeijstraat instead. A few blocks down, she got off her bike and pretended to rearrange the groceries. And out of the corner of her eye she watched the young Nazi riding past with his comrade. She realized that they had been tailing her and thanked God that she had not led the wolf to the door of the Annex.

HOUSE AND TABLE COMPANION

During the first several months of hiding, in the summer and fall of 1942, Otto tried to establish a routine in the Secret Annex to combat isolation and minimize the chance that the hideout would be discovered. Each day began promptly at 6:45 a.m. The Franks washed and used the toilet in a carefully prescribed order set by Otto, who was sometimes called "the Prussian officer" by Anne because of his talent as a taskmaster. Then they ate breakfast before settling in for the silent hours: no talking, no opening of windows (even in the summer), absolutely no flushing of the toilet.

Bep arrived at work around 8:30, and the warehouse employees came in around nine. In the office, it had to look like business as usual. Bep typed up the orders, Miep answered the phone, Jo balanced the books. But the undercurrent of fear made it hard to concentrate. A reprieve came at lunchtime. The warehouse workers went home, and Bep climbed the *helperstrap* and entered the Annex to join the residents for a bite to eat.

Anne was often the first face my mother saw—beaming, curious, impatient. "What is happening outside?" she would ask.

Anne sometimes referred to my mother in her diary as the ninth resident or "Number nine," since she was in the Annex so often. "Number nine is not part of our Annex family, although she does share our house and table. Bep has a healthy appetite. She cleans her plate and isn't choosy. Bep's easy to please and that pleases us. She can be characterized as follows: cheerful, good-humored, kind and willing."

While she ate, Bep made notes about what food and essentials the residents of the Annex needed. The rest of the time was spent discussing news from the outside world: the war, politics, gossip. Bep oscillated between listening to the adults and listening to Anne, who always demanded that Bep sit next to her so they could whisper into each other's ears. That was how Otto would remember my mother and his daughter years after—always together, whispering.

I don't think it took very long for Bep to start to feel as though the Franks were family. It was the same kind of connection she felt for her parents and siblings—in which love and affection mixed with loyalty and obligation.

After lunch, if there was time, Bep would follow Anne back to the tiny room she shared with a loudly snoring German Jewish dentist named Fritz Pfeffer. He had joined the Annex in the fall of 1942; Anne would later nickname him "Dussel" (German for *doofus*). A middle-aged man was not an ideal roommate for an adolescent girl, but Anne tried to carve out a space of her own in the room, however minimal. Above the small divan where she slept, she decorated the walls with pictures of Hollywood stars cut from magazines: Greta Garbo, Ginger Rogers, Rudy Vallee.

My mother knew that, in addition to movie stars, Anne idolized the Dutch royal family, who were now living in exile in Canada. So she bought Anne a special postcard with a portrait of Queen Wilhelmina; Princess Juliana and her prince consort, Bernhard; and their three children, Beatrix, Irene, and Margriet. The postcard was contraband, having been printed by the resistance newspaper *Trouw* to raise funds for its activities. Anne thought it was "incredibly nice of Bep" to risk buying it for her. She pasted the postcard on the wall of her room, where it can still be seen to this day.

My mother knew that the isolation of the Annex was especially hard for Anne. But she also knew that it couldn't be easy for Anne's sister, Margot, or Peter van Pels, who were just a few years older. So my mother brought to the Annex a brochure listing correspondence courses from a popular school, the Leidsche Onderwijsinstellingen, and encouraged the youngsters to pick out a course for themselves. She then signed them up under her own name. That was how Anne, Margot, and Peter learned stenography during their time in hiding. Margot also started a course in elementary Latin. The courses were not cheap, although Otto probably considered his girls' education a very worthwhile expense. Anne noted that the Latin course alone cost 90 guilders (about $650 in today's money). Two lessons were sent every fourteen days. The instructors would grade the homework and send it back with comments. By October 1942, Anne had already mastered the basics of shorthand.

Though schoolwork and a sense of routine helped pass the time, it was also important that the Annex residents be allowed to have a bit of fun. In December 1942, Bep and Miep prepared a surprise to mark the Dutch Sinterklaas holiday, a celebration of Saint Nicholas (from whom the American Santa Claus was derived).

After the workers went home and all was quiet at 263 Prinsengracht, Anne, Margot, Peter, and the other residents of the Annex were led down the wooden staircase into a pitch-black, windowless room. They flipped on the lights, and Otto—who had advance knowledge of the plans—opened a large cupboard to reveal a big basket wrapped in festive paper and filled with gifts and handwritten poems for each resident. The German Jewish hiders had little knowledge of Sinterklaas, so the gesture came as a complete and delightful surprise. Anne received a baby cupid doll. Many of the other gifts—an ashtray for the chain-smoking Hermann van Pels, a photo frame for Fritz Pfeffer, and bookends for Otto—had been carved by hand by my grandfather Johan. "How anyone can be so clever with his hands is a mystery to me!" Anne wrote.

About a week into the hiding, my grandfather had been informed about the existence of the Secret Annex. It is not clear who told him, perhaps Bep or Otto or Victor. In any case, everyone immediately recognized how valuable it was to have someone trustworthy on the ground floor, watching the workers in the warehouse and keeping an eye on the street. They all seemed to breathe easier having Johan on their side, especially my mother. "He's been most helpful," Anne wrote.

WHISPERS IN THE DEN

Outside work, Bep and Johan tried their hardest not to be heard speaking about the Secret Annex. My mother was terrified of making a mistake, of "letting something slip," as she always put it. Anne worried about the same thing—an argument overheard, a pan that was dropped on the floor at the wrong moment. She wrote in her diary that it was tempting to rationalize those things away, to tell yourself that no one had heard, that no one had been paying attention. "Easy to say, but is it true?"

Even though Bep was close with some of her sisters, she obeyed her boss's order and didn't say a word about the Secret Annex—as much for her family's safety as for those in hiding. Nevertheless, she sometimes had her sisters help her without their knowledge. She asked Willy, who worked as an invoice clerk for the Amsterdam drug company Brocades & Stheeman, to get medicine and calcium tablets "for a friend and her mother." She eventually had her sister place so many orders that the company's warehouse manager jokingly asked whether Willy wanted to start a store of her own. It was not until after the war that Willy discovered that the "friend and mother" had been Anne and Edith Frank.

My aunts Corrie and Annie were also unwitting helpers. They often made simple clothing with leftover fabric taken from Corrie's job as a seamstress. Bep asked them to sew a few practical outfits that she could use to barter for food for the family. The clothes were actually for Anne Frank, who was quickly growing out of her old things. My mother then took Anne's hand-me-downs and gave them to her younger sisters. That was how my aunt Diny received a velvet summer dress from Anne Frank during the war. Bep told her sister that the cobalt-blue dress embroidered with roses—a remnant of happier days—had belonged to Otto's young daughter, who had "managed to escape abroad" with her family. Bep had even wrapped the dress in a wrinkled package with labels on it to lend credibility to her story that the Franks had sent the dress as a gift from abroad. Diny was overjoyed, as most people were dressed in rags at that point of the war: "I felt like a princess wearing that dress, and I even wore it in the winter."

Though Bep and Johan took great care not to be overheard talking about the Secret Annex, they often gathered together after dinner in the sitting room for private discussions. As the girls cleared the dishes, Johan would give Bep a meaningful glance and then get up from the table. He would walk into a little den adjacent to the dining room, where he would sometimes sit reading in an old armchair or whittling something at his heavy wooden desk. Bep would wait a few minutes, then quietly excuse herself, entering the room and closing the sliding doors behind her. There were two small chairs near the coal stove, where father and daughter would speak in hushed tones, usually for an hour or so.

That mysterious behavior did not go unnoticed by the rest of the family, who assumed that Bep and Johan were talking about work, but they didn't understand why such secrecy was required.

"Ah, they're at it again," Nelly would say whenever Bep left the room to be with her father. The comment was designed to rankle Christina, who also hated being left out.

"Why does Father always whisper like that?" Diny asked her mother.

"I don't know."

Diny told me that Christina's fury over the secrets would build and build until she would explode in a wild outburst. Bep was spared the worst of Christina's harangues, which were directed at Johan. Sometimes she would even attack him physically. Johan never laid a finger on his wife, only raising his arm to shield his face. Diny doesn't remember how Bep reacted during those violent arguments, but she will never forget crying with her twin sister, Gerda, and begging her parents to stop.

CHAPTER 5

Concealment

Victor Kugler was the acting boss at Opekta, the man who had taken Otto's place. Perhaps more than anyone else, he was responsible for keeping the Secret Annex a secret. Each morning, when he got off the tram at Westermarkt and walked to the office, he asked himself the same question: "Will they still be there?"

Victor lived in Hilversum, a city surrounded by marshland thirty minutes to the east of Amsterdam. There he could indulge in his greatest pleasure: bird-watching. On the weekend, he liked wading into the tall grass to spot ducks that had migrated west from Siberia. At such moments, he could pretend he was living a normal life. But then the workweek would resume, and so would his anxiety.

I can almost picture him in his tailored wool suit, the veins in his carefully shaven neck pulsing as he stepped onto the cobbled streets, scanning for green uniforms, trying his hardest to look ordinary and businesslike—as though his only care in the world was thickening jam. During the three-minute walk from the tram stop to the office, he would see the Westerkerk tower, note the time on its famous black-and-gold clock, walk past street vendors selling pickles or Italian ices, rush past the steel urinal on the corner of Prinsengracht, and then catch his breath in front of the heavy wooden door at Number 263.

Will they still be there?

Anne could tell it was Victor from his "short but solid knock on the door" of the Annex. She could even discern what kind of mood he was in by looking at his hands as he entered. If he was rubbing them together, he would be happy and talkative. If he had scrunched them into fists, he would be taciturn and worried.

Victor cared for all those in hiding, but he had a soft spot for the youngest resident. He loved seeing Anne's big eyes light up each week when he brought her *Cinema & Theater* magazine. Anne would read it cover to cover and cut out pictures of stars to add to the ever-expanding mural on her wall. She was so well versed in movie news that whenever my mother mentioned that she planned to see a film over the weekend, Anne would announce the cast members and summarize the reviews. *Cinema & Theater* represented the world she loved best, and it was Kugler's pleasure to give her a glimpse of it each week. In an interview years after the war, he recalled how Anne used to look at him with anticipation until he presented her with the latest issue. Sometimes, he said, "I would hide it in my pocket, so that I could watch those questioning eyes for longer."

THE NEW BOSS

Victor was born in 1900 in Hohenelbe, a Bohemian town at the mouth of the Elbe River, which is today located in the Czech Republic and known as Vrchlabí. But in Victor's youth it was part of the Austro-Hungarian Empire and positioned at the fractious crossroads of various ethnic groups. Victor grew up in a very tribal German-speaking enclave known as the Sudetenland. Though his family was relatively prosperous, he had been born out of wedlock and had never known his father, a fact that had produced in him a sense of shame about his background that, according to his biographers Eda Shapiro and Rick Kardonne, accounted in part for his sympathy for outsiders.

As soon as he could, Victor left the Sudetenland, disgusted by the incipient blood-and-soil nationalism that would in a generation curdle into fascism, making the Sudeten Germans some of the most fanatical of Hitler's followers. He settled in the Netherlands in 1920. Before joining Opekta, he worked in the food business for a large bakery and restaurant supplier. On a business trip to Berlin in 1933, he saw firsthand the rise of Nazism: swastikas flying on every block, brownshirts "leading away little groups of men," kicking in the back those who did not move fast enough. When Victor returned to his birds in peaceable Holland, he said, "I was glad to come back home."

Little is known about Victor's wife, Laura Buntenbach, a sickly, shadowy presence throughout the Secret Annex period. The child of German immigrants to the Netherlands, she was born in 1895 in the small Dutch village of Neer. She married Kugler in 1928. Though "full secrecy" meant that no one outside the Circle could be told about the Annex, an exception was made in the case of Jo Kleiman's devoted wife, Johanna, who everyone on Prinsengracht believed could be trusted—and who eventually even visited the Secret Annex on the weekends. Yet Victor decided not to give his wife even a hint of the pressure he was under. He would claim later that he had kept Laura in the dark for her own good. "My wife was in poor health, and, not wishing to worry her, I did not tell her of the Secret Annex plans," he said.

Whatever the reasons, I think it must have been very hard keeping such a secret to oneself. Miep could talk about the Annex with her husband, Jan, since he had been in on the plot from the beginning. And my mother could unpack the events of the day with my grandfather. But Victor seemed to have no one to confide in, and his responsibility was in some respects the greatest of them all.

Victor would visit the Secret Annex on an almost daily basis, bringing not only magazines for Anne but newspapers and other necessities and trying to maintain the group's morale by being optimistic, which sometimes meant withholding bad news. To outsiders, he had to be convincing as the new figurehead of the company.

"I had to put on a good 'act' for Mr. Frank's former business associates, customers and neighbors," he said. Some he befriended; others he bribed or avoided altogether. "You constantly had to be able to react instantly. Comprehend matters immediately. You were the chess player who always had to be two moves ahead."

Anne wrote that the work of watching out for the eight of them sometimes left him speechless "from pent-up tension and strain." Under such stress, he could become touchy, occasionally venting his frustration at the Annex residents for their carelessness. He often thought they were taking too many risks: making noise during the day, leaving the Annex to roam about the office at night, when, they hoped, no one would be around to spot them.

In addition to running Opekta in Otto's absence and looking out for trouble, Victor managed to find counterfeit ration coupons, which he would give to my mother to buy food. But his most important role, according to Otto, was selling bulk orders of spices under the table so that he could pass the money on to the Annex residents, who were going broke from buying food and supplies at the usurious prices demanded by black marketeers. "Kugler never said a word to his wife during the whole two years," Otto said. "He kept it all to himself and bore everything alone; he is a nervous person himself and suffered from it."

Yet what was unknown to Otto and everyone else in 263 Prinsengracht was that Victor did have someone to turn to for help, understanding, and ultimately love: he had my mother. The romance between those two guardians of the Secret Annex had never been reported before Jeroen and I began the research that led to this book.

My mother first told me about her relationship with Victor when I was eighteen years old, although she made it seem like little more than an office flirtation. She was more candid with my aunt Diny—about how handsome Victor was, how smart a dresser, how gentle and kind, how they were able to understand each other "without words." It was the terrible pressure they were under that pushed Victor and Bep into each other's arms. Sometimes they would steal a kiss or allow themselves a silent embrace in the dark and cramped rear office where Kugler worked.

My mother told her sister Diny that though she could feel herself falling for Victor, their romance had been shackled from its inception. Though she did not know Victor's wife, Laura, she absolutely did not want to break up his marriage. Even more important: she did not want to cause conflict or intrigue among the members of the Circle. She and Victor had an understanding that whatever feelings existed between them would have to wait—till the end of the war, till Laura died, or perhaps indefinitely. There was too much at stake to take a chance on love.

VULNERABILITIES

From the moment the Annex was occupied, the helpers fretted over its security. Sounds rattled through the walls and pipes of the old canalside building. The rule inside the Annex was that the inhabitants had to whisper during the workday, and they had to wear slippers instead of shoes to muffle their footsteps. Yet despite such measures, arguments and even loud shouting would sometimes break out and echo loudly. The tension among the hiders was natural, with eight strong personalities sequestered in such a small space. Whenever my mother heard a row in progress, she would run up the *helperstrap* to tell everyone to quiet down.

We can hear you!

Despite her efforts to keep the peace, sometimes the voices would carry all the way down to the warehouse, where my grandfather worked. Whenever Johan overheard Anne squealing or a fight between Mr. van Pels and his wife, he would try to create a diversion. He would walk up to the closest warehouse worker and start screaming at the poor man for some imaginary infraction, trying desperately to drown out the noise.

An even bigger vulnerability than noise was the plain gray door leading to the Annex. Anyone who came to search the office would naturally wonder what lay beyond that door. And two years into the Occupation, raids on houses in Amsterdam were becoming more and more common. The Germans were rampaging through buildings looking not only for Jews but also for a particular kind of Dutch contraband: bicycles.

In the summer of 1942, the Nazis had ordered great numbers of Dutch people to turn in their bikes.* The request was unthinkable for most Amsterdammers, who considered the bicycle not only their primary mode of transportation but a source of identity. Yet the Germans claimed that their army urgently needed a hundred thousand bikes for the war effort. A huge roundup of bicycles in public storage sheds was scheduled for July 20, but most owners had been tipped off in advance and were able to hide their bikes the previous night.

Though Jewish residents of Amsterdam had been forced to give up their own bicycles even earlier in the Occupation, many had also flouted the order, including Peter van Pels, who kept his bicycle wrapped in paper on the wall of the little room where he slept in the Annex.

As the bicycle raids swept through Amsterdam, the helpers huddled to figure out how to better protect the Annex. According to Anne, it was Victor who thought it would be a good idea to have a bookcase built in front of the entrance to the hiding place.

The question then became: Who could build it? Everyone knew

---

* The so-called bike robberies were not quickly forgotten. In the postwar years, the phrase "First I want my bike back" became legendary and was chanted often during soccer games against Germany.

that Johan had a talent for carpentry. Jo Kleiman asked him whether he could rig something, and my grandfather said he would try. In August 1942, he began work at home, boiling glue on a gas range, erecting the bookcase in secret in the attic on Lumeijstraat.

In a normal house, the drafty space below the roof would have been used to store old furniture, clothing, and other odds and ends, but in the Voskuijl home there was no space to spare. Four of Johan's daughters—Willy, Nelly, and the twins, Diny and Gerda—slept in the attic. Attached to their room was a small walk-in closet that Johan kept locked during the day. He raised pigeons there, something that was forbidden by the Germans, but, my aunt Diny told me, "Father didn't care." The space was also Johan's workshop, the same place where he crafted toys for the children and Sinterklaas gifts for the hiders.

Johan could not tell anyone except my mother what he was up to during those hot weeks in August. After dinner, he would say to his wife, "Stien, I have to feed the pigeons," then disappear for a few hours without any explanation.

The girls could smell the glue cooking and hear the sawing and hammering. Just finding enough wood to build a large book-case during the war was no easy feat, yet somehow my grandfather managed it. The simple-looking piece of furniture concealed the ingenious mechanism that made it work: a hinge with a hidden catch that could be operated from either side of the door. To avoid arousing suspicion by transporting a large piece of furniture in the street, Johan dissembled the bookcase and smuggled it into Prinsengracht piece by piece, installing it there when no one was looking. A map of Belgium—nominally part of Opekta's territory—was hung above the bookcase, and ring binders were placed on the shelves so it looked like an ordinary filing cabinet. The result was that the entrance to the Annex was completely obscured.

"Things are getting very mysterious round here now," Anne noted impishly in her diary. "Now our Secret Annex has truly become secret."

My mother never spoke publicly about the bookcase, but years after the war she confessed to my aunt Diny that she had never felt prouder of their father than in the moment he agreed to take on the challenge despite the risks involved. The bookcase worked its magic. Over the next several months, a carpenter would brush up against it while doing repairs, and the police would examine it while searching the office after a burglary. Yet in neither case did anyone suspect what lay beyond those three wooden shelves.

CHAPTER 6

Sleepover

Though they meant no disrespect, the adults in the Secret Annex sometimes treated my mother a bit like a child: they lectured her, they pitied her, and always they gave her unsolicited advice along with their shopping lists. As the Annex residents grew to see Bep as a member of their extended family, Anne in particular felt an almost sisterly sense of protectiveness over her, a feeling of solidarity that came from dealing with overbearing grown-ups who, as Anne once put it, "don't understand the first thing about us!"

Much of the unsolicited advice given to my mother came from the loud mouth of Auguste van Pels, the quarrelsome, high-strung, tenderhearted matriarch of the other family who lived in the Annex. Mrs. van Pels had fled Germany in 1937. Though she had Dutch nationality through her husband's family, who came from Groningen, she never had more than a shaky grasp of the Dutch language. Yet that did not keep her from speaking freely about Bep's love life.

She would tell Bep, for instance, that she should not wait around until another woman scooped up the eligible bachelor who, until the outbreak of the war, had worked in Opekta's warehouse, a handsome young man by the name of Henk van Beusekom. Never mind that Bep wasn't interested in him; that Henk never seemed to take notice of her; or that she might have dreamed of settling down with someone who had more to offer than a factory worker, someone who could pull her out of the mire of Lumeijstraat.

When word of Henk's engagement to a woman named Aagje Pronk reached the Annex in March 1944, Mrs. van Pels tried to use the news as a teachable moment, lecturing my mother about how she should have made her move when she had the chance. As Mrs. van Pels spoke at the lunch table, Anne watched Bep shrink further and further into herself. After they had finished eating, when my mother had finally returned downstairs to the office, Anne decided to give Mrs. van Pels a piece of her mind. "I don't understand, Mrs. v.P., why you keep saying these things about Henk to Bep all the time. I find it incomprehensible that you don't realize how unpleasant it is for Bep."

It was characteristic of Anne to be blunt, to say what was on her mind, even if it might ruffle feathers. My mother told me that Anne "always had an opinion—an uncompromising opinion. It was either this or that." She used the word "explosive" to describe Anne's personality. Such bracing candor was a quality that my mother did not possess herself but that she seemed to admire.

Mrs. van Pels blushed, not expecting such impertinence from a teenager. "Surely I know best what to say to Bep; if she finds it unpleasant, she shouldn't talk about Henk so much herself!"

Yet Anne did not back down. Recalling the event in her diary later, she said her rejoinder to Mrs. van Pels had been calculated to be "rather disdainful and cool": "All I know is that Bep finds this sort of talk very disagreeable!" Then she stormed off.

The diary is full of such moments in which Anne rushed to the defense of "Elli," as Bep was called in the first published version of the diary. Taken together, they have given readers the understandable impression that my mother was too shy to stand up for herself. The truth, however, is that Anne, an adolescent with keen observational powers but also a vivid imagination, sometimes exaggerated such moments and often assumed that Bep's silence betrayed a wounded heart, when in fact she was merely being respectful and attentive.

Though Anne's description in the diary often paints Mrs. van Pels as a nettlesome character, my mother remembered a different woman: courteous, kind, and dignified. She also thought of Edith Frank as a caring and nurturing mother and told me she had been "surprised" to read how harshly Anne sometimes treated her in the diary. A striking example is Anne's reaction to a conversation between Edith Frank and Bep that took place in the spring of 1944.

My mother was doing the dishes in the Annex. She was exhausted and depressed, worn down by all the work she had to do—in the office, in the Annex, and at home caring for her sisters. Washing up in the kitchen with Mrs. Frank and Mrs. van Pels, she confessed that she felt discouraged. Would the war ever end? Was there any hope for the future? Unlike many girls her age, she was still unmarried.

Anne overheard the conversation, and she anxiously waited to see how the two older and presumably wiser women would reply.

What help did those two offer her? Our tactless mother, especially, only made things go from bad to worse. Do you know what her advice was? That she should think about all the other people in the world who are suffering! How can thinking about the misery of others help if you're miserable yourself? I said as much. Their response, of course, was that I should stay out of conversations of this sort. . . . Oh, I wish I could have said something to poor Bep, something that I know from my own experience would have helped. But Father came between us, pushing me roughly aside.

Anne was, of course, much younger than my mother, but she seemed more comfortable playing the role of the big sister. As the months in seclusion wore on, my mother was astonished to find herself relying more and more on the chatty fourteen-year-old and her open heart. One day in the Annex, when my mother nearly fainted from exhaustion, Anne came running up to her with eau-de-cologne to revive her.

"She sat by my side like a real little mother," Bep recalled in a letter to Otto years after the war. Whenever she felt low, Anne was always there to raise her spirits. "Isn't that remarkable for such a young girl?"

Yet just as Anne protected Bep, my mother would more than return the favor. Her special talent was being able to calm Anne down when no one else could. I remember a story my mother told me that was never recorded in Anne's diary. The Franks had gotten into an argument over some now-forgotten subject, and Anne butted in to give her unvarnished opinion—"she certainly had a sharp tongue," my mother said—but before she could finish speaking, Otto sternly cut her off.

More than anything, Anne hated being shut up. She burst into tears and ran to her room. When neither Edith nor Margot followed, Bep took it as her cue to step in. As Anne sat on her bed, tears streaming down her face, my mother walked up to her and—either because of the pent-up stress they were both under or because of some deep empathic connection between them—she spontaneously started crying as well. Then my mother bundled the girl in her arms and to the surprise of both of them began to dance, twirling and bopping around the tiny room. In seconds, tears were replaced with hilarious laughter.

As Bep left Anne's room, Otto motioned for her to come over. "What on earth have you done with Anne?" he asked. "She goes to her room crying and emerges all smiles!"

Bep knew how to deal with Anne's tantrums; they reminded her of her younger sisters'. But there was also something about Anne's nature that seemed to make her wise far beyond her years. After the war, my mother wrote to Otto that she had always admired Anne "because she was the youngest and those difficult circumstances must have been terribly strenuous to her. But she never let this be noticed, she didn't complain, was always cheerful, joked, was satisfied, and settled in her fate with the sensibility of a grown girl."

The thing that my mother admired most was the way Anne used her irrepressible zest for life and her storyteller's curiosity to experience the period of captivity not as a prison sentence to be endured but as "one big adventure." My mother once said that Anne had an "unwavering confidence in the future" and never doubted that she and the other hiders would make it through the Occupation unscathed. It was not a matter of *if* but *when*. During their private conversations, Anne spoke without any inhibitions about life "after the war": the babies she would have, the career as a writer she would pursue. In her diary, she even composed a list of things she would do right after being liberated.

"Ah, the plans we made in those days!" my mother reflected wistfully years later.

PORTRAIT OF THE AUTHOR

A turning point in my mother's relationship with Anne Frank came on October 30, 1942. That night, Bep joined the family for dinner and, after dessert, Anne refused to let her leave. She begged her to spend the night *just this once*. Surprising them both, Bep agreed to an impromptu slumber party in the Secret Annex.

Before bedtime, my mother sat with Anne and Margot, chatting quietly, and at one point the subject turned to Anne's writing. Margot asked permission to read out loud something her sister had written— not her diary, but a fairy tale written with such verve and imagination that Bep was amazed it had come out of Anne's head.

Though she had only just begun to write in her diary, Anne was beginning to experiment with short fiction as well. Most of the early drafts of her stories were composed on loose sheets of paper that have since been lost, although a few were written in the pages of her diary. Over the next several months, she would revise the stories, and sometime in 1943, she would copy the more or less finished versions into a notebook. The thirty-four stories were later published in English as *Tales from the Secret Annex.*[*]

Anne's earliest stories were romantic and a bit childish, written in the style of the young adult novels from the 1920s and '30s that she loved to read. Yet for a girl of her age, they were quite accomplished. Some were clearly autobiographical, such as "Kaatje," a tale about a young girl who had a black cat (just like Anne's cat, Moortje) and who was punished in school for being an incurable chatterbox (just like Anne). Other stories were fantasies, such as "The Fairy," about a young girl with magical powers named Ellen. When her parents died, she inherited their fortune and dedicated the rest of her life to sharing her wealth with others.

My mother was surprised when Anne asked her if she could help her find a way to get some of the stories into print. She must have had no idea how to publish the fairy tales of a thirteen-year-old girl in wartime, but the question would stick with her. It meant that even in the early days of Anne's writing life, long before she had conceived of the project that would turn into *Het Achterhuis*, she was writing with an audience in mind. Yet in 1942, Anne's commitment to writing was still only developing. Though she enjoyed scribbling in her diary—and began addressing her entries to several imaginary correspondents, including the now-famous "Kitty"—sometimes she wouldn't write in it for weeks at a time. And her entries were much shorter than they would be in the coming years.

Throughout the war, my mother played an important role in Anne's literary production by supplying her with notebooks, paper, and writing materials—and when she could not find these things in stores, she would give the young girl extra supplies from the office, in-

---

[*] The stories were first published in the Netherlands in 1949, two years after the Diary itself appeared.

cluding carbon paper that Anne would later use to revise her journal. Bep never witnessed Anne actually writing, as she carefully screened her notes from the eyes of others. She also liked to announce in the Annex that she was going off to write, in the hope that it would prevent her fellow hiders from entering her room unexpectedly.

"Her diary was her greatest secret," my mother said.

Nevertheless, Anne was proud of her work and occasionally showed off a diary passage that she thought my mother simply had to read. That was especially true late in the war, when Anne was revising her journal with an eye toward publishing after the Liberation. My mother told me that she vividly recalled reading Anne's description of July 5, 1942, the day Margot had received her summons to go to a "work camp" in Germany, the day before the family went into hiding.

My mother was not an intellectual—but she was a reader. I remember that she would tear through thick paperback novels in a matter of days. And she cherished her copy of the famous Dutch encyclopedia *Winkler Prins*, which she sometimes spent hours flipping through. She particularly liked articles on geography. I think she enjoyed reading about places she could not visit herself. She also kept a box with note cards on which she wrote down quotations from books and poems that she liked. Anne had done something similar in her *Mooie-zinnenboek* (Book of Beautiful Sentences), which she wrote in a blank ledger likely given to her by my mother.

Whatever her literary sensibility, Bep had enough sensitivity to recognize something in Anne's words that was exceptional. In a postwar letter to Otto, she recalled the first time she had heard Anne's prose during that sleepover in the Annex: "I couldn't believe what I was hearing. I could not believe that Anne had written those words. I can still see Margot's face: *Yes, Anne wrote these all by herself.*"

As much as my mother encouraged Anne's literary ambitions, she knew that the girl often recorded details of their intimate conversations—things my mother told her in confidence about her love life, her family, even her efforts to find food on the black market. If the Annex was ever raided and the diary fell into the wrong hands, such passages could prove extremely dangerous.

My mother tried to encourage Anne to be more discreet about such matters in the diary, but she eventually realized that her efforts were in vain. All she could do was warn the other people in the Secret Annex that they'd better be careful: "You shouldn't tell her so much. She writes everything down in her diary!"

A PRETTY QUIET GIRL

The sleepover occurred a few weeks before Anne's roommate, Fritz Pfeffer, moved into the Secret Annex. At the time, Anne was sharing her room with Margot. Bep slept on an air mattress between the two girls' narrow beds. Anne's bed was actually a chaise, less than five feet long, with a pair of chairs placed at the end for the girl's growing feet. There would have been so little space between the beds that my mother would hardly have been able to turn in her sleep.

She must have tried to put on a brave face. After all, she was older than Margot and Anne, more mature, so she should have been tougher. Yet when the lights went out, she had to use every bit of strength to keep from panicking. She couldn't handle the noises outside, the creaky beams and pipes that echoed through the wooden floors, the gusts of wind blowing over the canal, the sound of a car in the distance that seemed to be getting closer and closer. Every fifteen minutes she was startled by the ringing of the clock in the Westerkerk tower. Years later she would remember that night in the Annex as "horrifying."

Yet it wasn't only the tight quarters and the creepy noises, the idea that men in jackboots could be coming for them, that kept my mother awake that night. Just a few weeks earlier, she had made a decision, perhaps thoughtlessly, to tell Anne that one of her schoolmates, Bertha "Betty" Bloemendal, had recently been rounded up in a raid and deported to Poland. We don't know how Anne reacted to the news, the look on her face when my mother told her, but we know that Betty was the first person whom Anne knew personally who had been sent to the camps and that the "horrible" news weighed heavily on the young girl. Anne wrote that she felt guilty for being comparatively "so well off" in the Secret Annex.

Betty had been one of Anne's classmates during the 1941–1942 school year at the Joods Lyceum, the Jewish secondary school that Anne had been forced to attend after she had been kicked out of her Montessori school. Just a few months earlier, in June 1942, Betty had been eating cake and laughing with Anne's other friends at her thirteenth birthday party, the same birthday for which Anne had received her red-checkered diary.

Anne described all her classmates in her diary, and she painted a sad portrait of Betty as a striving girl from a poor family who struggled to fit in: "Betty Bloemendaal [sic] looks kind of poor, and I think she probably is. . . . She does very well at school, but that's because she works so hard, not because she's so smart. She's pretty quiet." And that was it. A photograph from the early 1940s shows Betty, with dark hair, squinting in a floral jumper as she sits on the grass, her big brother kneeling at her side.

Betty lived in a second-floor apartment in Amsterdam West with her parents and brother. Her Polish-born mother was a housewife; her father was a clerk in an insurance company. Her family was more religious than the Franks, although they lived in a mostly Gentile neighborhood, with only one small synagogue and a few scattered Jewish neighbors. The Bloemendal home was just one street over from Lumeijstraat, and every day my mother rode her bike past Betty's block on her way to work.

If my mother did not see the raid in which Betty and her family were arrested with her own eyes, she would have heard about it from her mother, Christina, who had friends on Betty's block who kept a close eye on everything that happened on the street.

The Nazis had begun actively rounding up Jews in Amsterdam in the summer of 1942, following the general order for all Jewish residents in the Netherlands to report themselves. Many Jews had ignored the order or gone into hiding. Husbands were sometimes arrested separately from wives and children, but they would all usually be reunited at Westerbork, the notorious transit camp in northeastern Holland that served as a relay station for the concentration and death camps in the east.

By all accounts, the September raid in which Betty was arrested was typical. Suddenly, police vans would come to a screeching halt in front of a chosen address, and then hordes of men in navy tunics (the Dutch policemen) and green uniforms (the Germans) would emerge. Sometimes people screamed and panicked; other times they were preternaturally calm. A raid could happen in the morning, in the afternoon, in the evening, or late at night. Sometimes Jews were literally lifted from their beds.

Anne couldn't have witnessed such raids from the window on Prinsengracht, but she had cobbled together enough information about them—some based on facts, others on rumors—to describe them in all their terror: "No one is spared. The sick, the elderly, children, babies and pregnant women—all are marched to their death."

By the time Anne and Bep lay down on their little beds in the Secret Annex, Betty's march had already come to its end. On October 1, 1942, immediately after arriving at Auschwitz, she was murdered in the gas chambers along with her mother and fourteen-year-old brother. Anne already knew at that point what it meant to be "packed off to Poland," as she put it, and she knew how many of her former classmates were on the verge of sharing Betty's fate. "I feel wicked sleeping in a warm bed, while somewhere out there my dearest friends are dropping from exhaustion or being knocked to the ground," she wrote.

No matter how depressing the news, Anne and the other hiders always tried to stay positive. Yet as word of more deportations filtered into the Annex over the fall of 1942, the mood of the residents became inescapably gloomy.

"Every now and then Miep used to mention what had happened to a friend, and Mother or [Mrs. van Pels] would start to cry," Anne wrote, "so [Miep] decided it was better not to say any more."

My mother must have made a similar decision. After the news about Betty, Anne never again reported that Bep told her about actions against Jews, even as more and more of them were deported. Instead, the stories Anne heard from Bep that made their way into the diary were almost exclusively about happier, or at least lighter, subjects: drama in the Voskuijl family, gossip from the milkman, a new hairstyle that my mother was trying out, concerts, weddings, or films she went to, and of course her love life.

Yet Anne and the other residents of the Annex didn't need the helpers to know what was happening to the Jews. They had a radio tuned to the BBC, which on July 9, 1942, had reported that Jews in Nazi-occupied territories "are regularly killed by machine-gun fire, hand grenades, and even poisoned by gas." In an interview that Bep gave in the late 1970s, she also said that Dutch journalists had been able to sneak past the Nazi censors hints about the death camps, which people could understand by reading "between the lines."

In other words, there was no way my mother or the other helpers could have kept the residents of the Annex from knowing what was in store for them if the Nazis discovered the hiding place.

"They knew everything," my mother said. "At least they suspected everything."

CHAPTER 7

One Small Act of Carelessness

Anne called it a "disaster." In May 1943, my grandfather Johan went into the hospital to have surgery for an ulcer. He had been suffering from stomach trouble for years. Usually, he just gritted his teeth and "carried on," as was his motto in the face of any difficulty. But at some point, the pain got worse. He would keel over in the warehouse or have coughing attacks after grinding a batch of nutmeg or pepper.

When the doctors cut his stomach open, they found a large malignant tumor—"a carcinoma, the size of the palm"—which was "clearly festering" and deemed "inoperable." So they just sewed him back up and, after explaining to the fifty-one-year-old that he probably had only months left to live, sent him home. Anne thought it had been "an unforgivable error" for him to be told that his situation was hopeless; now all he could do was brood over his imminent death. Yet as sorry as my grandfather felt for himself, I think what truly ate him up inside was the knowledge that because he could no longer continue his job as warehouse manager, he could no longer protect the Secret Annex.

In the end, Johan Voskuijl would live a bit longer than his doctors expected. He survived until the Liberation and died in November 1945, four years before I was born. Though we never got the chance to meet, I've always felt a special connection to him. I remember learning about his role as the self-appointed watchman of the Annex when I was fifteen years old. There was a man about my father's age who lived next door to us, a friend of the family we called *Ome* (Uncle) Piet. He taught me how to play chess. I loved seeing the pieces dance across their black-and-white board, and once I learned how each one moved, I could somehow think several steps ahead.

Ome Piet had played this game his entire life, but it took only about ten games for me to beat him.

"You're just like your grandfather," my mother told me.

Johan had also been a skilled chess player, and he had also been someone who always thought several steps ahead. He didn't only build and reinforce the bookcase that camouflaged the entrance to the Annex. He didn't only keep watch downstairs and covertly dispose of the rubbish from the Annex. He also cultivated a network of like-minded gossipers around Prinsengracht whom he would visit on his lunch break. That "little crew of loyal informants," as my mother put it, kept track of the movements of people on the street. They told Johan what the neighbors were up to, who was smiling at the Germans, who might have been feeding information to the police. Johan's spies kept him abreast of the Nazis' mobile checkpoints, enabling him to safely guide Bep and Miep on their shopping trips.

Anne called my grandfather "our greatest source of help and support when it came to safety measures," and now he was gone from the office. Otto seemed to be most affected by the news of Johan's illness. Comforting the sick came naturally to Otto. On that frightful Sunday when the Franks received the deportation order for Margot—the very letter that caused the family to go into hiding—Otto was making a goodwill visit to the De Joodsche Invalide, a Jewish nursing home.

In July 1943, just a few months after Johan's diagnosis, the hiders played a game in which they discussed the first thing that each of them would do if they somehow regained their freedom. Most of the Annex residents, quite understandably, chose to indulge in some personal pleasure long denied them. Margot and Hermann van Pels wanted to take a hot bath. Mrs. van Pels wanted to taste a freshly baked cream cake. The dentist Fritz Pfeffer wanted to be reunited with his beloved wife, Charlotte (who, as a Christian, did not have to hide from the Nazis). Edith Frank wanted a real cup of coffee. Peter wanted to spend a night on the town and watch a movie in a theater. Anne wanted to do so many things at once that, she wrote in her diary, "I wouldn't know where to begin." But Otto Frank said that the very first thing he would do after stepping into the blue light of Amsterdam would be to visit my sick grandfather at home.

SIDELINED

My aunt Willy said that for her and her seven siblings, the news of their father's illness was "almost impossible to digest." Willy's sister Diny, who was eleven in 1943, remembered that Johan came home from the hospital looking as "pale as a sheet." He was understandably depressed, but there was a smoldering edge to his depression, as though he was outraged to be sidelined so early in the game. Diny remembered the disgusted look on her father's face as he stared down at the dinner his wife prepared one night. He took three bites, then pushed the plate away. "That's all, Stien."

Diny's memories from that period are as specific as they are traumatic. She vividly recalls feeling the blood drain from her head when she saw her father for the first time after his surgery at the Binnengasthuis hospital in central Amsterdam. The sight of him in so much pain made her throw up and lose consciousness. In the coming weeks, she tried her best to make sense of what was happening, to comfort not only her dying father but also her increasingly hopeless mother.

"The two of them didn't talk with each other anymore," Diny said of her parents. "And I remember I got on Mother's lap and she let me slip off—she didn't feel like it. So I thought, *Then I go to Father*. He was sitting on the other side of the table. I felt so sorry for him—he looked terribly pale. I thought, *My goodness, how sick you are!* So I got on his lap and said, 'Father, I really love you. You'll always be my father!'"

When Diny was recalling that part of the story to me, some seventy years later, she broke down in tears. I think it was remembering Johan's reaction that made her so emotional. After she told her father how much she loved him, he barely said a word. Johan's idea of fatherhood was to embody everything solid, strong, and upright; if he did not know what to say, it was better to say nothing. This self-destructive reticence is a family trait, and unfortunately, it was something that Johan passed on.

My grandfather's illness had at least one positive consequence; it caused my grandmother to become less aggressive toward her husband. A measure of peace grew up between the warring partners. My grandmother must have realized, however enormous her worries about the future of her family, that there was nothing more her husband could do to help.

As for their daughter Bep, she was heartbroken. She was Johan's eldest child and the one who understood him the best. Their relationship had only deepened when they had become coworkers and coconspirators. Yet my mother hadn't the time that spring to comfort Johan or to process her own pain. There were problems everywhere she turned. The black market was drying up, which made finding enough food for the Annex almost impossible. Several of her colleagues were out sick: Miep had a bad cold, and Jo Kleiman had stomach troubles, likely a result of the stress he was under. It was left to Bep to keep the office running, all the while making sure that the hiders who depended on her for their survival had everything they needed. Often they would send her out several times a day, exploiting her natural kindness and risking her safety.

In September 1943, she collapsed from the stress. "A nervous fit," wrote Anne, who immediately went to my mother's side to provide comfort and advice. She encouraged her to "put her foot down" and say "no" once in a while, and then "the shopping lists would shrink of their own accord." But my mother was like her father; she didn't complain. Her only real relief would come later that fall, in the form of diphtheria. The doctor ordered six weeks of bed rest. It must have felt to my mother like a vacation. During that time, Miep and the others covered for her. Anne wrote that she missed my mother's companionship.

THE MAN DOWNSTAIRS

The man who replaced my grandfather as warehouse manager was named Willem van Maaren. The only known photographs of him, published in a Dutch tabloid newspaper in the early 1960s, show a scowling old man in glasses chomping on a cigar.* Van Maaren started working at Opekta when he was forty-seven. He had previously run a cigarette shop. Victor and Jo knew that he had experience working in a warehouse, but what they didn't know was that he had been fired from his previous job for stealing. Shortly after van Maaren showed up at Prinsengracht, he started snooping around the office. He *noticed* things: the sound of footsteps, the way the cat's empty drinking bowl seemed to be miraculously filled during the night. He began to set little traps, leaving pencils on the edges of door frames to see if anyone was entering the warehouse after dark. He even once, according to a story my mother told my brother Cok, placed a pencil on the top of the bookcase, indicating that he suspected it was a hidden door.

---

* The pictures, which seem to have been taken secretly, were published in 1964 in the Dutch tabloid *Revue* alongside an article about how the Amsterdam Criminal Investigation Department was reopening the case into the betrayal of the Secret Annex. At the time, Willem van Maaren was considered a major suspect.

Soon inventory began to go missing: baking soda, jam, potato flour. Whoever the thief was, he must have had a key or a way of accessing the building, since there was never a sign of forced entry. When Kugler asked van Maaren to explain the thefts, he tried to pin them on my mother.

"He spreads the most barefaced lies about her," Anne wrote.

My mother was outraged, and she told Jo Kleiman she wished they could slip poison into van Maaren's coffee. He posed a grave danger, yet she knew she had to tread very carefully in dealing with him. The two of them had regular contact, as she was the one responsible for paying van Maaren's wages and writing up the orders that he and the workers in the warehouse had to fill. She found his behavior alternately distant and threatening and his attitude toward his coworkers "unsympathetic."

Van Maaren always presented himself as the victim, an innocent colleague whose feelings were hurt because he was perpetually left outside the circle of trust for no apparent reason. He could sense, my mother said, that she and the others were hiding a secret from him. Sheer curiosity, or perhaps something more sinister, drove him to discover what it was.

Anne noted ominously that you didn't have to be Hercule Poirot to realize that something fishy was going on. "A person with any brains" would have noticed that Opekta's employees were always making flimsy excuses for why they had to disappear into the bowels of the building several times a day. Miep claimed she had some mysterious "work" to do in the laboratory, Bep was always searching for "files" that were never found, and so on. It was only natural for him to be suspicious.

One morning, van Maaren appeared in Kugler's office holding a man's wallet. "Is this your wallet, Mr. Kugler?"

Van Maaren had found it lying near the scale in the warehouse. Hermann van Pels, the night before, had been roaming around downstairs after all the employees had left for the day. A portly man who watched his weight, van Pels must have removed his wallet before stepping on the scale to weigh himself and forgotten to pick it up again. It was unclear whether the wallet contained his identity papers—with the telltale *J* marking him as a Jew—but, according to Anne, it contained about 100 guilders in cash.

Kugler stared at the wallet and turned pale when he realized that it belonged to van Pels. "Oh, yes, of course!" he said, taking it from van Maaren. "I must have left it there last night." When Kugler returned the wallet to Mr. van Pels, they discovered that the 100 guilders was missing—a devastating blow for the cash-strapped family. They assumed that van Maaren had pocketed the money for himself.

As van Maaren grew nosier, his coworkers became more careful. Kugler began to try to conceal his comings and goings, even appearing to leave once on an errand during his lunch break only to stealthily double back to 263 Prinsengracht, sneak through the ground-floor doorway (avoiding van Maaren, who was in the office), and then take the long staircase that led directly up to the Annex. An hour later, he tiptoed down the *helperstrap* to return to the office for the afternoon, but my mother, hearing his footsteps, met him in the corridor. "Not now," she whispered. "Van Maaren's still here."

So Victor turned around and waited with the Franks for another thirty minutes or so before finally making a run for it. Rather than risk returning to the office, he removed his shoes and walked back down the long stairway in his socks until he reached the door facing the street, where, presumably, he put his shoes back on.

"What must the passersby have thought when they saw the manager putting on his shoes outside?" Anne wrote. "Hey, you there, in the socks!"

By the spring of 1944, both the Annex residents and their helpers realized that something had to be done about van Maaren. He was a major security risk; they had traded their protector for a predator.

Could they fire him? They wanted to, but such action was deemed "too risky." It would confirm his suspicions and give him the motive to air his grievances. Anne understood the risks of eliminating van Maaren, but she wondered, "Isn't it even riskier to leave things as they are?" In the end, all they could do was redouble their efforts at concealment. There could be no more mistakes. "One small act of carelessness," Anne wrote, "and we're done for!"

The tension in the Annex became almost unbearable in that period. After my mother recovered from diphtheria and returned to work, she joined the Franks for dinner one night. There was a loud clang at the door. It was nothing, maybe an old pipe, but Anne turned white, her stomach twisted in knots, and her heart beat wildly. I have no idea what, if anything, my mother could have said to reassure her in that moment, but I'm sure she tried.

As for my grandfather, lying at home at Lumeijstraat, his condition was quickly deteriorating. In April 1944, Anne noted that he had been running a temperature of almost 104 degrees for more than ten days. "They think the cancer has spread to his lungs. The poor man, we'd so like to help him, but only God can help him now!"

RUMOR MILL

Van Maaren wasn't the only source of danger lurking in the building. There was also a suspicious cleaning lady named Lena van Bladeren. She was married to Lammert Hartog, who worked with van Maaren grinding and packing spices down in the warehouse. (Because he had ignored a summons for forced labor in Germany, he was technically working at Opekta illegally, making his position vulnerable.) My mother once described Lena to me as a "simple, pushy woman" with an appetite for gossip, and she spent a lot of time with her husband and van Maaren talking together in the warehouse.

Lena would visit my mother every two weeks to collect her wages for cleaning Opekta's offices. At one point in July 1944, Lena asked her straight out whether people were hiding in 263 Prinsengracht. Around that time, Lena asked the same question of Anna Genot, an acquaintance of Jo Kleiman whose house she also cleaned. Lena said she was asking only out of fear. She believed that if it was discovered that fugitives were sheltering in the building, everyone who worked there, including herself and her husband, might be in danger.

My mother told Lena that she was only imagining things, that no one was hiding in the building. But Lena's comments meant one of two very unpleasant things: either van Maaren was airing his suspicions down in the warehouse, or there was more than one source of rumors about the Annex. Either way, the news was devastating.

My mother and the other helpers put their heads together. Were they now sitting ducks? Was the existence of the Annex an open secret in the neighborhood? Or were they exaggerating the risks, paying too much attention to idle gossip? They talked about moving the hiders from the building on Prinsengracht, but that seemed practically impossible and far too dangerous. The summer sun didn't set until 10:00 p.m., and there were countless Nazi informants lurking who made a living out of denouncing their neighbors. How on earth could they smuggle eight people out of the building unseen?

The helpers decided, once again, that all they could do was do nothing. They had made it this far—if they could only hold on a little bit longer. Yet they also decided not to tell Otto and the other hiders about Lena's ominous questions. They knew, as Victor Kugler wrote in a 1964 letter to Otto Frank, that "if the secret was already known in our neighborhood, it would soon be circling throughout the whole city." But until they found a solution, they assumed that telling the hiders would only cause them unnecessary stress.

As Kugler put it in his letter to Otto, "Mr. Kleiman thought it was better not to tell you about it for the time being, so as not to worry you. But then, it was all suddenly over."

A few years after the war, my mother sat down with the German writer Ernst Schnabel, who authored one of the first historical accounts of the Secret Annex. There are strengths and weaknesses to his 1958 book, *The Footsteps of Anne Frank*, but one of its great strengths is that he reached many people before the diary became a world-famous document, while the details were still fresh in everyone's minds. Among the people whom he spoke to was my mother, who, despite her proximity to the story, gave very few interviews over her lifetime for reasons that will soon become evident.

My mother told Schnabel that as much as the helpers and the hiders could try to keep the secret from being discovered, the math was never in their favor. "Twenty-five months [is] a long time," she said, "and eight persons are eight individuals. If each one of them committed a single slip each year, that would be sixteen telltale signs. How many would van Maaren have needed?"

Van Maaren or Lena van Bladeren or, for that matter, anyone else.

CHAPTER 8

Invasion Fever

April 15, 1944, was a warm spring day in Amsterdam. The temperature reached 65 degrees Fahrenheit, and the light wind from the south carried the scent of cherry blossoms. It was Saturday, a half day of work at Opekta. On her way into the office, my mother must have wanted to share that lovely day with the people locked inside, so she stopped at a florist and picked out a bouquet of narcissus for the Annex as well as a bunch of grape hyacinths meant especially for Anne.

It was Anne's second spring in hiding. Through the window, the fourteen-year-old girl (who would turn fifteen in two months) could see the chestnut tree in bloom, and she thought it was even more beautiful than the year before. There was still much to worry about: the shifty van Maaren down in the warehouse, the impossibility of finding decent food, the ever-encircling enemy, the daily deprivations. Yet the spring of 1944 also seemed like a time of hope, of possibility.

"Every day I feel myself maturing, I feel liberation drawing near," Anne wrote. She was struck in that period by the simple beauty of nature, by the goodness of the people around her, even by the excitement of the drama she was living through. She felt that its long-awaited dénouement, the happy ending, would be coming soon.

On the English radio she heard her beloved Queen Wilhelmina describe the royal return as imminent. The war was turning in the Allies' favor. Since the Soviet victory in Stalingrad, the Russians had been clawing their way across Eastern Europe, and it seemed like only a matter of time before the Allies made their long-hoped-for invasion a reality. When it finally happened, on the beaches of Normandy on June 6, 1944, everyone in the Annex embraced.

"Oh, Kitty," Anne wrote, "the best part about the invasion is that I have the feeling that friends are on the way."

She wondered whether the war could be over before the end of the year, even whether she might be back in school by the fall. Her excitement in that period was not only about the future, which appeared bright, but also about the present, which was enchanted by the new feeling of being in love. Anne had earlier dismissed the "shy, awkward boy" upstairs, Peter van Pels, saying his company "won't amount to much." Peter read little, spending most of his time lazing on his bed, doing chores in the attic, and taking an occasional English lesson from Otto.

Though Anne had my mother and her diary to confide in, she was still starved for human connection. She always yearned for a sympathetic ear, for understanding and consolation. In the spring of 1944, she started making nightly visits to Peter's room. As the two teenagers spoke, she noticed a new quality in his "dark blue eyes," a strange force pulling her toward him. They sat for hours discussing religion, family, what they would do when the war came to an end. Peter dreamed of running far away, of living on a plantation in the Dutch East Indies, where "no one would ever know he was Jewish"; Anne wanted to study in Paris, maybe London, and to work hard as a journalist before she made her name as "a famous writer."

It was Anne who made the first move. She had never been kissed before. She felt the experience aged her in some profound way, that the silly "overconfident [and] amusing" little girl was now taking a back seat to a "second Anne"—gentler, more affectionate, a girl "who wants only to love." She knew that Peter, poor, unassuming, shy Peter, needed tenderness in his life, perhaps even more than she did.

Yet as she got closer to him, as she looked into his soul, expecting to find some hidden depths, she saw only shallows. She began to think about her ideal husband and how much Peter fell short of the ideal.

"Anne, be honest! You wouldn't be able to marry him."

My mother told me that Anne never would have fallen in love with Peter van Pels "if there had been a wide selection." He was "a sweet boy," my mother said, but they were driven into each other's arms "by circumstance." And although Peter was three years older than Anne, my mother told me that Anne was actually "so much more mature than him." She described their relationship as little more than puppy love, the kind of sentimental education that is formative in the life of an adolescent but that in most people's lives is later subsumed by more serious and meaningful connections.

Yet curiously Anne thought there was something about the experience of feeling both attracted to and repelled by Peter that made her understand my mother's own love story, which had recently taken a dramatic turn. "Oh, now I understand Bep," she wrote on April 28, 1944. "Now, now that I'm going through it myself, I understand her doubts."

"A TRUE GENTLEMAN"

Throughout the Annex period, while my mother was in love with her much older colleague Victor, there was another man in her life. His name was Bertus Hulsman, and he was the source of the great "doubts" mentioned in Anne's diary. A "nice, steady, athletic young man"—that was how Anne described him. He had been born in Amsterdam in 1918, a year before my mother, and, like her, he came from a poor family and didn't have much in the way of schooling. Before the war, he had served in the Dutch Army and then worked as a printer for a newspaper, and after the war he worked as a doorman at a Heineken beer hall.

Bertus liked music and he liked girls, which together explained his enthusiasm for dancing. My mother met him in 1939 at the Instituut H. Eyckholt, a well-known dance school in central Amsterdam. Bertus was in a carefree mood in those days, footloose and in search of a date. He and my mother paired up during class one night, and Bertus was struck by how gentle and especially cheerful she was. I barely recognized the effervescent woman he described; it was my mother before the war, before the losses of the Annex had sapped her spirit.

"When I'd tell the occasional double entendre, she would laugh heartily," he told me. "I can still picture the details of her face. Beppie wore glasses, and when she took them off, I'd say: 'Love, you've got beautiful eyes!'" After class, Bertus walked my mother home to Lumeijstraat, escorting her to the door "like a true gentleman."

Growing up, I never heard much about Bertus. When I would ask my mother about her love life before she had met my father, she would always turn red and clam up. Once when I pressed, she told me there had been someone, "a handsome, tough guy with a great sense of humor—but it didn't work out." Yet I never realized until I spoke to Bertus myself, seventy-five years after he had dated my mother, how close they had actually come to ending up together and how the Secret Annex, in many respects, had stood in their way.

"Joop," he told me the first time we met, "you could've been my son."

In 2014, while researching this book, Jeroen and I tracked down Bertus Hulsman through a stroke of luck. He happened to give an interview to the in-house newspaper at his Amsterdam nursing home, which we discovered via Google. The article mentioned that during the war, Bertus had nearly married Bep Voskuijl, one of the guardians of the Secret Annex.

Bertus had just moved into the nursing home and was overjoyed to have a visitor and an opportunity to share his story. When my wife, Ingrid, and I emerged from the elevator and saw the towering old man in his crisp white shirt and ironed jeans, he held his arms wide open and embraced us like his lost children. At ninety-five, he appeared full of life—and it was easy for me to picture that sweet and playful character cracking jokes on the dance floor a lifetime before.

Contrary to the dim-witted jock Anne described in her journal, Bertus struck me as being quite intelligent, and he had a direct, plain-spoken way of expressing himself that made him a natural storyteller. He had lost touch with my mother after the war, but the Secret Annex had always remained close to his heart. He carried a photo of Anne Frank in his wallet and took his three children on annual visits to the Anne Frank House. "And all those times I had this odd feeling when I was buying my tickets. I thought, *Do I have to pay for this, just like everyone else?* After all, I had been there before all those millions."

I couldn't immediately understand what Bertus meant by that. And I had no idea during that first meeting that he would help me unlock some of my family's long-hidden secrets. At the time I was most interested in his perspective on my mother's wartime love life. Millions of readers had read about the ups and downs of my mother's relationship with him in the published edition of Anne's diary (where he was given the name Dirk), but here was a living witness whose own account had been missing for generations.

Bertus explained that he and my mother had both quit dance school in 1942, the same year the Franks had gone into hiding. My mother had had neither the time nor the money to spend on dance lessons. And Bertus had been ordered to report for the *Arbeitsein-satz* (forced labor). He would be one of a half-million Dutch people pressed into backbreaking menial jobs in Germany.

Bertus did not dare ignore the order to report for the *Arbeitsein-satz*. He knew that the Nazis often punished the families of those who went into hiding. So he agreed to be shipped to Berlin, where he worked for about a year in a factory making electric parts. My mother feared that something terrible would happen to him there during an air raid, but when she shared her worries with the people in the Annex, whose safety was much more precarious, they mocked her for being overdramatic. But the munitions factories in which many Dutch people worked essentially as slave labor *were* the targets of repeated bombing attacks, and Anne wrote that the jokes made at my mother's expense were "hardly appropriate in this situation."

While in Germany, Bertus slept in a poorly heated barracks overstuffed with seventy-five other men. The experience left him feeling "hopeless," and when he was allowed to return to the Netherlands on a short leave sometime in 1943, he went underground, taking shelter on a farm in the Dutch village of Heino, about seventy-five miles from Amsterdam. He told me that the farmer who had taken him in "earned a golden seat in heaven, because he gave me a bowl of watery porridge every day. People were looking forward to that—that's how bad the hunger was."

While Bertus was in hiding, his family continued to receive letters summoning him to return to Berlin. Yet suddenly, the letters stopped. Bertus never knew why for sure, but he credited the intervention of an anonymous civil servant with a conscience "who made the files of random Dutch people disappear from the records, including mine." While hiding out in Heino, Bertus often sneaked into Amsterdam and stayed with his parents on Hoofdweg, a main thoroughfare in Amsterdam West.

Once back in his native city, Bertus noticed that many of his Jewish friends had vanished, including one of his close army friends, Henri Elias. Many years later, Bertus would discover what happened to him when he visited the Hollandsche Schouwburg (Dutch Theater), which had served as the main relay point for Jewish deportees in Amsterdam before they were shipped to Westerbork and then the camps. "When I looked at the list with the names of the Jews who had been deported, I suddenly saw Henri. 'Murdered in Auschwitz on August 19, 1942.' I cried like a baby."

At the time, however, Bertus had no idea what had happened to Henri and the other Jews he knew. But he was relieved to learn from Bep that her kindly Jewish boss, Otto Frank, had managed to escape with his family, first to Belgium and then to a neutral country such as Switzerland or Spain.

As close as my mother got to Bertus, during the twenty-five months that she watched over the Secret Annex, she never even gave him a hint about its existence. But Bertus claimed that he could detect an "immense aura of tension" surrounding her, which he attributed to the other very real hardships in her life: her sick father, her hungry siblings, the deprivations of the Occupation, and so on.

Bertus saw his role as trying to take my mother's mind off her problems. They tried to have fun together. They went swimming. They went to the movies. They walked around town. But sometimes on Sunday, her one day off, Bep would say she had to stop by 263 Prinsengracht "to feed the cat."

"Wait here," Bep would tell her boyfriend, instructing him to stay in the front office while she headed toward the Annex, "so as not to frighten the cat."

A LONG ENGAGEMENT

When Bertus and my mother's relationship began to get serious, he was invited over to Lumeijstraat to meet the Voskuijl family. "They wanted to know who they were dealing with," he said with a smile. "But they liked me, and I got along very well with Bep's father." Though Johan was "coughing all the time," Bertus said, he was never too tired to play a game of chess (on a chessboard that he had made himself) or talk politics.

Johan quickly took a shine to Bertus, and the reasons why were not complicated. He liked the boy's quick-witted humor, the fact that he was a worthy opponent in chess. He respected Bertus's family, which had a similar background to his own. He liked that he was a patriotic Dutchman who shared his own hatred of the occupier. As for whether he and Bep were in love, Johan didn't care about such things—but he knew that Bertus would be a source of much-needed stability in his daughter's life. As for my grandmother, she was just happy that Bertus was male and had four limbs. Though my mother was only twenty-four years old, Anne wrote, Christina teased her "about being an old maid." She wanted to marry off her eldest daughter, the sooner the better, and the unobjectionable Bertus seemed to fit the bill.

Though Bertus and his would-be in-laws were rooting for the engagement, my mother was unsure. And in fact she had tried to break up with Bertus earlier in the spring but had only felt "even worse" when she contemplated her future alone. Anne wondered "how long she will be able to keep" the relationship going. The problem was as old as time. She liked Bertus, genuinely enjoyed his company— but she didn't love him. Their connection could not come close to the bond she had with Victor, who, she told my aunt Diny, was "the better match." But who was she kidding? Victor was married. He was her boss. He was her *coconspirator*. She couldn't get involved, and she didn't have time to wait around for the world to change. As her mother and Mrs. van Pels constantly reminded her, she was not getting any younger.

On May 25, Anne took to her diary to report that "Bep's engaged! The news isn't much of a surprise, though none of us are particularly pleased," Anne wrote, adding that my mother probably said yes to Bertus only to "put an end to her indecision." Anne thought it was a mistake. "Bep doesn't love him," she wrote. All she wanted for Bep was a nice man "who knows how to appreciate her."

My mother was more practical than Anne when it came to matters of the heart. She knew that circumstances prevented her from having a serious relationship with the man she loved—Victor—and since she didn't have any other attractive prospects at the time, she probably reasoned that being with Bertus, who was at least kindhearted and adored by her father, was better than being alone.

There was an engagement party at Lumeijstraat with drinks and music. Miep and Jan Gies were there to raise a glass. So were Bertus's parents. But after the party, nothing changed, at least for the moment. Because Bertus was hiding from the Nazis to avoid being sent back to a labor camp, the engagement had to remain a secret until the war was over. Only then could they get married. In the meantime, the plan was for him to lie low. Whatever the future held, it would have to wait until the Liberation. Anne wished that my mother's life were turning out differently, that she could find someone to love, somebody who could make her truly happy. "What a sorry prospect for Bep, for whom we all wish the best."

Around that time, Bertus took Bep on a vacation to the small seaside farming village of Hierden seventy-five miles east of Amsterdam. Though he was in hiding, unemployed, and suffering the same privations as most other Dutch people during the war, Bertus was happy: happily engaged, happy by nature, hopeful for the future. My mother, though, must have felt the weight of the world on her shoulders. She knew that the Annex was vulnerable; she was powerless to plug all the holes in that leaky ship. Her father was dying; her fiancé would have wanted to help but had to be kept in the dark.

Lying in the grass with Bertus, far away from her colleagues and the hiders in the Annex, she suddenly felt alone and frightened. She told Bertus that she had to go to the bathroom but then disappeared for more than a half hour. When he finally found her, she was weeping uncontrollably at the side of a country lane. He asked what was wrong, what was torturing her so, but she would not say a word about it.

CHAPTER 9

All Was Lost

Of course she thought about the end. She couldn't help but think about it—*if* it would happen, *when* it would happen, *how* it would happen. But all the mental preparation, all the nightmarish dress rehearsals that played out in her mind over two years and one month, did not remotely prepare her for the moment when it finally arrived. On August 4, 1944, that muggy Friday morning when the hypothetical became actual, when she came face-to-face with the end, she could barely recognize it for what it was. The only thing that entered her mind was a question—*Is this it?*—and before she could reply, the answer grabbed hold of her, and then she could not speak, she could not move, all she could do was stand there—and watch.

She had heard the car pull up by the canal just a few moments earlier. She hardly looked up from the accounts book in which she was making notes; cars came and went on Prinsengracht all day long. But then she heard the heavy footsteps in the hallway—four, maybe five men. The first to enter had a shriveled yellow face; he was dressed in plain clothes; but all my mother noticed was the gun in his hand.

"Quiet!" he shouted in Dutch. "Stay in your seats."

Dazed, my mother was unable to comprehend what she was seeing. It was Miep, tough-as-nails and matter-of-fact Miep, who explained it to her in a whisper. "Bep," she said, "we've been caught."

One of the men had asked at the warehouse door who was in charge, and van Maaren had pointed up, toward the office, toward the Annex. They wanted to speak to "the boss." They were not interested, at first, in the two female secretaries in the front room. They grabbed Jo Kleiman and pushed him down the tiny hallway leading to Victor's office.

My mother couldn't see what was going on, but she heard shouting and Victor's muffled, trembling replies. Then someone lost his patience, and started screaming, in German, *"Wo sind die Juden?"* Where are the Jews?

So they knew. Of course, that question could have been a bluff, standard operating procedure for the secret police: pretend that you know a suspect is hiding something or someone, and see if they take the bait. Maybe that was how it happened. Or maybe the Nazi who spoke those words was operating on a tip, information given by someone who was not supposed to know the secret of the Annex.

There is some confusion about exactly what happened next—whether Victor, assuming that the Nazis already knew everything, led them to the entrance of the Secret Annex, or whether he played dumb and hoped vainly that somehow they would search the space and not discover that there were people hiding behind my grandfather's bookcase. But it doesn't really matter whether he showed them the door or they found it themselves, because in a matter of seconds they were all inside.

With a gun at his back, Kugler entered first. The terrified Edith Frank came to the door. When their eyes met, all he could do was whisper the word "Gestapo."

COMMON CRIMINALS

I don't want to dwell too much on the four men who conducted the raid on the Secret Annex. But one thing you should understand about those men is that they were not only foot soldiers in a genocidal army; they were also bounty hunters, in it for themselves, who were paid up to 40 guilders (about $285 in today's money) for every Jew they brought in. On top of that, they were thieves who plundered the homes of the people they preyed on.

Their leader, the man speaking German, SS-Oberscharführer Karl Silberbauer, is someone we will be forced to discuss at length soon enough. But allow me first to say a few words about his three Dutch henchmen. The identities of two of them, Gezinus Gringhuis and Willem Grootendorst, have been definitively established; the third man is still something of a mystery, but historians have speculated that he may have been Maarten Kuiper, a Dutch police officer and a particularly brutal villain of the Occupation who was eventually sentenced to death for murdering seventeen members of the Dutch Resistance and for rounding up *hundreds* of Jews in hiding. With so many corpses credited to him, Kuiper doesn't need to have arrested Anne Frank to ensure himself a special place in Hell.

Though there is no hard evidence linking Kuiper to the raid on the Secret Annex, the two other Dutch detectives, Gringhuis and Grootendorst, were positively identified after the war by Otto Frank (as well as by Victor Kugler and Jo Kleiman). They were both members of the NSB, the Dutch Nazi Party, and longtime veterans of the Amsterdam police force, and they enthusiastically partnered with the Sicherheitsdienst (SD), the German secret police organization charged with tracking down Jews and other "enemies of the State" during the Occupation. Grootendorst and Silberbauer actually became something of a tag team late in the Occupation; they are known to have terrorized many other people in Amsterdam in 1944.

In fact, just two months before the raid on the Secret Annex, the two men had ransacked the home of Wolf Tafelkruijer, a wealthy Jewish merchant. When they couldn't find him there, Silberbauer and Grootendorst savagely beat Tafelkruijer's non-Jewish, German-born wife, Erna Olofsson. She was arrested, along with a fifteen-month-old grandnephew of her husband, José, and a Jewish friend of the family, Cecilia Hüsfeldt, who was living in the house. Silberbauer ordered that the "Jew child" be sent off to Westerbork and then to a death camp in Poland. A day before his scheduled deportation, a Dutch lawyer managed to get José released on humanitarian grounds. But Cecilia was not as lucky; she died of typhus on October 31, 1944, in Ravensbrück.

Even under Nazi rules, Silberbauer's decision to arrest Mrs. Tafelkruijer, a Gentile, seemed legally dubious; the move was likely motivated by his desire to rob her home. On a follow-up search of the Tafelkruijer house, Silberbauer and Grootendorst helped themselves to a wristwatch, two diamond pins, a pair of pearl earrings, a small safe, and even a few pieces of furniture. Silberbauer also used the house to entertain his lover, Everdina Hartemink, a young Dutch secretary who worked with him at the SD. Silberbauer and Grootendorst's criminal behavior seemed to grow increasingly flagrant in that late period of the Occupation, perhaps because they were aware that the war was turning against Germany, that the days of Nazis in Amsterdam were numbered. It was time to get while the getting was good.

In the Annex, Silberbauer refused to believe that the Frank family could have been hiding there for so long—*more than two years*. To prove it, Otto showed him the marks on the wall measuring how much Anne and Margot had grown in that time.

As the Annex residents packed up a few essentials, Silberbauer and his men rifled through the rooms, looking for more valuables to steal. At one point Silberbauer found Otto's old briefcase in which Anne's diary was kept, along with the papers on which she had been revising her entries, editing them into a kind of epistolary war novel she called *Het Achterhuis*.

The idea had been formed that spring after Anne had heard on Radio Oranje, the official broadcaster of the Dutch government in exile, a speech by the Dutch minister of education, arts, and sciences, Gerrit Bolkestein:

History cannot be written on the basis of official decisions and documents alone. If our descendants are to understand fully what we as a nation have had to endure and overcome during these years, then what we really need are ordinary documents—a diary, letters from a worker in Germany, a collection of sermons given by a parson or priest. Not until we succeed in bringing together vast quantities of this simple, everyday material will the picture of our struggle for freedom be painted in its full depth and glory.

By May 20, she had begun furiously working on her novel (which would be known to scholars of Anne as Version B of the diary, whereas the original text, far less mature and written contemporaneously with the events described, is known as Version A). In her head, she wrote, the novel was already finished, yet in reality it was still a work in progress when Silberbauer grabbed the briefcase.

The Oberscharführer thought there might be money inside the briefcase, so he turned it upside down and shook it, spilling out the contents. The carefully edited drafts, on multicolored A4 and A5 sheets my mother had given Anne, were covered with an elegant schoolgirl's cursive handwriting. Some pages had inkblots from a runny pen, others had lines carefully crossed out marking deletions—all of that hard work now scattered on the floor. Anne barely bothered to look up.

"She was very quiet and composed, only just as dispirited as all the rest of us," Otto said later. "Perhaps she had a premonition that all was lost."

DAMAGE CONTROL

In the first few minutes of the raid, my mother had been frozen in a state of shock. But when she realized that there were Nazis in the Secret Annex, when she came to terms with the fact that Anne and the others were about to be shoved inside a police van and taken away, something inside her broke. "I can't, can't describe it to you—it was so horrible," she told the writer Ernst Schnabel in the 1950s. "I prayed and prayed, and cried, and fell on my knees, and wished for only one thing: Let it be over quickly."

Just the day before, my mother had sat down with Anne in the Annex. They had had a little chat, girl to girl, in her room. It was nothing special, those parting words, nothing like the haunting last entry in Anne's diary, in which she described herself as a person "split in two." Anne often presented herself as "an amusing clown," but this childish mask obscured a "purer, deeper and finer" person, one she hadn't quite yet found the courage to show to the world.

One of the last lines in her diary reads, "Before I realize it, she's disappeared."

With my mother, on the day before the arrest, Anne hadn't been confessing so much as asking questions. She wanted to know about the Voskuijl children, the different sports my uncle Joop loved to play, the new clothes that Diny and Gerda had recently received: trifling stuff, but my mother would remember how intently Anne listened to her in an almost investigative way, as though she was searching for new material, some little flourish she could record or embellish in her diary. During their conversation, my mother noticed that Anne had outgrown her clothes and that her face had become "awfully pale." She hadn't seen a ray of sunshine for more than two years.

While the Nazis were busy interrogating Victor, Jo Kleiman went back into the front office. He told my mother and Miep what they already knew: it was over. The Franks, the van Pelses, and Fritz Pfeffer had been arrested and would be sent off to Westerbork and then—who knew?

Kleiman had just been questioned by Silberbauer, who seemed intent on interrogating everyone in the office. Miep was next. "Just keep denying," Kleiman told her. The important thing now was limiting the fallout, hiding the evidence, making sure the Nazis wouldn't arrest everyone who worked at Opekta—and their families.

Later, when it was Miep's turn to be questioned, she noticed that Silberbauer had a Viennese accent, and as someone born in Vienna herself, she tried to use their shared heritage to appeal to him: Couldn't the Franks be released? Would he take a bribe?

"Aren't you ashamed of yourself, helping Jewish trash?" Silberbauer snarled. "You deserve to receive the worst punishment."

Before he was taken into custody by Silberbauer, Jo Kleiman was able to quietly take my mother aside and give her his wallet. It was stuffed with forged and stolen ration cards, some likely purchased on the black market, others obtained by Jan Gies through his Resistance connections. They were evidence that he and the other Opekta employees had all been in on the conspiracy. He told her to leave immediately and take the wallet to a friend who worked in a nearby pharmacy for safekeeping.

It didn't occur to my mother that she could just walk out of the office. Or run.

Yet once she stumbled downstairs, her legs refused to carry her. The street was empty, yet she thought there were Germans waiting by the front door, that they would shoot her in the back as she fled. She pushed herself down the block as if crawling through hardening concrete, but halfway there her muscles kicked in, and her pace quickened.

It took her just a few minutes to reach the drugstore on Leliegracht Canal. Kleiman's friend understood as soon as he saw my mother's face that she was in trouble. He took Bep to the back room, away from the curious glances of customers. Bep gave him the wallet, but she didn't know whether the pharmacist could be entirely trusted, so she only told him that the Germans had found an illegal radio at

Opekta and were now searching the building. Then, her voice quivering and barely audible, she called the office to ask what she should do next.

"Just come back," Kleiman said. "You can't escape your fate."

FAREWELL

Jo was insane if he thought she was going to go back to Opekta, back to "the belly of the beast," just so that Silberbauer could rough her up. If the Nazis wanted to talk to her, they would have to find her. But she had no idea where to go. She stayed, crying and praying, in the back of the pharmacy for about an hour, and then she began aimlessly wandering through the city, her cheeks wet with tears. By late afternoon, she knew, at the very least, that she needed a friend.

She went to see her boyfriend, Bertus, who that day was staying at his parents' house two miles away from Opekta on the Hoofdweg. As soon as they were together someplace private, the long-hidden truth came pouring out. She had been lying—lying to him, lying to everyone. Her Jewish boss and his family hadn't escaped abroad; they had been hiding in the back house of her office for more than two years. She and her coworkers had tried, day after day, to keep them safe, and now, after 761 days, it was all over. Bertus was stunned, but he finally understood "the aura of immense tension," as he put it to me, that had seemed to surround my mother. She had worked so hard, had sacrificed so much, to keep all those people safe. The war seemed to be ending, the Liberation was in sight. They had *almost* made it.

My mother and Bertus spent a few hours together that night. He tried to handle her carefully, gently; he didn't know exactly what to say. What could he have said? *You did everything you could. You tried your best. You couldn't have known. You'll see them again, maybe. . . .* At a certain point, they realized that there was nothing more to be said.

It was around 9:30 when Bertus dropped my mother at home. The late-summer sun had only recently set, and the house was dark but sweltering. It was almost time for the twins, Diny and Gerda, to go to sleep. Diny was playing in the living room, and she remembered seeing her sister Bep slide open the door and enter Johan's room. He was lying in bed, sweating and groaning in pain. It was an unusually hot summer, and the atmosphere in the city was buoyant and hopeful. People could feel the possibility of Liberation everywhere, the strictures of the Occupation beginning to loosen. Yet the atmosphere inside my family's house was very different: dark, cold, verging on hopeless. And now this.

Bep had gone into her father's room to tell him the news. It would be the last of their little father-and-daughter tête-à-têtes as protectors of the Annex. After she explained what had happened, Johan didn't say anything. But suddenly he stood up, despite his great pain, and asked for his clothes. Then he got dressed, walked out the door, and jumped onto his bike. Did my mother try to reason with him? Did my grandmother scream that he was out of his mind? Or could they just tell that whatever he was going to do, there was no stopping him?

It was after curfew, you couldn't be seen on the street without an official exemption, but Johan didn't care. He was a ghost, a dead man riding through the streets of Amsterdam. He passed the Bilderdijk Canal and the Singel Canal and rode into the Jordaan quarter, today the most exclusive district of Amsterdam but then a teeming working-class quarter of factories and warehouses. He used the company key that he had never given back to unlock the door to 263 Prinsengracht. He would later tell his daughter that the reason for his visit had been to get rid of whatever evidence connected her and her colleagues to the hiding. But she thought there was another reason her sick father had ridden through the night to the Secret Annex: he wanted to say goodbye.

PART II

NELLY

They are sure here that Nelly is not one hundred percent right in the head.

—Anne Frank, May 11, 1944

CHAPTER 10

The Voice of a Young Woman

In 1963, it was open season on Nazis. Adolf Eichmann, the architect of the Final Solution and the man who had called the efficient Dutch shipments of Jews to the death camps a "joy to see," had recently been put to death in Jerusalem. Now frail and graying, the exterminators who had presided over Auschwitz, Belzec, and Chelmno were finally shackled and put on trial in high-profile court cases across Germany. But the SS officer who had arrested Anne Frank, the most famous victim of the Nazi genocide, remained at large.

For five years, the Nazi hunter Simon Wiesenthal had been trying to track him down. In comparison to many of the other men whom Wiesenthal targeted—men such as Eichmann, who had played important roles in organizing, overseeing, and executing the mass murder of six million people—Karl Silberbauer was a small fish, "a nobody, a zero," as Wiesenthal put it in his memoir, *The Murderers Among Us*. But none of that mattered, he wrote, because "the figure before the zero was Anne Frank."

The fact that Silberbauer had arrested Anne, who in the intervening years, thanks to the fame of her published diary, had become the most identifiable victim of the Holocaust, made him important, if only by association. Six million was just a number. But Anne's story gave you the Holocaust in miniature, a crime that people could understand, a victim they could love. And once that little girl broke your heart, you could multiply the atrocity over and over again and the scale of the thing hit you in a deeper way that reached across cultures, making the Holocaust matter even to people who had never known the difference between a Gentile and a Jew.

"Anne Frank's diary has had a much greater impact than the whole Nuremberg trials," Wiesenthal once said. "For no one is able to identify themselves with piles of corpses. But this ordinary, fourteen-year-old child . . . People who read the diary will think, *This could have been my daughter or my grandchild or my sister*."

By 1963, Anne had become a global cultural phenomenon. In the eleven years since her diary had first appeared in English, the book had become an international best seller, spawning a popular Broadway play and a 1959 blockbuster film directed by George Stevens. People were invested in Anne; they had come to know her and her family; now they wanted justice on their behalf; they wanted those who had touched her to answer for their crimes.

Wiesenthal was a survivor in more ways than one, a man who, as he put it, had "decided to live for the dead." He had first understood what it meant to be a Jew in the twentieth century when, as a boy in Galicia, he had been slashed in the face by a Cossack's saber. Two decades later, he and his entire family had been swallowed up in the Nazi camps. His mother had been murdered in Belzec, one of eighty-nine family members Wiesenthal and his wife, Cyla, would lose in the Holocaust.

In 1943, Wiesenthal escaped from the Janowska concentration camp in present-day Ukraine, but he was eventually recaptured and sent back to toil away in execrable conditions. At one point he grew so desperate he tried to slit his wrists with a rusty razor blade. Another time he attempted suicide by hanging but was too weak to hoist himself into a makeshift noose. He survived a death march across Poland and ended the war at Mauthausen, where he was left to die in a block for the mortally wounded. When he was finally liberated by the Americans on May 5, 1945, he weighed just ninety pounds.

It's contested to this day how much of a role Wiesenthal played in tracking down Eichmann in Argentina, but he was unquestionably successful in smoking out other important Nazis in hiding, from the commandant of Treblinka to the sadistic female guard at the Majdanek death camp who had herded Jews into the gas chamber with a whip. He was a stubborn man, stolid, courageous; he didn't move from his house in Vienna even after it was firebombed by neo-Nazis.

So when a mob of teenagers screaming anti-Semitic epithets interrupted a performance of the play *The Diary of Anne Frank* in the Austrian city of Linz in October 1958, and began distributing leaflets that said "Anne Frank never existed," he took it as a call to action. The teenagers were not alone. A few weeks earlier, a schoolteacher in the German city of Lübeck had publicly declared the diary to be a forgery. The closer Wiesenthal looked, the more he realized that a whole generation of Austrians and Germans was growing up among seeds of doubt about whether the Holocaust had really happened.

Wiesenthal met one of the boys in a café, and, after he talked to him for a while, the boy admitted that he would believe that Anne Frank had been a real person and that her diary was genuine if Wiesenthal could offer him proof in the form of the Gestapo officer who supposedly had arrested her in the fabled Secret Annex.

So he set out to find the man, just one of tens of thousands of "anonymous handymen of death," as he put it.

In 1958, practically nothing was known about Karl Silberbauer except his surname. Miep had noticed his Viennese accent during her interrogation, but the helpers didn't know whether he had survived the war or where in Austria (or anywhere else, for that matter) he might be found.

As he hunted Nazis around the globe, Wiesenthal always maintained that he was after "justice, not vengeance." Yet to Otto his crusade seemed like salting old wounds. Otto had no stomach for retribution; he was interested in reconciliation for the living, peace for his murdered daughters. He wanted to forgive, if not forget. During those five years, while Wiesenthal tried to track down Silberbauer, Otto actively hoped that he would *not* find him. Otto even requested that Ernst Schnabel, in his 1958 book on the Secret Annex, use the name "Silberthaler," perhaps to protect the Nazi's anonymity, since Schnabel's personal notes clearly show that he had discovered the correct name of the SS officer.

Otto had his reasons for wanting Silberbauer to be left alone. He was magnanimous and tolerant by nature, and he knew that no investigation or score settling could ever bring his girls back. But I think the biggest reason he wanted to avoid tracking down Silberbauer was because he hoped the last word on the case of the Secret Annex would be Anne's—and only Anne's. He wanted the diary to stand alone, unchallenged by other voices and witnesses. He was not wrong to think that if the perpetrators were found, they would only muddy the story.

HE WAS ONLY FOLLOWING ORDERS

For nearly two decades, Silberbauer did not have to answer for the crimes he had committed on Dutch soil. After returning to his native Vienna in April 1945, he served a fourteen-month prison sentence, not because of what he had done to Dutch Jews and Resistance members but because of his brutal treatment of Austrian Communists even before he had been transferred to the Netherlands in the middle of the war. Almost immediately after his release from prison in 1946, he was recruited by the West German Federal Intelligence Service, and spent nearly a decade as an undercover agent in Austria and Germany spying on neo-Nazi groups, the dregs of the fascist system who no doubt invited him into their inner circles because of his credentials as an SS man.

By 1954, he was rehired by the Vienna police department, where he had worked before the war, and given the rank of inspector. At that point his rehabilitation seemed complete; he lived openly in Vienna, without any fear that his past would come back to haunt him. Yet Wiesenthal was on his trail. Since 1958, the Nazi hunter had been scouring the Austrian countryside looking for him, yet he had been misled by Otto Frank and thought he was looking for a man named "Silberthaler," or perhaps "Silvernagl," an alternative spelling provided by Victor Kugler. Yet late in the spring of 1963, Wiesenthal had a breakthrough. On a visit to Amsterdam, he met with a high-ranking Dutch police official named Ynze Taconis, who gave him a photocopy of a 1943 telephone directory of Gestapo personnel in occupied Holland. On the flight back to Vienna, Wiesenthal studied the names closely. There were about three hundred in total, divided into different sections. His eyes landed on Referat IV B4, the Gestapo section responsible for deporting Jews:

KEMPIN

BUSCHMANN

SCHERF

SILBERBAUER

There he was. It would take a few more months to track down Silberbauer in Vienna, to confirm that he was the man who conducted the raid, and to reveal his identity to the world. Wiesenthal said that after the news had been announced, he had received "more cables and letters than I had after Eichmann's capture." Yet in this case there would be no high-profile war crimes trial and certainly no execution or prison sentence. Silberbauer was placed on temporary leave from the Vienna police and an inquest was held, but he was cleared of any wrongdoing, since he had been merely "following orders" and had not tried to "conceal his past." Remarkably, during the proceedings, Otto spoke out in Silberbauer's favor, telling the authorities that he had "only done his duty and behaved correctly." Perhaps he was thinking of how Silberbauer, after discovering that Otto had been an officer in the German Army during World War I, had given the Frank family extra time to pack and told his men to put away their weapons—actions that, to my mother, revealed "a shred of humanity."

"The only thing I ask," Otto added in his statement to the Austrian authorities, "is not to have to see the man again."

"IF HE HADN'T CALLED US,
WE WOULDN'T HAVE COME"

"SD Man Who Arrested Frank Family Tracked Down in Vienna."

On November 20, 1963, my mother saw that headline on the front page of what was at the time one of the largest Dutch newspapers, *Het Vrije Volk*. I know this because she clipped the article out and pasted it into a scrapbook she kept that documented every aspect of the Anne Frank case. The fact that Karl Silberbauer had been tracked down made headlines around the world, not just in the Netherlands. Victor Kugler, who had moved to Toronto after the war, wrote my mother to say that his phone had been ringing nonstop ever since the story had been picked up in Canada. After speaking to reporters throughout the day on November 21, he had finally unplugged the phone at midnight to get some rest.

"The next morning, it started all over again at 7," Kugler wrote. "They called me constantly at the office until I had the telephone exchange say I was out. But then the TV people wanted to come by with big lamps to film me. . . . And that's why I was featured in the news on two stations that day. . . . The two most prestigious newspapers printed photos of me on the front page, with thick red letters."

The Austrians had wanted Silberbauer's privacy protected and his personal life kept out of the papers. But Wiesenthal saw no reason why he should be shielded from public scrutiny; if he was not going to be judged in a court of law, he should at least be judged in the court of public opinion. He gave Silberbauer's private address in Vienna to the Dutch journalist Jules Huf, and on November 20, 1963, Huf showed up at Silberbauer's front door. His wife answered. She claimed that her husband wasn't at home and that what he had done in the Netherlands nearly twenty years before should be of no interest to anyone. "Please leave us alone," she said.

Yet as she moved to close the door, a skinny, graying man emerged from the kitchen and said, "Let the gentleman come in."

Huf noticed that Silberbauer, though pretending to be suave and unafraid, was trembling and smoking one cigarette after another. Huf explained why he had come, how he wanted to hear Silberbauer's side of the story, his own account of the now-famous raid on the Secret Annex.

"For God's sake," Mrs. Silberbauer interrupted. "What do we have to do with this Anne Frank?"

After calming his wife's nerves, Silberbauer sat down for an extended interview, which quickly turned into a portrait of the banality of evil. The fifty-two-year-old Austrian thought he was being victimized by powerful interests, that there was some elaborate conspiracy that explained why that one case was being dredged up after all this time. "I wonder who is behind all this. Probably that Wiesenthal fellow or someone at the ministry trying to get on the Jews' good side."

He did not offer a shred of contrition. He said that the Franks, like all the other people he arrested, "didn't make an impression on me." One of the first things he remembered about the raid on Prinsengracht was that it had interrupted his lunch break. He made light of Anne's diary, joking that, had he known it would become so famous, he might have "picked it up off the floor." He said that his suspension from the police had been unjust and that the scandal had caused him to lose face among his neighbors. "No badge, no gun. I was suddenly forced to buy a ticket on the tram. You can imagine how the conductor looked at me."

Yet Silberbauer did not only air personal grievances; he also gave Huf a major scoop, claiming unequivocally that it was Willem van Maaren, the mistrustful warehouse manager, who had betrayed the Annex in a phone call on the morning of the arrest.

"One of my men spoke to the warehouse employee in Dutch," Silberbauer recalled. "He quietly motioned with his thumb, as if to say: You need to be upstairs. He was the one who had given us the tip by telephone, half an hour earlier. . . . I'm sure that he was the one. Because when we arrived, he stood ready and pointed in the right direction, without saying a word. If he hadn't called us, we wouldn't have come."

For years after the raid, my mother believed that van Maaren was the man who had betrayed the Annex. She never forgot his unpleasant manner, how he had been so demanding in his questions, so intrusive and nosy, so threatening. I remember her telling me that she would "bet almost anything" that he had *known* that there were people hiding in the building. She even told Schnabel that she believed he was the most likely betrayer when he interviewed her in 1957.

Yet something changed around the time that Silberbauer was found in Vienna. Just as the world was given a remarkable eyewitness testimony confirming that van Maaren had indeed been the betrayer, my mother, for the first time in her life, seemed uncertain. A month later, in December 1963, she told the Dutch magazine *Panorama* that she had "had no reason to suspect" van Maaren. Around the same time, she was questioned by the Amsterdam police, who had opened a new investigation into the betrayal of the Annex following Silberbauer's comments. She was asked the straightforward question if she could state who the betrayer was.

"Unfortunately, I can't," she replied.

The Amsterdam police also interrogated Silberbauer and van Maaren. Yet Silberbauer, after having told the newspapers just five days earlier that the betrayer was van Maaren, now backtracked on his story. "I want to make clear that I was never made aware of who-ever reported the Frank family," he said.

Van Maaren, meanwhile, finally admitted to investigators that he had stolen from Opekta during the war and that he had heard gossip in the neighborhood about the possibility of people hiding in the Annex. But he passionately defended himself against the betrayal charge. And it seems to me that he might have been telling the truth. *If* the alleged phone call had occurred thirty minutes before the raid, as Silberbauer claimed, it would have been practically impossible for van Maaren to have been the one making the call. According to his colleagues, he had spent the entire morning of August 4 downstairs in the warehouse, and the only phone at Opekta was in the office up-stairs, near Miep's desk.

So was it van Maaren or wasn't it? In late 1963, for whatever rea-son, Silberbauer told a journalist one thing (that it was van Maaren) and the police another (that he didn't know). Which story was true, and which was false? Or perhaps *both* were fabrications? Because shortly after Silberbauer's identity was revealed, he was visited by someone close to Otto Frank, and with that person he shared a third, very different story about who had betrayed the Secret Annex.

THE CONFIDANT

Cornelius "Cor" Suijk was born in a village near Amsterdam in 1924. He joined the Resistance while still a teenager and helped hide Dutch Jews during the war, until he was caught by the Nazis and sent to the Vught concentration camp near Den Bosch. He was a skeleton upon Liberation and became one of those people, like my mother, for whom the war never really ended, who remained haunted by the ghosts of the past.

A few years before his death in 2014, he told a journalist that far from being proud of his conduct during the war, he was ashamed—

ashamed that he and people like him hadn't stood up in greater numbers and taken more risks to save innocent lives when they'd had the chance.

"Our small group saved thirteen Jews in the war," Suijk said. "But how many more could we have saved! How many more could the Dutch Christians have saved! . . . I did not do enough. And I will live with that for the rest of my life."

In the early 1960s, one of Suijk's Resistance friends introduced him to Otto Frank. The two men became close, and in 1965, Suijk was invited to join the board of the Anne Frank House, where he later became the director and the head of international programs, working closely with the Anne Frank Center in New York City.

Otto trusted Cor implicitly; the most stunning evidence is that he gave Suijk five unpublished, previously unknown pages from Anne's diary—including entries about sensitive subjects (such as her parents' relationship problems) that Otto thought should be kept private—along with instructions not to release them to the public until Otto and his second wife, Elfriede, nicknamed Fritzi, had passed away. When the pages were finally made public in 1998, after Fritzi's death, they caused a sensation and were front-page news around the world. Though Suijk's role in that incident is well known, his interaction with Karl Silberbauer remained for decades an open secret among his colleagues at the Anne Frank House.

Sometime after Silberbauer was found in 1963, Otto asked Suijk to go to Vienna and talk to him in person to discover whether he had any more information about the betrayal. Suijk was personally motivated to find the betrayer. After interviewing my aunt Willy for the Anne Frank House in the 1980s, he said that he had planned to leave "no stone unturned" when it came to investigating the case.

According to one of Suijk's colleagues at the Anne Frank House, when Silberbauer met up with Suijk in Vienna, he told Suijk a third version about what had happened on August 4, 1944.

1937 • My mother at age eighteen, right after Otto Frank hired her at Opekta. *van Wijk-Voskuijl family*

1938 • Bertus Hulsman, my mother's wartime fiancé. Before the war he served in the Dutch Army. *van Wijk-Voskuijl family*

July 1940 • My mother with her twin sisters, Diny (right) and Gerda, on their eighth birthday. The Occupation had just begun. *van Wijk-Voskuijl family*

December 1940 • My grandparents Christina and Johan Voskuijl, and my aunts Nelly (at top) and Willy. *van Wijk-Voskuijl family*

May 1941 • The Nazis used this map of Jewish homes in Amsterdam—which was provided by Dutch civil servants—to round up Jews during the Occupation. One black dot equaled ten Jews. *Resistance Museum Amsterdam– Public Domain*

July 1941 • My mother and Anne Frank (second and third from the right) among other wedding guests on Miep and Jan Gies's wedding day. Otto Frank is on the left of Anne. *Getty Images*

November 1942 • The Stock Exchange board game, which was given to Peter van Pels for his sixteenth birthday. After the raid on the Secret Annex, my mother kept it as a keepsake. *van Wijk-Voskuijl family*

December 1942 • The underaged Nelly Voskuijl's application for a "Greater German" visa, which indicates that she received parental consent to leave the country—something which my aunt Diny said was not true. *Amsterdam City Archives–Public Domain*

1943 • A woman in Amsterdam wearing the yellow star, which all Jews in the Netherlands over the age of six were forced to wear from May 1942. *Bundesarchiv–183-R99538*

1945 • My grandmother Christina, still recovering from hunger edema, with her eldest daughter. *van Wijk-Voskuijl family*

May 1946 • The only time Otto Frank and my aunt Nelly are known to have crossed paths was at my parents' wedding in Amsterdam. Otto can be seen in profile, to the left of the groom. Nelly is three heads to the right of the bride, looking down, her face shadowed by a large hat. My aunt Diny, the bridesmaid, is holding a small bouquet and standing to the right of my mother. *van Wijk-Voskuijl family*

March 1949 • My mother and father, Cor van Wijk, with their first child, my brother Ton. At that moment my mother was three months pregnant with me. *van Wijk-Voskuijl family*

1957 • The wedding of Nelly and Uncle Carl. Left to right: my parents, my grandmother, and the bride and groom. *van Wijk-Voskuijl family*

November 1960 • The van Wijk family with newborn daughter Anne-Marie, named in memory of Anne Frank. Seated below on the left my brother Cok, my mother and me behind my father. On the right my brother Ton. *van Wijk-Voskuijl family*

September 1963 • My mother, my sister, and me at the beach in Zandvoort.
van Wijk-Voskuijl family

Spring 1965 • My mother and me in the kitchen.
van Wijk-Voskuijl family

November 1965 • The last ballroom dancing competition before I had my accident, which left me seriously injured. *van Wijk-Voskuijl family*

September 1967 • Sonja and me dancing on my eighteenth birthday. *van Wijk-Voskuijl family*

1973 • The helpers with their spouses after the war: (from left) Miep Gies, my parents, and Loes Kugler, with Jan Gies and Victor Kugler standing behind them. *van Wijk-Voskuijl family*

1972 • Otto Frank recommended my mother for the title "Righteous Among the Nations." She received this certificate from Yad Vashem in Israel, as well as a medal. *van Wijk-Voskuijl family*

תעודת כבוד
ATTESTATION

Le présent Diplôme atteste qu'en sa séance du 8 mars 1972 la Commission des Justes près l'Institut Commémoratif des Martyrs et des Héros Yad Vashem a décidé, sur foi de témoignages recueillis par elle, de rendre homage à ELISABETH VAN WIJK-VOSKUYL

qui au péril de sa vie a sauvé des Juifs pendant l'époque d'extermination; de lui décerner la Médaille des Justes et de l'autoriser à planter un arbre en son nom dans l'Allée des Justes sur le Mont du Souvenir à Jérusalem;

Fait à Jérusalem, Israël, le 1er septembre 1972

POUR L'INSTITUT YAD VASHEM   POUR LA COMMISSION DES JUSTES

UNE VIE SAUVÉ L'UNIVERS TOUT ENTIER

1978 • My mother and Otto Frank during one of his visits to the Netherlands.
van Wijk-Voskuijl family

May 1983 • Death notice from the Anne Frank House regarding my mother in the newspaper *Het Parool*. Her last name was misspelled. "She was a courageous woman."
van Wijk-Voskuijl family

Bedroefd nemen wij afscheid van
ELLI VAN WIJK-VOSKUIL
Zij was een van degenen die Anne Frank en de andere onderduikers in het Achterhuis van dag tot dag hebben bijgestaan.
Zij was een moedige vrouw.

Anne Frank Stichting

September 1990 • Nelly tending her mother and husband's grave.
van Wijk-Voskuijl family

August 1997 • My brothers (from left), Cok and Ton, my sister, Anne, and me, united in a rare moment of peace.
van Wijk-Voskuijl family

1997 • My mother's medallion, with
a photograph of her three eldest
children. My sister gave this to me in
August 1997, and I wear it every day.
van Wijk-Voskuijl family

1997 • My first meeting with Nelly in thirty years.
van Wijk-Voskuijl family

2003 • Scrapbook with pictures from my
youth, compiled by my mother. Twenty
years after her death, I was given this
scrapbook by my brother Ton.
van Wijk-Voskuijl family

2012 • Jeroen and me after our first
interview with Diny.
van Wijk-Voskuijl family

2014 • Me in front of the bookcase that hid the Secret Annex from view, made by my grandfather Johan in August 1942. *van Wijk-Voskuijl family*

2016 • Bertus, happily reunited with Diny after seventy-one years. This photo was taken shortly before his death in July 2016. *van Wijk-Voskuijl family*

2017 • Ryan and Kay-Lee, the twins of my daughter, Rebecca. My mother's great-grandchildren were born on August 4, 2011—exactly sixty-seven years after the raid on the Secret Annex. *van Wijk-Voskuijl family*

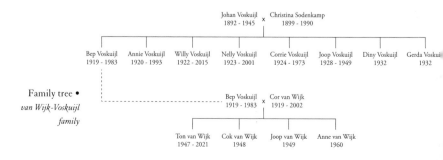

Family tree •
van Wijk-Voskuijl family

Johan Voskuijl 1892 - 1945 x Christina Sodenkamp 1899 - 1990

Bep Voskuijl 1919 - 1983 | Annie Voskuijl 1920 - 1993 | Willy Voskuijl 1922 - 2015 | Nelly Voskuijl 1923 - 2001 | Corrie Voskuijl 1924 - 1973 | Joop Voskuijl 1928 - 1949 | Diny Voskuijl 1932 | Gerda Voskuijl 1932

Bep Voskuijl 1919 - 1983 x Cor van Wijk 1919 - 2002

Ton van Wijk 1947 - 2021 | Cok van Wijk 1948 | Joop van Wijk 1949 | Anne van Wijk 1960

Now, Silberbauer admitted, the phone call tipping off the Nazis on that morning couldn't have come from van Maaren, because he had been told at the time that the informant on the line had had the "voice of a young woman." As for who the young woman might be, Silberbauer told Suijk he didn't know, or at least he wouldn't say.

Suijk never broadcasted the statement about the "young woman," and Silberbauer, who died in 1972, never repeated it. But Suijk must have shared the information with Otto and the other members of the Opekta Circle, because soon Otto, Kugler, and my mother all became convinced that van Maaren should no longer be considered a serious suspect. Until his dying day, Otto seemed to believe the information given to him by Suijk. In an interview with *Life* magazine in 1979, a year before his death, he said, "I still have my own theory on how our arrest has come about. It was said that a woman's voice betrayed us on the phone."

Fritzi Frank, in an interview with the Anne Frank House in the early 1990s, confirmed that, although she didn't seem to know (or didn't want to disclose) the source of the information, "[Otto] said all the time that it was a woman's voice on the telephone to the Gestapo. So that went against the idea that it was van Maaren. The Gestapo said it was a woman's voice, whoever it was who knew such a thing. 'Yes, a female voice called and said, "They are hiding there, in that house."'"

QUESTIONS WITHOUT ANSWERS

Why would Silberbauer lie to the press and the police only to tell the truth to Cor Suijk? Why would Otto, Fritzi, and my mother believe Silberbauer's third story but dismiss the first two? If there had indeed been a young woman on the phone, who was she? And how could one positively discern the age of a woman from the sound of her voice? Does a twenty-four-year-old woman sound so different from a forty-four-year-old woman?

These types of questions have dogged historians and journalists looking into the case and fueled much idle speculation. Ultimately, all of the evidence pointing to one suspect or another seems, upon further inspection, flimsy or circumstantial when it is not made up of whole cloth. Theories have blossomed and shriveled with the years; suspects have come and gone. In order to follow a line of inquiry, an assumption has to be made somewhere. The assumptions are based on a series of *if*s and *but*s, on hearsay, on misremembered conversations, on secondhand and thirdhand accounts. Much of it is suggestive; none of it is conclusive.

I can use the various bits of information that Silberbauer provided in his interviews or the rumors that were circulating around the Annex in the run-up to the raid to draw a sketchy portrait of this possible betrayer or that possible betrayer. But ultimately, to pin the crime on someone requires a leap of faith, a bout of magical thinking, which is irresponsible for those of us who claim to be writing history. I hope I've made it clear thus far that using *any* information provided by Silberbauer immediately puts us on shaky ground.

Take, for instance, his very basic claim that the SD received a tip on the telephone thirty minutes before the raid on 263 Prinsengracht. Silberbauer alleged that the person who had received that notorious phone call was none other than SS-Obersturmführer Julius Dettmann, the head of his SD unit in Amsterdam. Is it plausible that such a man would take a personal interest in a handful of people hiding in an Amsterdam canal house? That he, and not one of his many underlings, would be the one noting down information from an informant? Maybe, maybe not. But by saying that Dettmann had taken the call, Silberbauer chose somebody who could not contradict his story: Dettmann had died of suicide while in prison in Amsterdam in 1945.

Silberbauer's other boss was Willy Lages, the chief of the SD. He was, by all accounts, a monster who ordered prisoners to be tortured with hot iron rods, whips, needles, and nightsticks. Even Silberbauer called him "a true dog." He liked to sign the death sentences of his victims with a large *L*, a kind of trademark. As sadistic as Lages was, he did not have a hand in the Anne Frank affair. And when questioned about the raid on the Annex after the war, he claimed that the prospect of a squad of SD men jumping on a tip about hidden Jews the moment after it came through the transom was "highly illogical." His office had received hundreds of such tips every week from a large network of spies, and rarely had information been acted on so quickly. "Unless," he added, "the tip came from an informant who was well known to our service."

There were, of course, many such informants in Amsterdam, people who had made themselves useful to the occupier. Some of them did it for money; others to save their own skin. When Jews were caught in hiding, it was common practice for the Nazis to offer them a chance to avoid deportation by becoming a "V-man" or "V-woman" (*V* stood for *Vertrauen* in German, or trust), who stayed alive by sending other people to their deaths. One of them was Ans van Dijk, a Jewish milliner who pretended to be in the Resistance to gain information about the whereabouts of hidden Jews—150 of whom she ended up betraying, including her own brother. Van Dijk, the only Dutch woman to be executed for her conduct during the war, was one of many people over the years who has been accused, without evidence, of betraying the Annex.

I believe that we will never know with any certainty who betrayed the Secret Annex. Unless, after eighty years, a document from the SD turns up with the name of an informant and the address 263 Prinsengracht, it would be hard to imagine how one could prove definitively who betrayed the Annex. Jeroen and I are not sifting through the contradictory accounts of the betrayal in order to somehow "crack" this "cold case"—and using the tropes of detective stories to discuss

CHAPTER 11

Gray Mouse

Now I have to say something that still, after all these years, feels like a confession: my mother, Bep, and my grandfather Johan, who risked their lives to protect the Secret Annex, were not the only Voskuijls whom Anne Frank wrote about in her diary. There was also my aunt Nelly, who was twenty-one at the time of the raid and who appears in a much less heroic light.

I had always known that Nelly, like a lot of other Dutch people, had cozied up to the occupier. But compared to the misdeeds of the average collaborator, her story—as repeated by multiple members of my family over the years—always seemed understandable. Her mistake could have been made by any young person during the war, I thought, and it was a mistake for which she had already paid a heavy price.

At the beginning of the Occupation, when she was just seventeen years old, Nelly worked as a servant for a wealthy family in Amsterdam. The lady of the house happened to be a member of the NSB who frequently entertained German officers at home. It was there that Nelly met an Austrian noncommissioned officer by the name of Siegfried. She fell in love, causing tensions back at Lumeijstraat. Johan was vehemently opposed to his daughter dating a Nazi. Yet Nelly could not be dissuaded.

In 1942, Nelly followed Siegfried back to his home in Austria. Shortly thereafter, Siegfried was sent to the eastern front to fight the

Soviets. Nelly said she would wait for him. She lived with Siegfried's sister and played the role of devoted *Hausfrau*: ironing sheets, making knödel, and practicing her German. All was well until Nelly discovered that there was another woman in Siegfried's life. Heartbroken, she left Austria and returned to the Netherlands after a harrowing journey through occupied France. She did not arrive in Amsterdam until several months *after*—this last point was always emphasized—the raid on the Secret Annex.

That was our "family story," and for most of my life I had no reason to doubt it. I never even knew that Nelly had been mentioned in Anne's diary. All the entries about her had been redacted from every published edition of the diary in both Dutch and English. That was why in August 2009, when researchers from the Collections Department of the Anne Frank House came to interview me (as they routinely do with the family members of witnesses), I told them the old story about Nelly without having any inkling that it was wrong.

I now know not only that it was wrong but that it was a fabrication, designed to protect both Nelly and us from the truth.

A BIG BREAK

In 2010, a year after my interview with the Anne Frank House, Jeroen and I were in the early stages of researching our book about my mother's life. We usually met at a coffee shop in Den Bosch, a city about halfway between Antwerp, where Jeroen lived, and my house in the eastern Netherlands. The café was called 't Gerucht, which in Dutch means The Rumor—a name that became more ironic the deeper we dug into the story. We had a regular table by the window. I ordered tonic water and fried eggs with bacon; Jeroen got a Coke and a Caesar salad. After we ate, we took out our laptops and worked all day long. Much of the work, in the beginning, consisted of talking, remembering, clarifying. Every detail I recalled about the Secret Annex came freighted with some painful family story, usually one that ended with my mother in tears or my father in a drunken rage, and the more I shared with Jeroen, the more I realized that the very subject of the Annex was a family minefield. As much as we talked about why that was the case, neither of us could ever supply a satisfactory explanation.

I usually stopped talking around 5:00 p.m. I remember the feeling of pure exhaustion as Jeroen gathered up his notes and went off to catch a train back to Antwerp. I would stay at the café for an hour or so longer, drinking beer and chatting with the friendly owners, trying to unwind and putting off the long and lonely ride home. The journey took two hours, during which time I wandered through the rooms in my mind, long abandoned and boarded up, that Jeroen in his gentle way had asked me to break into. Each time, I told myself I would not get emotional; each time, I failed. The mixture of feelings was strange; there was pain but also relief, the kind of relief that comes after you set down a great burden.

Once we had discussed everything my mother had told me about the Secret Annex, everything she had told me about Anne and Otto and Johan, we began to talk about my mother's seven siblings, what each of them had done during the war. Jeroen kept getting stuck on Nelly, on the fights between her and Johan, on the questions he had about her whereabouts during the war and her love affair with Siegfried. It struck him as odd that so little was known about her besides the fact that "she did it with Krauts," as my father had once crudely put it. (My mother had been more decorous: "Nelly used to kiss Germans.")

The prospect that two protectors of the Secret Annex lived under the same roof with somebody who was literally in bed with the enemy troubled Jeroen. He noted that Nelly had been mentioned—glancingly but in a sinister way—in earlier books about the Secret Annex, including the German author Mirjam Pressler's 1992 biography of Anne Frank.

I must admit that at first, I didn't like the direction his questions were headed in. "This is my mother's story, Jeroen," I said. "What my aunt did during the war should have nothing to do with it."

I believed that at the time, but I was also, I now realize, *covering* for Nelly. A little voice in the back of my head kept saying that I had to be loyal to her, that she was one of us. Even though my aunt was hardly a family favorite and she remained a troubled and divisive figure until the day she died in 2001, my mother had always stood by her and tried to minimize conflict between her and other members of the family. Why shouldn't I follow her example?

Then, one day in March 2010, came the moment when everything changed, the moment when the scales fell from my eyes. Jeroen had been poking around on the website of the NIOD Institute for War, Holocaust and Genocide Studies, the Amsterdam-based organization that keeps extensive archives on the Second World War and the Holocaust. It has in its collection copies of every single surviving page from all the known versions of Anne's diary, including inaccessible pages that are marked "confidential," usually for privacy reasons.

By mistake, someone at NIOD had uploaded to the public server a confidential document titled "Statements from (and Correspondence with) Persons Who Are Mentioned in Anne Frank's Diaries." It contained mostly letters between the NIOD archivists and former classmates of Anne Frank, several of whom were described bluntly by Anne in the diary—and as a result wished that their true identities be concealed with pseudonyms, usually some made-up abbreviation. There was no correspondence with Nelly, but there was in the file a typescript of lengthy, never-before-published passages from the diary in which she was mentioned.

I had a strange feeling in the pit of my stomach when Jeroen gave me the passages to read. What Anne Frank had written in her famous journal proved that the family story I had grown up with was a fraud. Nelly was not some innocent girl who had merely fallen in love with an Austrian soldier and had her heart broken. She had had many other contacts with the Nazis, first in Amsterdam and then at a Luftwaffe airfield near Laon in the north of France, where she had worked almost until D-Day. But most shockingly, Anne's diary showed that in May 1944, after learning of her father's illness, Nelly had returned home to Amsterdam, which meant she had been living at Lumeijstraat with Bep and Johan at the time of the betrayal.

I cannot express to you the shock I felt at that moment, reading the sinister portrait of Nelly written in Anne's own words, a portrait that had been hidden from me and the rest of the world for some sixty years. I was spooked and uncertain about what to do, what it meant for the book we were working on. For a time, I considered abandoning the project altogether. Jeroen and I had set out to tell my family's story, to explain the *good* the Voskuijls had done; now I had stumbled on information that complicated matters, to say the least.

Around that time, I had a terrifying dream. I saw my mother sitting with her family at the dining table during the war. Nelly was there, in a rebellious mood, bragging about her German boyfriends and the food they had given her. My mother was embarrassed, she was blushing, she was ashamed. Then I noticed her eyes: they were *spinning*, spinning in all directions. The dream echoed something my mother had once told me. At one point during the war, she had been stopped on the street by a German soldier and forced, along with other passersby, to watch the execution of a group of five or six Dutch people who had been taken hostage by the Nazis. That was, sadly, not an uncommon occurrence. After an assassination attempt or act of sabotage by the Resistance, the Nazis would arrest random citizens and force their neighbors to witness the executions in order to deter them from joining the Resistance.

My mother had never seen such violence in her life. The Germans literally kept her from turning her head or averting her eyes as the shots were fired. She spared me more details but told me that afterward, she had felt as though her eyes were spinning, that she had wanted to "rip out her retinas," to unsee what she had just seen.

When I woke, I was full of old regrets and new questions.

HIDING IN PLAIN SIGHT

Why, after so many years and so many suspects, had Nelly Voskuijl never been investigated? The answer was complicated, but it was not for lack of evidence. It took only a little bit of digging for us to uncover a multitude of connections between Nelly and the Nazis: there was an arrest report from 1941 in which she had been dragged into an Amsterdam police station for having violated curfew while out late in the company of a noncommissioned German officer. We found a number of living witnesses who could confirm what Anne had written in her diary—that Nelly had had not just one but several romantic entanglements with Nazi officers during the war. We also learned that her contacts with the enemy had not been only social. Before she had gotten her job working for the Luftwaffe in France, she had worked in Amsterdam for the Wehrmacht as one of the militarized women—derisively nicknamed "gray mice" because of the color of their uniforms—who served as telephone operators, typists, and bookkeepers.

As we discovered more and more about Nelly, we couldn't help but wonder whether she had been the SD's informant, whether the "voice of a young woman" could have belonged to her. Did she offer up her information on the condition that her sister Bep would not be punished after the arrest? Was that why Silberbauer had left my mother alone after the raid, while Miep was harshly interrogated and Kugler and Jo Kleiman were arrested and sent off to prison?

I reviewed the facts in my mind, the statements by Silberbauer and Willy Lages, everything that was known or assumed about the person who had betrayed the Annex: the betrayer had been young and female; she had been well connected to the SD or at least "well known to our service," as Lages had put it, otherwise her tip wouldn't have been acted on immediately; she'd known that there were Jews hiding at Prinsengracht, but she had not known how many. In fact, one of Silberbauer's men, according to Miep Gies, had had to call for a bigger truck that could fit all eight of them inside.

I knew it would be impossible to learn for sure that Nelly was the betrayer; the evidence we had been gathering, at least so far, was all circumstantial and hardly conclusive. But the question that haunted me then and still haunts me today was *what my mother knew*, what she suspected. Did she think that she had been betrayed by her own flesh and blood? Was it that suspicion that had tortured her all those years, that explained why she had always turned away from the cameras, why she had asked Otto and the others to speak for her?

That suspicion would not only explain her reticence, it would also explain why Nelly had always been treated like the black sheep in my family—why my grandmother Christina would never sit next to Nelly at family functions, why my mother would suddenly turn red in her presence, why my father cursed his sister-in-law until his dying day. I had always thought such treatment was ridiculous, strange, even cruel. Sure, Nelly could be at times rude and sarcastic. But did she deserve to be called a "dirty whore," as my father sometimes called her under his breath?

"Cor, don't say that," my mother would snap back at him. "She's still my sister."

The day after one of my father's particularly vulgar drunken outbursts, I asked my mother what was behind his animosity.

"I can't tell you," she said. "Please don't ask me again."

When I asked my father if it was really so bad that Nelly had had a fling with a German soldier, he gave me a look to suggest that there was more to it than that, but he didn't engage further. "You heard your mother—the subject is closed."

A lifetime later, I was beginning to understand why. After weeks of indecision, I decided that the questions surrounding Nelly were too numerous and too troubling to leave unanswered. So Jeroen and I set out to interview her surviving family, the people who had known her, to track down old letters and missing documents, whatever we could find. I also did my own personal research, taking walks around Galileïplantsoen, the street where I had grown up, and passing by the train platform, where I would sometimes look down and see my mother hanging laundry in the backyard. I began rifling through my memories, things I had overheard her and Otto Frank say when I was just a boy, things I couldn't make sense of then that now clicked into place. I was still unsure about where all of it was headed, unsure of the path we were on, but I decided that we should keep going and that I would not make a decision about whether to publish what we found until we had the whole story. The question of family loyalty, at least for the moment, I simply pushed out of my mind.

CHAPTER 12

Exile and Return

Nelly was the kind of person you would instantly notice at a party. She was very tall and buxom, with broad shoulders and long painted lips that curled into a mischievous grin. She had a rebellious nature that seemed only to be heightened by the deprivations—and temptations—of the Occupation. Diny remembers how angry Nelly was in the early days of war—at her parents, at the food shortages, at the stifling, meager life her family led in the four-room apartment on Lumeijstraat. She wanted *more*.

According to "the family story" I grew up with, Nelly's first contact with German soldiers in Amsterdam occurred while she was working as a maidservant in the house of a rich Amsterdam family who supported the Dutch Nazi Party. Yet Jeroen and I, despite an exhaustive search, have not been able to independently verify this story or find any record of Nelly's wartime employment history. We did discover, however, that Nelly's older sister Annie worked as a live-in maid for a wealthy family from 1939 to 1941, according to a registration card in the city archives. Annie's employers, the Jacot sisters, were a trio of former couturiers who had once dressed the Dutch queen. Then in their seventies, they lived together in a grand fin-de-siècle villa at 50 Roemer Visscherstraat, overlooking the Vondelpark, which happened to be the Amsterdam neighborhood of choice for Nazi officers.

Diny said that Nelly came by the house often to visit Annie and would mingle with the soldiers who were quartered in the neighboring apartments. One time, Diny, who would have then been nine or ten years old, went along. Diny vividly remembers a "beautiful house with many levels," a "huge" basement kitchen where she met the butler, and a lovely garden that became a kind of open-air salon where German soldiers were entertained by "the ladies of the house."

"Those German soldiers were sitting very nice and cozily, with their feet on little tables," Diny said. "I didn't understand a word of what they were saying—I didn't speak German as a child."

That villa could have given Nelly her entrée into the world of Nazi Amsterdam, and it could have been the place where she first met Siegfried. But we cannot know for sure. In any case, it did not take long for Nelly's circle of contacts among the occupier to widen. Diny remembers accompanying her sister on a long walk around Amsterdam in 1940. She first shared this story during an interview with the Anne Frank House in 2011, before we spoke to her for this book.

Nelly hadn't announced the destination of their walk in advance, so when she stopped at a garage full of German military cars near Frederiksplein, a square in the city center, Diny couldn't conceal her alarm.

"Don't be too surprised," Nelly said.

There were soldiers relaxing on chairs outside the garage. As Nelly began to walk toward them, her sister stopped her, worried about her safety. Diny was just a girl, but she knew that German soldiers were the enemy, to be avoided at all costs, and that Dutch people who befriended them were called traitors.

"What are you going to do?" Diny asked.

"Take it easy. I'll go upstairs, wait here for me," she said. "I'm going to get some food for Mother." About half an hour later, she emerged with two loaves of dark bread. Her sister was speechless. "I know some German soldiers," Nelly said with a smile.

WINE, WOMEN, AND SONG

Nelly wanted more than just bread from the Germans. According to my mother's onetime fiancé Bertus Hulsman, she started spending most of her free time at social clubs frequented by occupying soldiers. One was a former ice-skating club revamped by the Germans into the Kameradschaftshaus Erika, a kind of recreation center known for *Wein, Weib und Gesang* (wine, women, and song), where Wehrmacht officers could blow off steam and meet a nice Dutch girl.

Some of the establishments were more or less brothels. Imagine a dark room, a series of tables, small pink lamps, men in uniform with iron crosses on their chests. The waiters would not only offer the soldiers jenever and brandy and dishes of beef and pork, but also, according to a period account in the underground newspaper *Het Parool*, young Dutch girls. Sixteen- and seventeen-year-olds were reportedly the favorites. The police vice squad knew of such establishments but turned a blind eye.

Some of the women who frequented those places may have been prostitutes, but many of them were ordinary girls who were taking a serious risk by dating the enemy. The Dutch derisively called them *moffenmeiden* (Krauts' bimbos). According to the historian Monika Diederichs, as many as 145,000 Dutch women had relationships with German soldiers during the war. Some did it because they were in love, some did it out of ideological affinity with Nazism, some were drawn to the glamour and power of the "conquering heroes." But many *moffenmeiden* sought German lovers because of the material benefits that such a relationship would confer on them and their families: food, protection, and a better quality of life, all of which were in short supply in wartime Amsterdam. Yet quality of life was in full display at a place such as the Erika, which by all accounts was a more wholesome and family-friendly place than the typical *Wein, Weib und Gesang* establishment.

The ballroom was decorated in German folk style. There were

wooden beams overhead. Tall windows filled the space with light, and a giant mural showed triumphant German soldiers marching beneath a giant swastika flag. It wasn't only soldiers who were welcome there but also NSB members, German personnel, and their Dutch "friends." The *Deutsche Zeitung in den Niederlanden* (German Newspaper in the Netherlands) described the club as a "home away from home" with "excellent food," German film screenings, concerts, and, every evening from eight to midnight, dancing.

The social club was located a stone's throw from the Rijksmuseum, next to a series of buildings that together symbolized the Nazi leadership in the Netherlands. Here were the Ortskommandantur, the headquarters of the German Army, as well as the Amsterdam police headquarters and the office of Arthur Seyss-Inquart, the Austrian-born Reichskommissar of the occupied Netherlands (who would later be sentenced to death in Nuremberg for crimes against humanity). Sometimes special events were held on the Museumplein. One such event occurred on June 27, 1941, to celebrate the Nazi invasion of the Soviet Union, which had begun five days earlier. Fifty thousand people attended the rally, and beneath a banner that read A NEW EUROPE WITH ADOLF HITLER they listened to Seyss-Inquart describe the importance of the battle against the Soviets "for the Dutch State and for every Dutch citizen in particular."

It's easy to imagine that a girl like Nelly—young, impressionable, defiant—would be seduced by the strength on display. Yet as invincible as she might have felt in the company of Nazis, she was still an underage Dutch girl living in her parents' home and subject to the same rules as anyone else during the Occupation. That was made very apparent to her after midnight on November 1, 1941, when she was arrested by the Amsterdam police for violating curfew. The police report noted that she had been out that night in the company of a German noncommissioned officer in the Nieuwendijk, a commercial row near the central station known for its cinemas and black markets.

My grandfather had to pick Nelly up from the police station, since, at eighteen years old, she was still a minor under Dutch law. After the arrest, Johan forbade Nelly to see Germans. "But she did it anyway," Diny said. "She had a mouth on her. 'I'll do whatever I like!' she would tell Father. That's how she was."

"HEIL HITLER!"

Diny doesn't remember whether my mother was home on that day in the winter of 1941–1942 when Siegfried, Nelly's Austrian boyfriend, visited the house on Lumeijstraat to ask Johan for permission to date his daughter. But she does remember her father's reaction. She and her twin sister, Gerda, were hiding in the room behind the sliding doors.

"There was this big crack we were able to peep through," Diny recalled. "I saw the table, with Mother on one side and Father on the other. The two of us were a bit giggly—a German soldier, you know! And there he suddenly came."

"Herr Voskuijl," he said, clicking his heels. "Heil Hitler!"

Diny remembers how "awful" it was, even as a child, to hear those words spoken in her own home. Johan did not shout, he wasn't rude, but he told the German flatly that he would never grant him permission to see his daughter. The soldier didn't stay for more than five minutes, but when he left, Nelly left with him. She would've probably liked to get her father's approval, but she wasn't going to let his opposition stand in her way.

In December 1942, when Siegfried left Amsterdam to return to his native Austria, Nelly applied for a "Greater German" visa to go with him. Little is known about her stay there. Although Anne would write in her diary that Nelly often sent letters home, none of the letters has survived in my family. I suspect that they may have been destroyed by Nelly herself or by relatives of mine who were keen on protecting Nelly's image and upholding the "family story."

"Nelly hardly spoke about the past," Diny said, but she did once share with her younger sister the sad story of how her stay in Austria ended. After Siegfried was sent to the eastern front, Nelly assumed that if he survived the war, their future together was bright. She hoped they would get married. But Siegfried's sister woke her up from that fantasy by placing a letter for her to find in the linen closet that revealed that Siegfried was engaged to someone else.

"This made her return home brokenhearted," Diny said.

The Siegfried episode did not sour Nelly on Germans, however. According to Bertus Hulsman, once back in Amsterdam, Nelly either lived or spent a lot of time at Huize Lydia, a former Catholic boardinghouse close to the Museumplein that had been turned into a dormitory for *Funkmädel* (German for "radio girls"),* the Dutch women who served as telephone operators, typists, or projection operators for anti-aircraft defense. Many of the women dated German soldiers. And compared to the average Dutch person, they were well provided for. A delivery of fresh food arrived every week, much to the envy of the neighbors.

FIRST ASSISTANT

Sometime in 1944, Nelly left Amsterdam and took a job at a German airfield near the city of Laon in occupied France, where she worked as the secretary and first assistant to the air force commander, according to Diny. It was during that period that Nelly made her first appearance in Anne's diary. Interestingly, Anne did not identify Nelly as "Bep's sister," which is strange since she always made a point of introducing new people and subjects—yet another indication that her

---

* The women were just as often called *Blitzmädel*. *Blitz* (flash of lightning) was a reference to the lightning bolt symbol on their gray uniforms.

diary was written with some future reader in mind. She merely wrote that "Nelly Voskuyl is in L'aône [*sic*] in France. There has been terrible bombing, and she wants to go home at any price."

The lack of introduction could have been just an oversight, but it is more likely that Anne wrote about Nelly in the 1943 A-version (first draft) of her diary, which was lost after the raid and never recovered. Judging by the 1944 passages, my mother clearly spoke openly in the Annex about her wayward sister, so it is quite possible that Anne made mention of Nelly's escapades in Austria or her work among the *Funkmädel* in one of the lost diary entries.

Nelly probably worked at either Laon-Athies or Laon-Couvron, two airfields north of the city from which German Junkers Ju-88A bombers launched raids on the English Channel coast. In the spring of 1944, the air bases were attacked repeatedly by Allied aircraft, including on May 5, when they were targeted by B-17 Flying Fortresses from the US Eighth Air Force. Anne wrote that during that period Nelly "did nothing over there but sit in an air raid shelter" and that she was "terribly frightened."

> She rang one of her many friends, an airman from Eindhoven, in the middle of the night and begged him to help her. The illness of her father would have been a good reason for her to get leave, but only when the poor man dies will she be allowed to come over. Nelly is deeply worried about her past behavior and has asked for forgiveness in her letters.

Anne wrote that Nelly and people like her who worked for the Nazis "will be punished after the war for treason," something she heard on underground radio reports. She thought that Nelly's best course of action to avoid reprisals would be to marry a German citizen, thereby essentially becoming German herself. Yet in the spring of 1944, Nelly seemed most concerned with getting back to her sick father in Amsterdam. She told her Nazi superiors that she would never forgive them if her father died while she was trapped in France. It is impossible to know whether she was genuinely "longing for home and her father," as Anne put it, or whether she was merely using his imminent death as an excuse to escape the Allied bombs.

Yet Nelly's desire to flee did not mean that she had switched sides. Anne joked that Nelly was so enamored of Nazis that she probably kept "a photograph of the Führer" in her wallet. She also wrote that the people in the Annex believed Nelly to be mentally unstable: "They are sure here that Nelly is not one hundred percent right in the head."

On May 11, 1944, Anne reported the "latest news" that Nelly had returned to Amsterdam with her "tin hat and gas mask." She may have tried to make things right with Johan, but it took only a few weeks of living under the same roof before Anne noted that the Voskuijls were having "the old trouble again. Nelly is never at home."

Nelly would disappear from the house for several days, then show up with no notice and expect to be welcomed back. It made Johan, who was sick and depressed, fly into a furious rage. There were bitter fights after which, Anne reported, Johan "stays in bed and weeps a lot." My grandfather knew that my mother was buckling under the pressure of watching over the Annex, and I suspect he couldn't stomach having one daughter protecting innocents from the Nazis and another working for the enemy.

Except for relating the details to Anne, who recorded them in her diary, it's not clear what role my mother played in the Nelly drama. Did she try to mediate? Did she shun her troubled sister? Did she confront her?

Besides Diny, the only other witness we found who had spent time at Lumeijstraat in the spring of 1944 was Bertus Hulsman. After Jeroen and I interviewed Bertus, we managed to obtain a video recording of another interview that he had given to Dineke Stam, a former employee of the Anne Frank House, in 2007, seven years before he sat down with Jeroen and me. That interview confirmed many of the details Bertus later shared with us.

During the interview, Dineke showed Bertus a 1946 photograph of the Voskuijl family. He recognized most of the people, yet he began to study the image closely, looking for someone in particular.

"The one who had an affair with that German seems to be missing," he said.

Actually, Nelly was in the photo, but she was wearing a large hat that shrouded her face. Then Dineke showed him a photograph of the family from the 1930s, and Bertus immediately pointed to Nelly. "That's the one. She had relationships with Germans. You know that, don't you?"

Bertus went on to tell Dineke a troubling story, one that he later repeated to Jeroen and me. At one point during the war, when my mother and Bertus were at the table, a fight broke out with Nelly. He didn't remember when the fight had occurred, what it had been about, or how my mother had reacted, but he said that he would never forget what Nelly had yelled at her before storming out of the house: "Just go to your Jews!"

"Nelly *knew* that Bep and her father were helping Jews," Bertus told Dineke. "That's obvious." He went even further; he wasn't sure, he said, but he believed that Nelly could have been responsible for the betrayal.

Dineke was stunned by the accusation. "Why would she betray them?" she asked. "What would she have gained from it?"

"Perhaps it had something to do with the interrelationships in the family," Bertus said. "Or maybe she wanted to score points, for that's how it went back in those days. And there were bounties for whoever was able to sniff out a Jew. Those kinds of people did exist at the time."

"But . . . why would she turn in the people her sister was protecting?" Dineke wondered. "In that case she must have hated Bep!"

"Because there was always this striking field of tension in the house," explained Bertus. "They were always having fights—not a day went by without arguing. And thus you start wondering. . . . It may have been some kind of revenge. For me it's clear she betrayed the Annex. And you probably think there's not enough proof. But why do I have these thoughts to this very day? I'm now eighty-nine, and I'm still talking about it. I've never stopped saying, 'Before I close my eyes, I'm going to unveil the betrayer's identity.'"

As it turned out, Bertus, who passed away in 2016 at the age of ninety-eight, was not the only one who remembered Nelly screaming "Go to your Jews!" In a letter sent years before I interviewed Bertus, my aunt Diny recalled her sister uttering almost exactly the same words. "Inwardly Nelly was very mad at Father and Bep. Always they had much to tell each other. They did this very, very softly, accompanied by gestures. Nelly didn't tolerate that. At one moment, when Nel had to leave, she said: 'Why don't you go to your Jews!' She suffocated from jealousy because of the special bond that Father had with his eldest daughter."

PUNISHMENT

Neither Bertus nor Diny remembered where Nelly had been on the day of the betrayal. But according to Diny, on the day after, August 5, 1944, she showed up at Lumeijstraat just after dinner.

Johan was an old-fashioned disciplinarian, a stickler for the rules, and before the war he had sometimes spanked his younger children when they misbehaved. But what happened that day was something entirely different. When he started hitting Nelly, he did not stop. She fell to the ground in the corner of the hallway, in the same place my mother had used to give Dutch lessons to Diny by candlelight. Nelly covered her face with her hands. Johan started kicking her; first he struck her legs, then her head, over and over again.

Diny remembers that her mother, Christina, just stood back and watched as Nelly cried out, "Please, Father, not my head! Punish me—but not my head."

All her life, Nelly never made a secret of the fact that her father had viciously beaten her, but she never told anyone why. I think she talked about that day because she was always looking for someone in the family who would care. And I *did* care. I was saddened that this had happened to her, heartbroken that Johan, whose self-sacrifice and moral bearing I respected so much, would have stooped to such a level, whatever his reasons.

I tried a few times in the late 1990s to talk to Aunt Nelly about her past, especially the war years. At the time I had no reason to suspect that she had somehow been involved in the betrayal of Anne Frank, yet I could sense—as much from her silence as from the hints from my family members—that the Occupation was an especially dark chapter in her life.

I suspected that the truth, once revealed, would not be so bad, that her silence was unjustified and unhealthy. She would be better off, I assumed, if she just dragged it out into the open. Yet the three times I summoned the courage to ask her what, exactly, had happened to her during the war, she said she felt dizzy. Her eyes fluttered, and she nearly lost consciousness.

I remember one time in particular when Ingrid and I visited her at home in 1997. Nelly would have been seventy-four at the time. We were drinking coffee when I brought up the war in an offhand way, and before I knew it her eyes were rolling to the back of her head and she was grabbing hold of the table to support herself.

I moved to call an ambulance, but she managed to stop me. "No doctors," she pleaded.

I grabbed hold of her by the arms as she tried to regain control of her body. It was very troubling, but she told me not to worry, as if it were a kind of seizure or spell that she had grown accustomed to. "It'll be over soon."

When she finally regained her composure, she explained that "This happens to me sometimes. I've never been the same since Father kicked me in the head."

I didn't dare to mention the war again that night. I felt too sorry for her. So we sat there in silence until Nelly noticed that our coffee had grown cold, and then she stood up and insisted on making us each a fresh cup.

PART III

BEP

Please know that I will do anything to uphold the symbol of the idealized Anne, which for me is combined with always thinking about what has happened, what I witnessed. This great pain never leaves my heart.

—*Bep Voskuijl to Otto Frank, 1958*

CHAPTER 13

Scraps

On August 5, 1944, the day after the raid on Prinsengracht, my mother decided to visit the Secret Annex one last time. She asked her boyfriend, Bertus, to accompany her because she couldn't face going in alone. Even though Johan, who had visited the Annex himself the night before, told his daughter that the place was now deserted, she knew that she was taking a risk by returning to the scene of the crime. She assumed that her colleagues had all been arrested and that Opekta had been shut down by the Nazis. She and Johan were in fact so worried that Silberbauer would soon come looking for her that she moved out of Lumeijstraat in the immediate aftermath of the raid and went into hiding in a friend's apartment.

Yet despite the risks, she later told my aunt Diny, she had to see the Annex once again with her own eyes to believe that the people she cared for and loved were really gone. Bertus was there to support her, but he was also curious about the hiding place and still amazed that my mother had kept the secret from him for the past twenty-five months.

They waited until it was very late at night, when all was quiet on Prinsengracht. My mother used her company key to enter the building. She led Bertus up the first flight of stairs to the front office. They climbed the *helperstrap* to the landing, where my mother showed Bertus how the bookcase could be unlatched and the door opened. Then they went inside.

The place was ransacked, all the furniture toppled over, the contents of cabinets and drawers spilled on the floor. The smell of food still hung in the air from the last meal the hiders had prepared. Anne wrote that they usually ate breakfast from 9:00 to 9:30 a.m. Food shortages made it difficult to find bread in the summer of 1944, so they breakfasted mostly on fried potatoes or leftover kidney bean soup, which created a pungent smell in the unventilated rooms—where it was always prohibited to open a window, even on a hot August day. Given the timing of the raid, the hiders had already finished their breakfast and were about to sit down for tea or coffee, which Anne noted that they often had around 10:45 a.m., when Silberbauer and his henchmen burst in.

My mother could see that the table had been set—there were cups and spoons and a white porcelain salad bowl with lime jelly in it—but that all the china was clean, unused. Bertus was ninety-five when Jeroen and I interviewed him, yet he remembered the moment as though it had occurred yesterday. He even remembered the look on my mother's face as she surveyed the wreck of the Annex.

"We were both shocked, you know. It was one big mess upstairs. You could tell that the people had left in a hurry. There were still pots and pans on the stove," he said.

Bertus watched as my mother lingered at the table, unable to move. She was beginning to understand the enormity of the loss. She would later tell the writer Ernst Schnabel that though the Annex had become like a second home to her, once inside she felt so paralyzed by fear and grief that "I scarcely dared to take a step."

Bertus said she did not say another word until they were back outside. "When, all those years, you've looked after these people and they're suddenly torn away, what is there left to say?"

FINDING THE DIARIES

The story of the Secret Annex is often told as a fable, in which gaps are covered up and jagged edges smoothed over. In this storybook version of events, Anne's complete diary with its girlish gingham cloth cover was lying on the floor in the wreckage of the raid until the heroic helper Miep Gies rescued it from oblivion. This version of events is implied by the original Hollywood adaptation of the Broadway play *The Diary of Anne Frank* and actually depicted in several more recent TV dramatizations of the story. But it is not true. What actually happened, according to what Jeroen and I could piece together based on historical documents, is both more complicated and more revealing.

On August 4, 1944, while searching for valuables in the Annex, Karl Silberbauer turned the leather briefcase in which Anne kept her writings upside down, spilling the contents onto the floor of the Annex. The next day, Miep Gies, still likely in shock, found the red-checkered diary lying on the floor along with a few notebooks. For some reason, Miep did not notice the loose bundle of heavily annotated sheets of paper lying nearby.

Maybe she didn't realize that those papers were also part of the diary. Or maybe she simply didn't see them. We know that she was moving through the Annex quickly, as Silberbauer had threatened her only the day before, saying he knew full well that she had been in on the secret and would be coming back to Opekta to "check on her." She hurried downstairs and hid the diary in her desk drawer.

What Miep found on August 5 was Anne's original diary, the "A-version," including the red-checkered book that has become the diary's iconic emblem, even though it contains only a small portion of the text that Anne wrote. The A-version was the more spontaneous, less mature draft of Anne's diary, written contemporaneously with the events described. Ingenuous, full of life, and charming, it nevertheless lacks the literary power of the B-version, the revised edition of the original diary that Anne conceived of as an epistolary "war novel" called *Het Achterhuis*.

In a great burst of creativity lasting from May 20, 1944, to sometime right before her arrest on August 4, Anne wrote more than three hundred pages of the revised edition on loose sheets of carbon paper given to her by my mother. That version of the diary was the one that she intended to share with the world, and it formed the basis of the manuscript that Otto later edited for publication, which scholars call the C-version.

"It's hard not to be continuously impressed," the German American literary scholar Laureen Nussbaum wrote about the B-version of Anne's diaries. "Full of self-criticism and literary insight, the barely 15-year-old Anne revised and complemented her original texts and transformed them into a fascinating, easily readable whole."

I sometimes wonder whether we would even know the name Anne Frank today if only the A-version of her diary had survived.

· · · · · · · · · ·

When my mother visited the Annex on August 5 with Bertus several hours after Miep had left, she also did not notice the B-version of the diary lying on the floor. She was probably too upset to search the space for items of sentimental value. That could have turned out to be a tragic mistake, since in a matter of days the Nazis sent a moving truck to the Annex to strip it of anything of value. That was standard practice. The Nazis even had a preferred Dutch moving company, run by the NSB member Abraham Puls, who did their dirty work, systematically pillaging Jewish hideouts after they were raided. When that happened, the people of Amsterdam would say that a house was being "pulsed."

It took my mother nearly a week after the raid to gather the courage to return to work. She spoke to Miep on the phone and discovered that although Jo and Victor had been arrested, Miep herself had been released by Silberbauer after a harsh interrogation in German. As Miep later recalled, he considered her a *Landesverräterin* (traitor to her country) and let her go only *aus persönlicher Sympathie* (out of personal sympathy). My mother also learned from Miep that Opekta had not been seized by the Nazis and was, in some shape or form, still in business.

On her first day back in the office, my mother went to the Annex together with Miep. Remarkably, the table with the empty cups was still standing. The lime jelly in the porcelain salad bowl had grown moldy. The Puls movers had taken almost everything else inside the Annex, leaving behind only books and papers, which had been swept into piles. Miep and my mother walked through the space, making an accounting of what was left. They were still heartbroken, but their heads were clearer. The worst was over, it seemed. When they reached the attic, the place where Anne and Peter had often held their private conversations, my mother noticed a pile of papers "in a jumble" on the floor.

"Look, Miep," she said, "there is Anne's handwriting!"

They sat down on the floor and began to leaf through the papers. They were all Anne's: colored carbon paper taken from the office, tied together with a string. It was the working text of *Het Achterhuis*, the manuscript that would later be known as the B-version.

Interestingly, the very last fragment of Anne's written work to be recovered from the Annex was found not by Miep nor by my mother but by Willem van Maaren. A few days after the B-version of the diary was found, he was snooping around in typical van Maaren fashion when he showed up at my mother's desk. My mother still suspected him of the betrayal at that point, and she could barely conceal her fury when he delivered the pages to her, saying that he had found "more stuff" in the Annex.

That you of all people are the one to give this to me! she thought, snatching the pages from van Maaren and placing them in the drawer with the rest of Anne's writings. My mother still hoped with all her heart that she would be able to return the texts to their author.

In addition to the diaries, my mother rescued a few other things of emotional value from the Annex. She later offered those things to Otto. But he wanted only his portable typewriter; the rest, he said, she could keep for herself. The things included the porcelain salad bowl, which she washed out and took home to Lumeijstraat, as well as the Stock Exchange board game, a Dutch cousin of Monopoly, which Peter van Pels had been given for his sixteenth birthday. My mother had sometimes played the game in the Annex with Peter, Anne, and Margot. And when I was a boy, I played it as well. I still remember sitting in the living room with my mother and brothers and turning the dial that determined whether your stock price was low (*baisse*) or high (*hausse*). But I had no idea, as I counted up my imaginary winnings, whose fingerprints were on the game. Many years later, my mother donated that board game to the Anne Frank House.

MAD TUESDAY

My aunt Nelly did not stay in Amsterdam for long after the raid on the Secret Annex. In fact, she left the city for Germany almost exactly a month later, on Tuesday, September 5, 1944. It was a fateful day in the history of the Occupation, known as Dolle Dinsdag (Mad Tuesday). The BBC had reported that the British had invaded the southern Dutch town of Breda, some sixty-five miles from Amsterdam. Euphoria immediately gripped the city; people took out their Dutch flags and gathered in the streets. Everyone, including German soldiers and their Dutch collaborators, thought the Liberation was imminent. Many Germans rushed toward the border, as well as approximately sixty thousand NSB members, who, fearful of reprisals, simply abandoned their homes.

There was a German family, the Reiches, who lived one floor down from the Voskuijls at 18 Lumeijstraat. Ernst Reiche was a technician who worked at a photo shop in Amsterdam. He and his wife, Flora, came from Weissig, near Dresden, but they had been living in the Netherlands since the early 1920s. They had two children: a boy, Hermann, who was eleven in the fall of 1944, and a girl, Louisa, who was nineteen—nearly the same age as Nelly. It is likely, given Nelly's interest in German language and culture and her proximity to the Reiche family, that she and Louisa became friends. Diny remembers that Nelly would often spend her free time with the Reiches, particularly when she was bickering with Johan or her sisters.

Though the Reiche family spoke Dutch fluently and had been long established in the Netherlands, and though they had no clear connection to the occupying forces, they may have feared that their German origin would make them a target once the Liberation came. Or, like a lot of Dutch residents with ties to Germany, they may have actively supported the NSB and the occupier. In any case, in the mad rush of Dolle Dinsdag, the family hastily packed a few bags and took off, leaving everything else behind. According to Diny, Nelly decided to go with them. Perhaps even more than the Reiche family, she had reason to flee ahead of the Liberation; her romantic entanglements with Nazis and her work for the German Army were widely known.

Diny remembers that Nelly didn't even leave a note.

We don't know how the rest of the Voskuijl family reacted to Nelly's sudden departure, but the departure of the Reiches provided them an opportunity to leave their cramped upstairs apartment and occupy the much larger downstairs apartment, a move that was recorded in the city archives. Diny said that the Reiche family had left nearly all of their furniture and clothes in the apartment, so she and her sister Annie helped themselves to some much needed things.

As it turned out, the Dolle Dinsdag celebrations were premature. The BBC report had been incorrect. There would be no Liberation— at least not yet.

THE LAST WINTER

The Dutch call the winter of 1944–1945 the Hongerwinter, a season of starvation. Food supplies plummeted, malnutrition was rampant, mothers scavenged through trash bins looking for food for their families. People ate tulip bulbs and candle wax. My mother's family couldn't afford to heat their house, so the twins, Diny and Gerda, spent most of the winter shivering beneath their covers. Though Opekta was nominally in business, its operations ground to a halt; there were no more raw materials with which to make food products.

The Allies had almost liberated the Netherlands in the months after the Normandy invasion. They made it as far as Maastricht on the Belgian border by September 1944 and landed more forces near Arnhem, a city in the eastern Netherlands, a gateway to the Rhine. But the expected invasion was repulsed after a fierce battle, dashing hopes that the Occupation would be over before the onset of winter. Everyone knew by now that the Nazis were *eventually* headed for defeat; the question was who would be alive to celebrate the victory.

There was no coal to heat homes; railway workers were striking; airports and harbors had been destroyed. Not a single tram was running in the entire city of Amsterdam. Schools were shut down. The Germans plundered apartments and rounded up any men under the age of fifty who could be pressed into forced labor. It felt like the end times. And then the harsh winter weather set in; the IJsselmeer Bay north of Amsterdam froze over. People began stripping historic buildings for scrap wood and anything else that could be burned as fuel. According to the historian Geert Mak, some 20,000 trees were cut down and 4,200 homes destroyed that winter alone.

If the Annex had not been betrayed, I can't imagine the difficulties my mother and Miep would have faced finding food for the hiders during that period. During each month of the winter, more than a thousand Amsterdammers perished from starvation or exposure. The Resistance fought harder than ever, but as their sabotage and assassination attempts grew more audacious, so did the Nazi reprisals. Public executions became a ghastly routine. The Voskuijls did not escape the suffering. Christina developed hunger edema, the swollen belly that is often a symptom of starvation, because she gave every scrap of available food to her children.

Black-market prices doubled, then tripled, then quadrupled. My mother and Miep didn't dare ride their bikes to work anymore; it was too dangerous. A German or even a Dutchman, seeing a functional bike, might steal it on the spot. Everyone was weak, on the edge of fainting. What little business Opekta received came mostly from butchers, who wanted imitation sausage fillings.

"We were using filler made from ground-up nutshells purchased in bulk and bottles of synthetic scents from a chemical factory," Miep recalled in her memoir.

> When these two products were mixed, they looked and smelled almost like the real thing. Naturally, they had no taste, but the smell and consistency created the suggestion of sausage filling that would bind together with ground meat to make sausage. These butchers were making sausage from God knows what, there was so little meat around. Never did we ask questions; it was better not to know.

"FORMALITY, BUREAUCRACY, AND COLDNESS"

By the time the Liberation came in May 1945, the local supply of sympathy for wartime suffering—especially suffering borne by Jews—was close to zero. The attitude of the average Amsterdammer was that *everyone* had suffered, *everyone* had lost—*what makes your pain matter more than mine?* The historian Dienke Hondius, who wrote a book about the treatment of Dutch survivors of the Holocaust, said that they were welcomed back by their countrymen with "formality, bureaucracy, and coldness." Jewish survivors often received little to no assistance from the Dutch state; they were told to apply to Jewish organizations for help. Fearing an outbreak of disease and lice, the government even quarantined many survivors, putting camp victims back into camps, where the conditions were often appalling.

In the summer of 1945, a former Resistance newspaper, *De Patriot*, told survivors that they should "feel humble" and not try to exploit their suffering: "There can be no doubt that the Jews, specifically because of German persecution, were able to enjoy great sympathy from the Dutch people. Now it is appropriate for the Jews to restrain from excess."

Some female survivors whose heads had been shaved in the camps were insulted in the streets as people mistook them for traitors, whose heads were often shaved as punishment for collaborating with the enemy. Jews returning to their old homes would find strangers living there who refused to move out. One awful story recorded by Hondius tells of a camp survivor who, while registering as a repatriated citizen, was greeted this way by a Dutch bureaucrat: "Not another Jew! They must have forgotten to gas you."

These may be extreme cases, but they speak to a general attitude toward Jewish victims in the aftermath of the Liberation. Many non-Jewish Dutch people were waiting for their own relatives to return from German forced labor camps. The country had been exhausted by the nearly five-year Occupation and bled dry by the Hongerwinter. That explained—but did not excuse—the wall of silence on the part of many Dutch, who had no appetite to hear about gas chambers, sadistic medical experiments, or death marches, things that seemed to make their own very real suffering shrink in comparison.

My mother experienced some of that coldness firsthand when she got in touch with the company that had provided Margot Frank with correspondence courses during the Occupation. She wanted to explain that though a course had been completed in my mother's name, it was a bright Jewish girl in hiding who had done the work and she should get credit, if she made it back.

Gentlemen,

Since the war has come to an end . . . only now I am able to explain to you the whole situation.

The lessons you have sent to me were not meant for myself, yet for a young girl in hiding. This girl was arrested and taken away by the Germans in August 1944 and hasn't returned ever since. You see, my address was just meant as a cover. You will understand that it is impossible for me to continue a course I actually had nothing to do with. Should the concerned girl return, then she will surely get in contact with you, as she found the greatest pleasure in her study.

I would like to ask you to inform Mr. A. Nielson about the case. I know that this gentleman corrected the lessons with great commitment and took pains to make the lessons as interesting as possible. . . .

I remain, with most sincere regards,

Ms. E. Voskuijl
263 Prinsengracht
Amsterdam

In response, the company said that it would stop sending lessons but noted that there was a bill of 7.50 guilders in tuition left to pay. "As soon as we receive this final payment, the course has been paid in full."

That was it. No condolences, no violins—just business.

MISSED CONNECTIONS

Though Bertus Hulsman was there for my mother in those painful, uncertain weeks after the raid on Prinsengracht, in the fall of 1944 he began to drift away. The worsening conditions in Amsterdam kept him on the farm in Heino where he had been hiding out from the Germans. He spent the Hongerwinter there, and in April 1945, the town was liberated by Canadian troops. Caught up in the excitement of the impending victory, he met a young Dutchman who was planning to sign up with the US Marines to take the fight all the way to Berlin.

When Bertus decided to join up as well, my mother was faced with a choice: to continue to wait for him, as she had been waiting all those past months, in the hope that one day soon they could get married and settle down, or break off the engagement. Her father was deathly ill, but she went to him for counsel. Johan told her that although Bertus was a good man, she had waited for him long enough.

In the end, Bertus's hopes of joining the marines were dashed. Germany surrendered on May 7, 1945. Bertus thought he could still be of some service to the Americans by fighting the Japanese. But after spending a few months in limbo waiting to be called up, he found himself in a scabies-infested camp for would-be recruits in Antwerp, where he learned that atomic bombs had been dropped on the Japanese cities of Hiroshima and Nagasaki. Less than a month later, the war was over. In September 1945, Bertus returned to Amsterdam, but he did not try to revive his relationship with my mother or even contact her.

It was difficult for me to listen to Bertus discussing that period because it was clear that though a lifetime had elapsed since the events he was describing, he still felt an enormous burden of guilt for having left my mother. "We were engaged, but I abandoned her, and that caused her so much pain. I really shouldn't have done that. Look, I'm getting goose bumps just talking about it."

Bertus felt that he had to justify his actions to me. "Back then, you wanted adventure, you wanted revenge against the Germans and to be able to fight back. I had been in the military before the surrender,

I had experienced the bombings of Rotterdam with all those victims. And I just wanted to do *something*."

When he got back to Amsterdam with nothing to show for his efforts, he told me, "I was ashamed. I couldn't bear to face Bep again."

In the spring of 1945, Victor Kugler returned to Opekta. He had suffered terribly in a succession of Nazi prison camps but had managed to escape when a chain gang he was marching in had been strafed by a British Spitfire. Relying on friendly farmers who had given him shelter, he made his way across the Dutch countryside and back to his hometown of Hilversum, where he hid out with his sick wife. After the Liberation, he returned to Opekta, resumed his old job, and tried to rekindle his romance with my mother.

My aunt Diny told me that in those first few weeks of freedom, Victor actually asked my mother if she would run away with him to America, to start a new life across the ocean. My mother still had feelings for Victor. And now that Bertus had broken off the engagement, she was unattached. Yet she told him to go home to his wife.

"She really liked Kugler," Diny told me. "But she couldn't break up a good marriage. 'There are choices in your life you simply shouldn't make.' I can still hear her say that."

I can't say, after all these years, that my mother made a mistake by telling Victor no. If she had gone with him, I wouldn't be here to tell this story. Yet I think she was haunted for a long time by the question of what her life might have looked like if she had said yes. Diny said that years later, my mother would sometimes stand still in her kitchen as a train ran past our house and wish that she was on it.

Victor's long-suffering wife, Laura, finally died in 1952, and shortly afterward, he remarried and crossed the ocean to start a new life, just as he had planned. It would be many years before he and my mother would see each other again.

CHAPTER 14

Uncle Otto

How can I begin to repay everything these people have done?

—*Otto Frank, May 1945*

I have already mentioned this statistic, but it bears repeating: 75 percent of Dutch Jews were murdered in the Holocaust, giving the Netherlands the highest death rate among Western European countries occupied by the Nazis. Most of those deaths occurred before September 6, 1944, the day the residents of the Secret Annex arrived at Auschwitz after a hellish seventy-two-hour journey on cattle cars.

At that point in the war, the machinery of the Nazi genocide, which had been working with terrible efficiency, was starting to wind down. In fact, the Franks, the van Pelses, and Fritz Pfeffer were on the very last train from Westerbork to Auschwitz. That fact did not improve their chances of survival. Only 127 of the 1,019 Jews aboard that train would make it out of the camps alive.

Otto was one of them. After arriving at Auschwitz, he and the other men from the Annex were separated from the women and sent to Block II in the main Auschwitz camp, known as Auschwitz I. There they were forced to do hard labor: building roads, slaving away in the mines, even peeling potatoes when they were too weak to do anything else. Hermann van Pels was the first to die; he injured his finger digging in the fall of 1944 and, unable to work efficiently, was gassed. Around the same time, Fritz Pfeffer was transferred to the Neuengamme concentration camp in northern Germany, where he died of an infection on December 20.

Otto nearly succumbed from exhaustion. One day in November 1944, he was viciously beaten by his *Kapo* (inmate overseer). He spent the following two months starving in the camp's infirmary. Peter van Pels, who had found himself in the relatively fortunate position of working in the mail office at Auschwitz, managed to visit Otto and take him scraps of food. As Soviet troops closed in, all Auschwitz prisoners who could still walk were evacuated to other camps farther west. Otto begged Peter to hide with him in the infirmary until the Russians arrived, but Peter thought he was strong enough to survive the death march. And he did survive. He made it to Mauthausen in Austria, where he was forced to do slave labor in nearby mines despite his progressively worsening health. He lived long enough to see US troops liberate the camp on May 5, 1945, but according to the camp hospital records, he died five days later of an unspecified illness. He was eighteen years old.

After his liberation from Auschwitz on January 27, 1945, Otto Frank, along with other survivors, was housed in an empty school in the city of Katowice, Poland, while he recuperated and gathered his strength for the long journey back to Amsterdam. In Katowice, Otto met a Dutch woman named Rosa de Winter, who had befriended his wife at Auschwitz. She told him of Edith's final days: how she had developed a high fever, been sent to the infirmary, then died "completely exhausted" on January 6, 1945, three weeks before the camp was liberated.

The last time she had seen Edith, Rosa wrote later, "she was only a shadow."

Even if part of him had suspected that news, Otto was devastated. He wrote his mother, "Only the thought of the children keeps me going."

In the spring of 1945, he began the journey home. He left Poland and traveled east into Ukraine, then south toward the Black Sea port of Odessa, where he boarded a steamer that took him through the Bosporus and Dardanelles and into the Mediterranean Sea. His boat docked in Marseille in late May, and he was back in Amsterdam by June 3. Having no place to live, he moved in with Miep and Jan Gies in Hunzestraat in Amsterdam South. There he learned that Miep and my mother had not been arrested after the raid and that Victor and Jo had survived the Nazi prison camps. The Opekta Circle was intact; now they closed ranks around their former boss.

The next day, June 4, Otto returned to the office on Prinsengracht. My mother remembered how "terribly nervous" he looked. He went into the Annex but could find barely a trace of the old life in the mostly empty space. He noticed five brown beans on the floor in Peter's room and recognized them as being from a bag of dried beans that had burst when Peter had tried to carry it to the attic for storage. Otto picked the beans up, put them into his pocket, and would hold on to them until the day he died.

On June 5, only his second day back in Amsterdam, Otto went to Lumeijstraat to spend time with my mother's family. Since word of Johan's illness had reached the Annex two years earlier, he had wanted to pay his respects. Now he finally had the chance. Diny remembered that moment, the emaciated Otto's almost spectral presence in the front room as the Voskuijl family gathered around him. He described what it had been like to say goodbye to his wife and children on the first day in Auschwitz, the chaos in the camp before the Liberation, the nervousness and abject misery.

"I really hung on his every word," Diny recalled.

It was hard for him to speak at times, and at one point, he became so overcome with emotion that he excused himself and left abruptly.

"Recalling memories for two hours was too painful," Diny said. "The events were still too fresh."

Though the war was over, that June of 1945 was probably the most anxious and terrifying month of Otto's life—waiting for news, hoping against all odds, then watching as those hopes slowly slipped down the drain.

"I just can't think how I could go on without the children, having lost Edith already," he wrote his sister, Leni. "It's too upsetting for me to write about them. Naturally I still hope, and wait, wait, wait."

But then the waiting stopped. On July 18, while searching a list of camp victims from the Red Cross, he saw the names Margot Betti Frank and Annelies Marie Frank. Someone had drawn a little black cross beside each name. Camp survivors were asked to add those marks next to the names of people they knew had perished. Otto asked who had supplied the information and was given the address of Rebekka "Lien" Brilleslijper, a thirty-two-year-old Dutch woman who, along with her sister Marianne, nicknamed Janny, had tried to help Anne and Margot in their final days. Otto visited the Brilleslijper sisters at their home in Laren in North Holland, and they told him what they had witnessed.

At the end of October 1944, Anne and Margot had been transferred to the German concentration camp of Bergen-Belsen. There had been so many people arriving at that time from camps farther east that most of the prisoners had had to live in tents, barely sheltered from the elements. Everyone was freezing, starving, and riddled with disease, which spread quickly because of the overcrowding and the total lack of sanitation. Margot was the first to succumb to typhus in February 1945; Anne died a few days later, just weeks before the camp was liberated by British troops.

Otto could not really process the information at first. He wrote to his younger brother, Herbert, that he was trying to distract himself as much as possible. "No one has to know how I'm grieving on the inside. Who would be able to understand anyway? My fantastic people here, but only that small group." About that period, Otto later wrote in his memoir, "My friends, who had been hopeful with me, now mourned with me."

My mother, who was in the small group around Otto, never in her life spoke about the moment when she learned that Anne and Margot would not be coming back. The only thing we know is that around that time she wrote a condolence card to Otto's elderly mother, Alice, in Basel, who was suffering greatly from the loss of her only granddaughters. That note did not survive, but we do know that Alice Frank replied at once and thanked Bep for her "sweet card."

Around that time, Miep gave Otto every page from Anne's diary that she and my mother had found in the Annex. For the moment, he put the bundle of papers and notebooks aside. "I still don't have the strength to read it," he wrote his mother in August.

On November 7, 1945, Otto made his final visit to my grandfather's bedside. Johan was then too weak to stand up and shake his old boss's hand. He must have known that his time was almost up. There is a story in my family that Nelly, who had recently returned from Germany and was living in the city of Groningen, two hours away from Amsterdam, was called to her father's bedside in the last days of his life and some kind of reconciliation occurred between them. My aunt Willy claimed that it was Nelly herself who had told her, "Father forgives me."

"Forgives her for what?" I once asked Willy. But she just brushed off the question.

No one else in my family has been able to confirm whether the reconciliation was a fact or wishful thinking on the part of Willy or perhaps Nelly herself.

On November 27, 1945, Johan finally died at home in his bed at the age of fifty-three. He was buried in Amsterdam on December 1. Otto went to the funeral. It is not known whether Nelly was also in attendance.

FATHER OF THE BRIDE

May 15, 1946, was the sixth anniversary of the German occupation of the Netherlands. It was also the day my parents got married.

Otto was there to give away the bride. I sometimes get choked up just thinking about that fact. It was only a year since he had returned from Auschwitz, a year since he had learned that he had lost his entire family. Yet there he was, forcing a smile while posing for pictures with my mother in her wedding dress outside the municipal building in Amsterdam. How must it have felt to be him in that moment, standing in as the father of the bride, knowing full well that his two girls would never have weddings of their own?

On top of grief, there was so much guilt. The economic situation in the Netherlands made it hard for Opekta to stay in business. In the beginning Otto went to work mostly to "divert myself," he told his sister, Leni. Yet it was difficult. There were virtually no basic materials. The firm was losing money, yet each week the employees' salaries had to be paid.

Otto was trying "to build a new existence in Amsterdam"—to rebuild the business, if not for himself, then for the people who had stood by him. But he was ashamed that some weeks he couldn't afford to pay my mother and her colleagues. Everyone understood why. They knew he was trying his best under difficult circumstances. But Otto thought his best wasn't good enough. He asked his relatives in Switzerland to send money, clothing, and food for my mother and her coworkers. And he looked for creative ways to keep the company afloat.

"How can I begin to repay everything these people have done?" he wrote to his relatives. "Here I'm surrounded by the people who were with us daily when we were in hiding, who risked everything for us in spite of all the dangers and the threats of the Germans. How often Edith and myself impressed on the girls to never forget those people, and to help them in case *we* didn't come back. We knew we owed everything to them."

Otto felt grateful to all the helpers for what he called their "unparalleled sacrifice," but he was especially devoted to my mother, perhaps because she was so young or fragile or because she had only recently lost her own father. That was probably why he couldn't refuse when she asked him to walk her down the aisle.

As painful as the wedding might have been for Otto, he was happy for my mother. Anne would have been happy for her, too. Anne had written in her diary that she hoped Bep would marry "a man who knows how to appreciate her." Bertus was probably too immature. Victor was married. But Cor van Wijk must have seemed like an ideal match.

A vigorous young man with a sharp nose and strong chin, he was optimistic, energetic, and fun-loving. He had trained as a furniture maker and before the war had started his own small upholstery and wallpaper business in Amsterdam. He came from an honest, hard-working family that was already close with the Voskuijls. My mother was friendly with his sister, Rie. And in the desperate, uncertain days after the Annex had been raided, she briefly moved in with the van Wijk family in case the Nazis came looking for her at home. They lived at 12 Joos Banckersweg, just a ten-minute walk from Lumeij-straat.

At the time, Cor was working at a forced labor camp in Germany, but when he came back to Amsterdam after the Liberation, Rie pointed out Bep to him one day when they passed her on the street. "Look, Cor, that's the girl who slept in your room!"

Introductions were made, and within weeks, the two were inseparable. Cor behaved like a perfect gentleman at first. He had a big heart and, like my mother, was warm and generous. He picked her up from work at Prinsengracht every day. He charmed Otto, who gave him a personal tour of the Secret Annex. Cor was deeply touched by the story and amazed that Bep, despite her retreating nature, had been so brave.

My parents had a big wedding, owing to the size of the Voskuijl family and the celebratory mood coursing through postwar Amsterdam; even with all the hardships people faced then, no one wanted to miss out on a party after five years of occupation. Miep and her husband, Jan, attended. So did Nelly Voskuijl. It was the first time that she and Otto came face-to-face, and it was likely the last. My aunt Diny remembers Otto staring fixedly at Nelly, trying to catch her eye. But she wore a large, drooping felt hat, and she seemed almost to be hiding beneath it.

Otto made it through the ceremony, but after posing for a picture with Bep, he left abruptly. He seemed troubled. Perhaps he had been overcome by emotion. Perhaps he could not stomach being in Nelly's presence. He had no reason yet to suspect her of betraying his family, but at the very least he knew—because my mother had spoken openly about it in the Annex—that Nelly had worked for the German military and had love affairs with Nazis.

Otto may have been forgiving by nature, but at least in the early years after his return from Auschwitz, he wanted to discover the identity of the person who had betrayed the Annex. He once even walked up and down Prinsengracht, ringing the doorbell of every house (as well as those on the side streets) to ask whether the occupants had been aware that people had been hiding in the *achterhuis* behind number 263.

"All the surrounding neighbors told us the same story," Otto said later. "'Yes,' they said, 'we knew all along that hiders were staying in the Annex.' But no one had said anything."

More stories came to light in the months after the Liberation. One employee at a neighboring upholstery store said he had heard voices coming from the Annex. Another worker in a nearby warehouse had heard water flowing through the drainpipes late at night, when the office was supposed to be closed. Otto and the others realized that their Annex had been anything but secret. Given that fact, the only surprising thing about the betrayal was that it had taken so long to happen.

SETTLING DOWN

In 1947, after a decade of service to Opekta, my mother resigned from her job to raise a family. She must have already been pregnant; my brother Ton was born that year. Another brother, Cok, arrived in 1948. I was born in 1949. We lived in a little house on Galileïplantsoen in Amsterdam East, in front of a pond where we ice-skated in winter.

Even though my mother always avoided talking about the war, my brothers and I could feel the legacy of those years in the way she scrimped and saved. Our plates had to be clean after every meal. We mopped up every morsel of food, just as she had done when having lunch in the Annex. Old bread was made into porridge or French toast. Clothes were patched and darned. Though the Nazis were no more, Bep maintained the quiet vigilance she'd had during the Occupation, an attentiveness to danger, as if part of her were still living that old double life.

The name Anne Frank was not to be mentioned at home. That became an unwritten rule, enforced by my father. His decision to prohibit all discussion of the Annex was rooted in kindness. He saw how distraught my mother would get when somebody asked her about the war, so he thought that she was better off not talking about it at all.

"Don't do it, Beppie," he'd implore. "You'll only get emotional."

He was not wrong. My mother was reduced to tears whenever she tried to recall the Annex or talk about Anne and Margot. Yet my father's rule had the effect of forcing her pain underground. As the years wore on, she would be more and more reluctant to dredge up the subject, even with close family.

"Usually, when I asked her anything about the Annex, she'd take a long time to think, and finally she wouldn't say more than a word or two," my aunt Diny recalled. "She said she would rather not talk about it because it had been so terrible. And that was the end of it."

Though my father didn't want my mother to be burdened by her past, his position was complicated by the fact that he also desperately wanted the outside world to recognize her for what she had done. As Anne Frank's fame grew, it infuriated him that Miep Gies and the other guardians of the Annex received more attention than she did.

When Otto visited us, he would tell my mother the latest news about the diary: the various documentaries, interviews, and memorials, none of which my mother wanted to take part in. Cor would stew quietly, thinking about how his wife was being left out. That reached a peak in the late 1950s, when the Hollywood film about the diary became a hit around the globe. My mother, my grandfather, and Jo Kleiman—all were erased from the story; Miep was credited by name, and Kugler was identified with his pseudonym from the early edition of the diary, Mr. Kraler.

When Otto visited us around that time, my father could barely contain his resentment. The many snide remarks he made under his breath made my mother terribly anxious, which often caused her to suffer a migraine the next day. My father knew the effect he was having on her, but he was unable or unwilling to keep his mouth shut.

THE OLD MAN AND THE SEA

My clearest memory of Otto Frank comes from the summer of 1963. I was thirteen, accompanying my mother on a visit to Noordwijk, a small resort town about thirty miles southwest of Amsterdam on the North Sea. It was a hot August day, and *Ome* (Uncle) Otto, as I called him, was waiting for us on the terrace of a luxury hotel.

A collar of tall grass separated the boardwalk from the beach, which was crowded with candy-striped tents and people sunbathing. Dutch flags blew in the wind, and at the end of the boardwalk there was a lighthouse. It was the peaceful Netherlands of my childhood, and I had no idea at the time that the beachhead had been heavily fortified by the Nazis, that just beyond the lighthouse were bunkers and pillboxes, the remnants of the Atlantic Wall defenses. Most of the guns were dismantled and the bunkers covered up with sand. The beach, like the country, was trying to move on.

Otto hadn't changed much from the newspaper photographs I had seen in my mother's scrapbook from the early 1950s; I recognized his beneficent smile, the push-broom mustache, and the sad, twinkling eyes. But now, in his early seventies, his eyebrows had turned white and there were sunspots on his bald head.

He loved the sun. In summer, he liked to arrange meetings with journalists and admirers here, in the fresh air, with the sea breeze blowing across the broad terrace. Perhaps being in a space that was open, free, and flooded with light somehow made talking about those dark, cramped days easier.

My mother explained to me that Uncle Otto was "an important person." Celebrities and politicians wanted to have their picture taken with him. Schoolchildren sent him thousands of letters. He tried his best to answer each one. Many people just wanted to thank him— for not giving up on humanity, for sharing his daughter's story with the world. He had moved to Switzerland by that point—the weight of the past in Amsterdam had been too much to bear—but he often came back to Holland on visits related to human rights work or the Anne Frank House, which had been opened to the public in May 1960. Despite his full schedule, he always made time to see us and to check in on my mother.

Otto realized that something was wrong with her almost immediately after we sat down. He took her by the hand and listened quietly. She was whispering to him. I'm not sure exactly what was said.

I remember that she mentioned her sister's name—Nelly—but not much else. I left at one point to go to the bathroom. When I came back to the terrace, I saw that my mother was crying. Otto decided that I shouldn't be there; perhaps he didn't want me to hear what was being said, or perhaps he just wanted to give her some space.

He motioned for my mother to stop speaking. Then he gave me some money as a gift for my birthday, which was coming up in September. I happily ran off along the boardwalk to buy myself a present. It didn't take me long to pick something out: a large kite called *Groene Valk* (Green Falcon).

Later that afternoon, Uncle Otto showed me how to fly the kite. By that point, we had moved to the beach. My mother was relaxing in a chaise longue, watching us play. I could see why she confided in Otto—he was so gentle and patient that I felt he would understand almost anything. I asked him why it was that my mother always cried around him.

He smiled. "Because she loves my family and me," he said.

Then he told me to run off and play with my present and returned to my mother's side. I watched them laugh together before turning my attention back to the Green Falcon. I remember feeling a surge of pride in that moment. It might have been because my mother was so close to such a special person, or it might have just been because I was now able to fly the kite high in the air all by myself.

TROUBLE AT HOME

My father's birthday fell on Christmas Eve. Despite my mother's best efforts, it was almost always an unhappy occasion. She would roast a turkey, decorate the table, take out our best china, wrap gifts. Papa didn't need a special occasion to get drunk, but on holidays he would not stop drinking until he passed out. It was not a question of *if* the night would take an ugly turn but *when* it would happen.

I remember one of his birthdays in particular. It was 1962, so he would have been turning forty-three. The night was unusually cozy. We had lit the oil heater, and my mother and brothers were in a happy mood, giggling as my father dosed himself with gin. Yet at a certain point in the evening, Papa got the idea that we were laughing about him. It was always some tiny, practically nonexistent slight that wormed its way into his pickled brain. Without warning, he exploded, standing up at the table in a fit of fury, grabbing the tablecloth, and hurling all the food and dishes onto the floor.

I screamed as he lunged at my mother and began cursing. Christina, my sixty-three-year-old *oma* (grandmother), was at the table that night, and she quickly sprang into action, pushing my father away from my mother. The woman had lived through hell and was not about to be afraid of a little tantrum by her drunk son-in-law.

"You wanna fight, Cor? Go ahead!" she said, rolling up her sleeves in a motion that would have been funny if she hadn't been deadly serious. "You go first!"

I was terrified. My mother, however, kept her cool. I'll never forget the way she reacted. She quickly removed her eyeglasses, shut off the oil heater, and scooped up the children. In a flash, she had assessed all the risks and was trying to minimize them. Using us as a shield was a smart move; it had the effect of defusing my father's anger, making him ashamed of himself. Later that night, after Papa had passed out, Mother and I made eye contact. She let a small smile escape from her lips. The message was that she was in control, that, come what may, I needn't worry.

Despite my father's many character flaws, I actually felt bad for him. He was a cheerful person by nature who was ill equipped to help my mother process her pain. He worked very hard to support his family, sometimes wallpapering five or six rooms in a day. He would come home exhausted and "grant" himself three shots of liquor, which he kicked back quickly before dinner. I sometimes think he drank to cope with my mother, who often spent her days feeling sad and lost, looking right through him.

Their marriage had started out strong, but cracks had emerged in the late 1940s, and as the relationship had deteriorated, my mother retreated deeper into herself. By the 1950s, she started to investigate the roots of her pain. She began writing long letters to Otto and the other members of the Opekta Circle, trying to make sense of what had happened. But all that seemed to do was to open old wounds.

"I'm stuck again," she'd sometimes say to me.

I now think what she meant was that she was back in the Annex, replaying the events, thinking about it over and over again. I couldn't understand what it was that so tortured her. Of course, what had happened to Anne Frank and the others in hiding was horrible, yet what more could she have done? Couldn't she give herself a break? Couldn't she be proud that she had managed to hold on to some of her humanity, that she had been brave in the face of such barbarism? Although she sometimes said that she and the other helpers had "failed" in their efforts to keep the Annex a secret, no one faulted her for what had happened, for how it had ended. To the contrary, the world seemed poised to *celebrate* her, if only she'd allow it.

"Why are you always so sad when you go back in your mind to that time?" I asked her when I was only ten years old. "It's just beautiful what you've done."

My mother started sobbing. "My dear boy . . . that grief will never leave my heart."

My father, seeing the tears stream down her cheeks, lost his temper. "Joop, can't you see that she can't handle talking about this?"

Around that time, I noticed that my mother would often sob quietly in the mornings while sitting at her writing desk in the living room. As the weeks passed and she grew more hopeless and forlorn, I began to watch over her, to worry about what she might do.

One Friday morning in the winter of 1959, we were home alone together. My father had gone to work early, and my brothers had already left for school. I thought I heard the same soft sobs coming from my mother's bedroom. I tried to ignore them—I'm sad to say that they were becoming rather routine at that point—but soon the sobs were replaced by a plaintive moaning that sounded almost as though she was in physical pain. I ran toward her bedroom, but she was not there. Next, I checked our small bathroom.

She was sitting on the edge of the bath, in front of the sink, and weeping. Her mouth was filled with small white sleeping pills. I lifted her up without thinking. All I knew was that I had to get those pills out. I slapped them out of her mouth. Many of them ended up in the sink, but I couldn't get them all out of her mouth, so I stuck my finger down her throat, making her retch. Afterward, I helped her back to the side of the bath, where we cried together for a long time. Then she stumbled to her bed. All she said to me was "Don't tell your father or your brothers."

I must not have gotten all the pills out of her mouth, because she quickly slipped into a sleep so deep that I could hardly see her breathing. I skipped school and stayed by her side all day. She was still sleeping when my father arrived in the evening, expecting dinner. I told him that she had had another migraine and had gone to bed early. I tried to put on a brave face, to act as though everything was normal, but inwardly, I was still crying, terrified that she would never wake up.

It's a strange thing for a ten-year-old to think, but that day I somehow knew that my childhood was over. Something radical and irrevocable had occurred, even if I wasn't able to fully process what the act had meant or why she had felt driven to it.

On Monday, Mother gave me a note to take to my teacher, explaining that I had missed school on Friday because I had been sick. She said that I had to keep what happened "between us," that it would be "our secret." I kept my word, so much so that years after my mother's death, when I was sixty and I finally decided to unburden myself about this to my siblings, they had trouble believing it. "Mom would *never* do that," one of them told me.

After my mother's suicide attempt, she began to tell me things. A secret trust developed between us. She would take me to her old office on Prinsengracht, the Anne Frank House, and tell me stories about the Annex. When visitors caught wind of who she was, what she had done, they asked her questions and I watched how attentively they listened to her answers. I began to see her in a new light as a rare but damaged person, somebody who needed and deserved extra care.

In the spring of 1960, just a few months after my mother tried to take her own life, I noticed that she was putting on weight and tiring more easily. She told me that, at forty, she was going to have another baby. She was often at the doctor's during the pregnancy. She had high blood pressure and kidney problems. She did not say it, but it was clear she wasn't ready, in body or mind, for another child. My father was more sanguine.

"God, let it be a girl at last!" he said. "We'll name her Anne."

My sister was born at home early in the morning of November 13, 1960. My father wasn't permitted by the doctor to be in the bedroom where the baby would be delivered, so he sat on the sofa with me and we waited together. My mother's awful screams had begun the night before. She lost a dangerous amount of blood during labor. At several points, I could hear the doctor yelling over her cries, telling her to push harder. I took some comfort in the fact that my grandmother Christina, who had become a midwife after Johan's death, was in the room to help.

As my mother's agony continued, I was shocked to see my father's reaction. He seemed totally unfazed by her pain and was only impatient to discover the baby's gender. When Anne was finally born at 6:05 in the morning, he exploded with joy. He put his coat on over his pajamas and ran out of the house, broadcasting the news throughout the neighborhood: "I have a daughter!"

I couldn't wrap my mind around the contradiction my parents presented: on the one hand, a happy father; on the other, a mother who might be dying, who a year or so earlier had tried to end her own life.

BROWN ENVELOPES

I have no idea if Otto knew about my mother's struggles with depression, but he always seemed to worry about her. He comforted her. He held her hand. He listened while she cried. He also tried to make her laugh, just as he did during that summer day in Noordwijk. He also helped her financially, long after she had retired from his company.

On one of his many visits to our house, while my mother was pregnant with my sister, Otto slipped a brown envelope in between the arm of the chair that my mother was sitting on and the seat cushion. I had been sent out of the room, but I was spying on the scene from the hallway.

"Mom, what's that envelope?" I asked later.

She turned red and told me that it wasn't important. That didn't satisfy me. I pressed her for more information, and eventually she decided to show me where she had hidden the envelope in the linen closet. It contained a large amount of money, she said, about 5,000 guilders (worth $20,000 in today's money). "I don't want you to share this with anyone, but that money is meant for tough times, if your father is ever out of work. You're the only one I'm telling this to—just in case something happens to me."

Jeroen and I later found letters that my mother had written to Otto, in which she thanked him for the monetary gifts. In one letter from 1957, she revealed that my father had actually once asked Otto for money without her knowledge, something that had evidently caused her much embarrassment.

Dear Mr. Frank,

We received your check for 500 guilders; once again, I want to express our heartfelt thanks. As I told you on the phone, Cor arranged this without telling me—I only heard about it after he'd visited you. . . . I'm really grateful you helped us financially once again, though I must say I feel burdened at the same time with all this money. However, if this is the way you want it, I will give in. I just hope I won't become ill from stress, for that won't do my family any good, of course. In any case, I do hope that Cor will pay you everything back, and I want to ask you to please not send any more money. I really hope I shall be able to repay you one day, for all of your help.

Several of my mother's letters to Otto are apologetic in tone. In another letter, following a meeting in June 1960, my mother wrote, "I just can't stop thinking about the fact that I wasn't able to hold back tears that morning, even ending up in a puddle of tears." Otto had given her a "large amount of money," a gift for the expectant mother that had likely taken her by surprise. Yet because my father could be generous to a fault—often treating his friends, especially after he had a few drinks—she seemed to want to keep the gift a secret from her husband.

I immediately deposited the money into our savings account. Because there was no other way, I told Mother and Cor that I'd received a small amount, which they thought was terrific. I would rather tell Cor the truth, but I don't, for I think it's better, given his generous behavior from time to time. . . . I don't have to tell you how infinitely grateful we are, Mr. Frank. I know you don't like me writing about that, but I still believe such things shouldn't be taken for granted. I simply can't separate your person and the thought of all that has happened.

I think the last line is particularly significant—my mother's inability to separate her friendship with Otto and the memory of what he lost. Otto probably felt that helping my mother financially was the least he could do, given all she had done for his family.* Yet on some deep level my mother felt she had "failed" him, as she often said, and the thought of receiving money for that failure was too much for her to bear. She accepted it, in the end, because she needed it and because she could never say no to the man who had become a second father.

But the gifts, I think, never sat well with her.

The night my mother showed me the money in the linen closet, I had trouble sleeping. I kept on hearing her words in my head: *in case something happens to me.* It sounded like a bad omen. While I lay awake in bed, a terrible fight erupted between my parents. Listening to them scream at each other, my concern turned into a kind of fury. When they did not stop after a few minutes, I got out of bed and ran to their room.

The intensity of the anger between them, my father's gratuitous unkindness, my mother's reticence and stubbornness, the stupid secrets she kept—all of it suddenly revolted me. Their bedroom was locked, as it always was when they wanted privacy, but I tried as hard as I could to break the door down with my eleven-year-old fists. At the very least, my outburst made them quiet down for the night.

I would see Uncle Otto give my mother the same kind of brown envelope on at least two more occasions. Thanks to his book royalties from Anne's diary, Otto lived well. He stayed at fine hotels, trav-

---

* Otto's gratitude toward the Annex's helpers led him to recommend Bep as well as Miep and Jan Gies, Victor Kugler, and Jo Kleiman for the title "Righteous Among the Nations," awarded by the Yad Vashem World Holocaust Remembrance Center in Israel. This title recognizes non-Jews who selflessly aided Jewish people during the war. In January 1973, Bep received a certificate and a medal from the Israeli ambassador in The Hague.

eled everywhere by taxi, and always arrived bearing gifts. Yet he was never careless with money.

"It was Anne's money and not his," said his son-in-law, Zvi Schloss. "That was his feeling until the day he died."

Given how careful a custodian Otto was when it came to his daughter's legacy, I think his gifts to my mother were even more significant than they appeared. He believed that helping her was what Anne would have wanted. And I like to think that as much as my mother saved Otto during the war, she was eventually saved by him as well.

CHAPTER 15

Denial

While I was growing up, Anne Frank was already world-famous, yet my mother hid from the cameras. That wasn't especially difficult for her to do. Though she had been a constant presence in the Secret Annex and the closest to Anne of all the helpers, very few people knew who she was or what role she had played in the story. From the day of the raid, she had been overlooked, first by the Nazis, who had never questioned her (unlike her three colleagues), and then by the Dutch police, who hadn't bothered to interview her for the first official investigation into the betrayal of the Secret Annex in the late 1940s.* When the play and film based on Anne's diary came out, my mother's character was erased and much of what she had done was attributed to Miep.

Nevertheless, beginning in the mid-1950s, a handful of journalists and historians investigating the Secret Annex began to figure out that my mother was an important witness and contacted her seeking more information about the now-famous story. Most often they would come away disappointed. Usually she refused to speak. And in

---

* For unknown reasons, Bep was the only one of the helpers who wasn't interrogated by the Politieke Recherche Afdeling (Political Investigation Department) of the Amsterdam police force, which carried out the investigation in 1947–1948. Miep Gies would later call that "a grave mistake on the part of the police."

the few cases when she did sit for an interview, she couldn't hold back tears and shared little that wasn't already known.

That she was now a person whom journalists even wanted to speak to came as an uncomfortable shock to my mother. She could not believe how much had happened since June 25, 1947, the day when Anne's diary had first appeared in print in Dutch. The first edition, printed on cheap grayish paper, had run to just three thousand copies. Against all expectations, the book had flown off the shelves. Otto had taken care to send copies to family members, friends, and people who were mentioned in the diary. So not only did my mother receive a personally inscribed copy of the book, so did my grandmother Christina.

"When sending you *Het Achterhuis* now," Otto wrote to her, "I am thinking particularly of your husband, who was always such a great support to us, and of Bep, who harmonized with Anne in a special way. May this book tell you something of the difficult years we have all experienced. It will also be a memory of all those who have not returned and whom you all knew."

My mother was curious about what Anne had written in her diary. But she delayed opening the book for a long time, and her grief prevented her from reading more than a few pages in a single sitting.

"She was overcome by everything that was going on inside her head," Diny said. "She had very mixed feelings. On the one hand, the diary made her relive the misery of the war; on the other hand, it made her remember the beautiful events in the Annex."

My mother probably disagreed with some of the things Anne had written. But she knew the author and understood that many of those things had been written in a moment of pique or were the result of Anne's teenage imagination running wild. Her overarching impression of the book confirmed the feeling she'd first had on the night of the sleepover in the Annex, when Margot had read from one of Anne's stories. Now she knew that the diary was the record of a brilliant young writer finding her voice.

As astonishing as the diary must have seemed to my mother, its publication felt like a small event, confined to their private circle in Amsterdam. It wasn't until the book was translated into German, English, and French in the 1950s that she began to realize that something special was happening. She bought each new edition immediately. She also made scrapbooks, in which she collected newspaper articles, photo reports, and reviews to which she added many handwritten comments.

As my brother Cok noted, even if she was reluctant to talk about the Annex, "Anne's story was always on her mind." Yet as the story was read more and more widely, as it touched more people, my mother began to realize that it no longer belonged only to the Opekta Circle but to the world at large. She, Otto, and Miep began to feel that "the legacy of Anne Frank" had to be protected from those who would seek either to profit off it for financial gain or slander it for their own twisted ideological reasons.

That became apparent to my mother after she met with the Dutch journalist Bob Wallagh in December 1958. At the time, he was at work on a book capitalizing on the public interest created by the movie adaptation of the play *The Diary of Anne Frank*. He wanted "the inside scoop" on Anne from someone who had known her. He had first contacted Miep, but she had explained that Bep "knew more about Anne" than she did, so she had given him my mother's phone number.

My mother wished that Miep had asked her permission before giving out her number, but she "didn't see any harm" in speaking with Mr. Wallagh. Yet during the interview she had an uncomfortable feeling. Wallagh didn't seem to know much about the story he was investigating. He had only recently decided to write his book and hadn't yet bothered to see the play. My mother thought his questions about Charlotte Kaletta, Fritz Pfeffer's still living widow, were particularly tactless.

Two days later, she wrote a long letter to Otto, saying that she hadn't been able to sleep after talking to Wallagh. She could not stomach seeing Anne's story turned into a commodity and wanted no part in such a business. She told Otto, as politely as she could, that she would rather not continue doing those sorts of interviews. It was too painful. She would rather "distance herself from everything"—not only speaking to journalists but also attending film premieres and receptions. Even those supposedly "pleasant things" she found "nerve-racking." *

Back in 1956, Otto introduced my mother to a few American admirers of Anne, but when they suggested meeting up for tea, she demurred, saying that if forced to speak about the Annex she would find herself at "a loss for words." She had apologized to Otto for her nature: "I hope you don't blame me. . . . I am just not a woman of the world."

Anyone who got close to my mother knew that she did not feel like a hero and she did not think her memories of the Secret Annex should be recorded. She craved a kind of erasure. Once, when she was moved to share with Otto some personal recollections of Anne, she asked him to keep her letter confidential, drawing a sharp distinction between her desire for privacy and Anne's desire to live on through her words. "I do hope you will keep everything for yourself," she wrote, "for I am no Anne Frank."

SPLITTING HAIRS

Since my mother found it excruciatingly painful to talk about the Secret Annex—to journalists, to ordinary readers of the Diary, even to her own family—she usually avoided opportunities to speak publicly

---

* Despite her reservations, Bep did attend the 1959 Dutch premiere of the movie *The Diary of Anne Frank* and met Queen Juliana of the Netherlands. Though initially nervous, she was put "at ease" by the queen's "humility," she told Otto, and the two women had a nice conversation about what life in the Secret Annex had really been like.

about her role in the drama. There was, however, one exception to the rule: when it came to standing up to Holocaust deniers.

In 1958, two residents of the German city of Lübeck, a high school teacher named Lothar Stielau and another man with neo-Nazi sympathies, Heinrich Buddeberg, claimed publicly that Anne's diary was a fiction, fabricated by "certain circles" in an act of "hate-mongering against the German people." Otto sued them for defamation, and in the ensuing trial, my mother was asked by the district court of Lübeck to give a statement confirming that Anne's diary had been written by the young girl while in hiding.

My mother's answer to the court's request was clear: "You can count on me. I believe my knowledge of the German language will serve me just fine."

In that case, her testimony and those of other witnesses proved decisive. Following five hours of deliberation, the defendants reversed their earlier position and claimed that the investigation had convinced them "beyond doubt" of the diary's authenticity. As a result, the slander charges against them were dropped. Otto was satisfied, but of course the attacks against the diary, and against him personally, did not stop.

And some slander, he realized, was better left unanswered. "I'm shocked that you as a father have published such a thing," read one letter that he received in 1959. "But that is typical of the Jew. You'd still seek to fill your pockets with the stinking corpse of your daughter. What a blessing to humanity that such creatures were exterminated by Hitler."

As the years wore on, the attacks against the diary's legitimacy became more sophisticated. In the late 1970s, Robert Faurisson, a Franco-British Holocaust denier and former academic, generated much controversy by writing articles and books that sought to contradict the accepted history of the Holocaust. Chipping away at the legitimacy of Anne's diary was central to his project. Early into his research on the Secret Annex, he was able to meet under false pretenses with Otto Frank, Miep Gies, and my mother.

In his loathsome book *Is the Diary of Anne Frank Genuine?*, Faurisson claimed that my mother was "totally incapable" of recalling key details about the Secret Annex and it was impossible that she had spent twenty-five months caring for the hiders there. He suggested that the story was a hoax and that the Franks had lived openly at Prinsengracht.

My mother later wrote that Faurisson "wasn't interested at all in the actual events from those days. . . . He was only looking to score points, splitting hairs, if you ask me."

As the years wore on, more conspiracy theorists would come out of the woodwork. And each time, it fell to the surviving helpers and to Otto to stand up to them, which often put them into the uncomfortable position of insisting, over and over again, that something that they wished had never happened had in fact happened. That took a toll on them emotionally. In 1980, when the diary's legitimacy was again called into question for spurious reasons, the journalist Jos van Noord of the Dutch newspaper *De Telegraaf* telephoned Miep Gies, who started to cry. "How dare they question the authenticity again," she said. "Thanks to Anne's diary, the hiders from the Annex form the only family of all those six million anonymous Jewish victims who won't be lost in oblivion."

THE NEW WORLD

In the late 1970s, something changed in my mother's approach to the outside world. It didn't become easier for her to talk about the Annex, exactly, but she was more willing to overcome whatever pain and discomfort she experienced in order to speak up. She was enjoying a rare period of good health. She looked more relaxed in photos. And she had taken a more assertive role in her marriage. Rather than retreating from my father, she now took a page out of her mother's book and fought back. She once even poured a glass of cold water over his head to stop a drunken outburst.

She was more assertive in interviews about the Annex, too. In 1978, in an interview with the Dutch *Trouw* newspaper, she complained about the many myths that had been created about the diary due to ignorance and journalistic laziness. "No one has ever asked us: How did you find that diary? Everyone who wrote about it would make up his own story," she said.

Also in 1978, my mother decided, for the first time in her life, to travel overseas. She planned to visit her old friend Victor Kugler. He had remarried a Dutch woman named Loes (or Lucy) van Langen and settled in Weston, a small neighborhood in Toronto with a large Dutch community. Because of the fame of the diary, he had become a minor celebrity there. He was often featured in the newspaper and invited to local schools to speak about World War II. Soon there would be a biography as well as a documentary about him.

For the most part, Victor welcomed the attention, although he drew the line when some acquaintances wanted to organize a "Victor Kugler Day" in his honor. I know from Victor's many replies to my mother's letters that they corresponded frequently after he left the Netherlands in the early 1950s. But only one of my mother's letters to Victor has survived. In that letter, from 1959, she spoke of her past almost as if it had happened to someone else: "Our time at the office, my marriage, the boys' births, the tragedy and the success of the Secret Annex . . . almost everything seems like a dream to me."

Victor had always been an extremely judicious and careful man, but by the late 1970s, his mind was failing. He had been diagnosed with Alzheimer's disease. A month before my mother's visit to Toronto in October 1978, his condition became so severe that Otto wrote to Victor's wife, saying that he wanted Victor to stop giving interviews for fear he might mix things up or say things that weren't true. Otto knew that any factual error could be exploited by enemies of the diary, such as Faurisson. He warned Victor through Loes to "refrain from giving interviews to anyone under any circumstances, because this could cause enormous damage. . . . I hope you understand what's at stake, also for you. . . . After all, Victor has received awards for his selfless aid to us."

Otto had good reason to be concerned. Alzheimer's had turned Kugler into an emotional man, unable to deal with whatever painful memories he held on to. His wife said that when he met with young people, he would often start crying uncontrollably. In 1979, one friend reported that Victor was experiencing time lapses, sometimes thinking he was back in Amsterdam: "Victor and Lucy Kugler were at our house, when, without warning, he went up the stairs. Lucy said, 'Where are you going, Victor?' To which Victor replied, 'I'm just going upstairs to check that the people are all right.'"

I don't know what my mother and Victor talked about on their visit or how painful it was for her to see her old friend in that state. I have a photograph of them sitting peacefully in Victor's garden. I suppose that my mother must have realized that it was the last time she would see him.

Though the Toronto visit was personal in nature, my mother found time while there to sit for an interview, which became the only extended interview she would ever give that was recorded on tape. Her interviewer, Oskar Morawetz, was not a journalist nor a historian but a composer. His orchestral piece *From the Diary of Anne Frank* set quotes from Anne to haunting melodies. In performances given around the world, he would often preface his work with a lecture, in which he showed pictures of the various survivors he had spoken to, including Otto, Miep and Jan, and Hanneli Goslar, one of Anne's best friends. When his piece was performed in Toronto, where Morawetz lived, he would often introduce his good friend Victor to the audience.

According to Morawetz's daughter, Claudia, my mother represented the "last piece of the puzzle" to the composer, the only person from the story he had not met. Their interview was conducted in Victor's home, although owing to his condition Victor didn't say much. Kugler's wife, Lucy, served as translator. Oskar asked all the questions.

After Jeroen found the tape, I was astonished, as I had never heard my mother speak about the Secret Annex so openly to outsiders. Parts of the interview were lighthearted, as when my mother described the interactions between Anne and her much older roommate, Fritz, who needed to "muster a lot of courage" merely to take a midday nap in the irrepressible teenager's presence. Morawetz also asked about Willem van Maaren, but my mother dismissed him as a serious suspect in the betrayal, saying that he was an "unreliable" character and ultimately "not important" to the story.

My mother remained mostly unemotional during the interview, but when Morawetz asked if she remembered Otto's reaction to the "sad news" about Anne and Margot, she began to sob lightly.

My mother had one more chance to unburden herself on tape in the late 1970s, when she agreed to be interviewed for a documentary directed by the Jewish Canadian filmmaker Harry Rasky. The interview was conducted by Harry's teenage daughter, Holly, who had been fascinated by the diary for years. Unfortunately, she made the mistake of interviewing my mother alongside the much more voluble and confident Miep Gies. As Miep spoke, my mother just sat there, nodding along and in one case repeating a few things Miep had said for emphasis.

"She wasn't a big talker," Holly recalled, saying that it had taken some effort to get my mother to sit on the sofa beside Miep. "I believe she felt she didn't deserve the attention for her helper's role." Holly experienced my mother as distant and rather cool. But after the interview was over and Holly was about to leave, my mother walked up to the girl and without a word embraced her.

"To me it felt like a thank-you," Holly said, "because I helped spread Anne's story."

CHAPTER 16

A Girl Named Sonja

I don't think I would have ever been able to understand how deeply the war affected my mother had I not suffered, at the age of sixteen, a terrible accident, a trauma of my own. It happened in December 1965. My siblings and I were home from school for the Dutch holiday of Sinterklaas, the same holiday that Miep and my mother had celebrated with the residents of the Secret Annex two decades earlier.

My mother was in the kitchen, frying batches of bacon in two large pans. She was exhausted, and she had a migraine, the result of the terrible fight she'd had with my father the night before. As she removed each batch of bacon, she left the fat in the pan, creating two big pools of grease.

At one point, she must have lost track of what she was doing and left the kitchen to go into my father's workroom. She was gone perhaps one minute, perhaps five. I was alone in the dining room, reading, when my brother Ton started screaming.

I hurried into the kitchen and saw that one of the pans had burst into flames. In a split second, I removed a large lid from the kitchen cabinet. My plan was to cover the pan tightly with the lid, starving the fire of oxygen. But as I approached the stove, Ton opened the kitchen door to let out the smoke, and a strong gust of wind blew the fire to the neighboring pan, which was closer to me, setting the entire stove ablaze.

The top half of my body was instantly engulfed in flames. Scalding-hot grease was all over me—in my hair, on my clothes, on my skin. I flung my arms about, desperately trying to put the fire out. My brother Cok was standing behind me; he put his arms around my chest, pulling me away from the fire and burning his right arm in the process. He almost certainly saved my life.

I didn't feel much pain, at first; I was in shock. I ran out of the kitchen into the dining room, then to the sitting room. I didn't realize that in doing so I was setting our curtains on fire. In my peripheral vision, I could see my father running after me. He was trying to help, but I thought that he blamed me for causing the fire and that he was chasing me down in order to punish me. When he finally caught up with me, he somehow managed to put the fire on my head out with his bare hands. I remember feeling embarrassed for having thought so little of him.

He sat me down on the sofa, and then my mother appeared. She was very quiet. She carefully removed my burnt clothes. Someone had called the emergency services, and the police arrived before the ambulance or firefighters. I know I was still conscious at that point because I remember a policeman asking me, "Did someone throw the grease over your head? Did someone harm you on purpose?"

I fainted for the first time while walking to the ambulance. They laid me down on some kind of stretcher. I remember the sound of the siren blaring. When we arrived at the emergency room, a doctor, seeing my condition, asked that I be admitted to the burn ward for special treatment. He was told that there was no room available for another patient. "If we don't help him," he said into the telephone, "I am certain he will die."

It's strange, but I felt in that moment as though it made only a small difference whether I survived or not.

As the doctors examined me, I fainted for the second time, and then I fell into a coma that lasted three days. When I awoke, I had a clear, strong feeling—similar to the feeling I'd had that day after my mother attempted suicide, when I'd realized that my childhood was over. Now I felt that in some decisive way I would have to take my life into my own hands, that I would have to choose for myself. I didn't know what I would do with the feeling, but it had the power of a revelation, a literal baptism by fire.

My spirit felt freed when I came out of my coma, but I was trapped in a badly wounded body. I had third-degree burns on my head, face, and arms and second-degree burns on my torso. The nurses refused to let me look at myself in the mirror. Several days went by before I was allowed to receive visitors from outside. When my parents and siblings finally came to see me, my face was completely bandaged, my head and neck were swollen due to edema—which occurs after severe burns—and I couldn't move. I watched as my father, my mother, my brother Cok, and my five-year-old sister walked straight past my hospital bed. (My eldest brother, Ton, was not there because the hospital limited each patient to only four visitors at a time.)

Initially, no one in my family recognized the wounded eyes peering out under the bandages. Then my sister, Anne, suddenly said to the three of them, "But that is Joop!"

My father didn't believe her, but Anne and my mother walked up to me and saw that it was true. My mother wept for a long time. "I'm so sorry," she told me. She had carelessly left the pans on the fire, and she blamed herself for what had happened.

I didn't fault her for my accident then, nor do I fault her now. I was just happy to be with her. She held my left hand, which had escaped the fire, as Anne, Cok, and my father took turns embracing me. For all the constant bickering in our family, it felt wonderful to be with them at that moment; it was a kind of reunion, a moment of togetherness and love that unfortunately would prove all too rare in the years to come.

A FRESH START

I had always done well in school, but I was painfully shy around my classmates. My only friends were the kids I used to tutor in math. Most of them happened to be girls, a fact that caused my brothers to tease me—probably out of jealousy, I realize now. Their teasing only got worse when I discovered, around age thirteen, a new passion in life: ballroom dancing.

I asked my mother to sign me up for lessons, and I mastered in rapid succession the English waltz, the Viennese waltz, the foxtrot, and the major Latin American dance styles, from the cha-cha to my personal favorite, the tango. By the time I was fifteen, I was competing and sometimes winning awards in dance contests with people of all ages.

I remember that one day, a few months before my accident, my mother was singing along to a Shirley Bassey record that she adored. I'm not sure what came over me, but I took her by the hand and led her through the steps of the English waltz. I think it was the only time we ever danced together. She smiled and told me that my grandfather Johan had also been a very good dancer and that for a moment while we were dancing she'd felt as though he was with her again.

About a year before my accident, I began working as an assistant dance instructor for a local youth group, which offered classes in ballroom dancing, as well as free dancing, the twist, and rock and roll. One of our best students was a girl named Sonja. She was smart and confident, and she had acquired a salty, ironic sense of humor from her Jewish mother. She was a bit younger than me, but she dressed less like a schoolgirl than a grown woman. She seemed far out of my league, even just as a friend. I remember how surprised I was, one night after class, by the mysterious way she smiled as I said good night.

I think I had been a rather good-looking boy before my accident.

I had wavy blond hair, blue eyes, and a wide grin. But the fire had given me a hideous makeover, leaving me with a crooked eye and a scar on my head that made me half bald. I felt ashamed, as though no one would ever love me, as though the pretty girls I had danced with in class would now keep their distance.

Then, one day, Sonja appeared at my hospital bed holding a box of chocolates. I couldn't believe my eyes. I had no idea that she even knew who I was. We mostly exchanged pleasantries that day, but she kept in contact during my rehabilitation: she wrote letters and sent cards, and when I was finally discharged from the hospital after six weeks, she visited me at home, where I continued the long healing process.

Because of my injuries, I had to miss a year and a half of school, and in that time I underwent seven plastic surgeries. The doctor told me that administering general anesthesia to me over and over again could be harmful to my brain, so he just gave me a local anesthetic and went to work. He excised the scar tissue from the top of my head and then stretched the healthy tissue with hair on it, gradually covering up the affected area. That ingenious but painful technique was repeated a half-dozen times. He also repaired my left eyebrow, which had been burned off. He tried as much as midcentury surgical techniques would allow to give me my old face back.

In June 1967, just as the school term was ending, I felt well enough to return. There was a dance to mark the end of the school year, and I decided to take Sonja. I was self-conscious around my peers, many of whom hadn't seen me since before the accident. But I felt safe and proud dancing with Sonja, and I think that was the night we truly fell in love.

As happy as I was to be with her, I soon became incredibly busy with schoolwork, trying to make up for all that I had missed. With great effort, I managed to graduate from high school on time. Sonja cheered as I received my diploma at the graduation ceremony. My parents, however, were not in the audience; they spent the day furniture shopping. I discovered, years later, that they had not come partly to avoid Sonja. They did not approve of her, for reasons that I will soon try to explain.

After high school, I began a five-year professional degree program in mechanical engineering, studying at night while I worked during the day. Whatever free time I had, I spent with Sonja. My mother was worried about that; she thought I was taking too much time away from my studies. Sonja had already quit school and was working as an assistant buyer for a large department store in Amsterdam. She charmed my siblings with all sorts of presents she brought home from work. My father was initially warm to her—I think he enjoyed looking at her, honestly. My mother was a bit colder but still correct and friendly. Yet I could detect some reservation, a watchfulness, and a sense of not wanting our relationship to go "too far." It may have been because, in my mother's view, Sonja dressed too provocatively or that she had a forceful way of speaking that could have seemed disrespectful.

"NOT THE RIGHT GIRL"

I think I decided to marry Sonja the instant we fell in love. She had been loyal to me after my accident; I felt I had to repay that loyalty. Sensing my mother's reservations, however, I did not disclose my plans right away. But sometime around my eighteenth birthday, my father and mother suddenly invited Sonja's only real parent—her mother, Roza van Weezel—to our house for drinks.

I was home that evening, but I gave my parents and future mother-in-law space to chat in the sitting room. I could hear short bits of their conversation. My father laughed at Roza's colorful jokes, but my mother just listened silently. The two women could not have been more different. Roza worked as a piano player in some of Amsterdam's less reputable nightclubs. She was flirtatious, irreverent, and very funny—the opposite of my shy, conservative mother. The meeting lasted about two hours. Afterward, I asked my parents if it had gone well. My mother said yes, but she avoided my eyes. I felt that there was something about Roza that she couldn't, or wouldn't, discuss with me. Over the next few days, I pressed her to explain. When she refused to, I finally broke down and told her that I was going to ask Sonja to marry me and wanted her blessing.

My mother told me that she wasn't the right girl for me.

"Why? What is wrong with her? I thought you liked her?"

"We do."

"Then why can't we get engaged? Is it because of Roza?"

"It isn't just that."

"Then . . . *what*?"

"Joop, I'm not allowed to say why your father and I can't agree to this engagement . . . but we can't."

I had been cleaning dishes in the kitchen during the conversation, and at that point I threw down the towel and stormed off. She wasn't *allowed* to say? What force was preventing her? And how was I supposed to explain any of this to Sonja or her mother?

I decided to stall for time; I was uncertain what to do. I still saw Sonja every week, although now we met at her mother's place or on neutral territory. But now that I had made my intentions known, my parents' position toward Sonja seemed to harden. And once we officially got engaged, not long after my nineteenth birthday, my father began to call Roza late at night, cursing into the telephone. He usually just told her that she was a whore or a slut and then hung up. It was the exact same kind of brutish language he used to describe my aunt Nelly under his breath. I could hear him in the hallway, drunkenly dialing each night on our old rotary phone, while I lay on the convertible sofa in the dining room, where I slept most nights.

Soon Roza stopped picking up, but that did not keep my father from calling every night. After a couple of weeks, an agent from the phone company appeared at our door with a log of phone calls made from our address. I answered the door and got my mother to speak with him. He said that "someone" in our house had been dialing Roza's number over and over.

"That's Pa," I said.

My mother's look of confusion turned to one of embarrassment and shame.

My father later admitted to us that he had indeed made the calls; he said he was sorry, but he never bothered to explain himself to me. Roza also never talked to me about my father's campaign of intimidation. She always treated me kindly, and we got along well—especially when I fixed a broken toilet or replaced a light bulb that was out of her reach. "It's nice to have a man around the house," she would say.

Though Roza turned the other cheek when it came to my father's insults, Sonja was furious about them. She could not understand the source of my father's hostility, and she thought I was not doing enough to stand up for her. I had given her an engagement ring after we had decided to get married, but at one point when we were at her mother's house, she became so enraged that she threw it down the stairs and told me to get out. She wanted nothing more to do with me.

I pleaded, I told her that I wanted to be with her, no matter what my parents said. And in time, I convinced her to put the ring back on her finger.

DIRTY LAUNDRY

Maybe my father had heard something. He often worked in and around Soembawastraat, where Roza lived, and had spent a week carpeting the stairs of her next-door neighbor. Roza often had male visitors come by late at night. And she and her daughter frequently got into loud, even hysterical arguments. Neither of those things endeared them to the neighbors. Perhaps my father picked up on a rumor about what Roza had done during the war—the kind of rumor that I also heard later in my life—and that explained why my parents didn't want her in our family.

Four people close to Roza told me that, despite the fact that she was Jewish, she had slept with Nazis or Nazi sympathizers during the war, just as my aunt Nelly had. That information came to me from two of Roza's daughters, Roos and Bettie (Sonja's half sisters), and Bettie's husband, Gerard. My aunt Diny also knew about Roza's alleged Nazi lovers.

I was and remain somewhat skeptical of those family stories. Yet the more I researched my mother's life, the more troubled I became about her attitude toward Roza. My mother had protected and hidden the most famous victim of the Nazi genocide against the Jews. Yet she opposed her son's decision to marry a Jewish woman, for reasons that she refused to discuss but that might have had some murky connection to the war. I could not flesh out my mother's portrait, I realized, without understanding why she'd felt as she did about the woman who became my mother-in-law.

So with Jeroen's help, I searched in the archives, but we could find no document proving that Roza van Weezel had collaborated with the enemy or had relationships with Nazis or NSB members during the war. Yet our search did reveal some details that were troubling when overlaid with things Sonja herself had told me.

According to government records, Roza van Weezel was born in Amsterdam in 1914. In the early days of the Occupation, her domestic situation was complicated: she was living on Paardekraalstraat in Amsterdam East with a certain Daniel Keizer, although she was married at the time to another man named Jacobus Campagne, whose child she was carrying. She divorced her husband and married Daniel in 1945. Neither of the men appears to have had any Nazi connections.

Roza had two more girls before Sonja was born: Bettie in 1942, who was given Daniel's last name, Keizer; and Roos in 1945, who for some reason was given Roza's maiden name of van Weezel, possibly suggesting that Daniel wasn't her father. Roza's personal record card listed her as a member of the Dutch Israelite Religious Community, meaning she was Jewish. But in April 1944, she had herself baptized and joined the Dutch Reformed Church. Almost certainly, her baptism was done to avoid persecution by the Nazis. Many Jews took such a step. If they didn't convert, they visited the city archives, hoping to find documents that could prove they had some non-Jewish ancestors in their family tree. Or they convinced a civil servant to falsify their birth or baptismal documents.

Roza's baptism, combined with the facts that she was living with a Gentile and the mother of two half-Gentile children, may have been sufficient to save her from the camps. There are many examples of people in similar situations who were spared. One of Anne Frank's best friends, Jacqueline van Maarsen, for instance, had a Gentile mother and a Jewish father. Jacqueline, her father, and her sister were untouched by the Nazis and even exempted from wearing the yellow star.

The rest of Roza's family was not as lucky as she was. Her sister Jeanette, along with Jeanette's Jewish husband and two children, were deported to Ravensbrück and eventually to Bergen-Belsen. They survived the camps, but one of Roza's uncles and four of her aunts were murdered in the Holocaust.

Whereas Sonja's mother was Jewish, her father, Raymond Fremdt, was German by nationality. He was born in 1913 in France, the child of a German father and Dutch mother, but his father died when he was just three months old, and he moved with his mother to Amsterdam, where he was living at the outbreak of the war. In the chaotic days just before the Occupation, when anyone with a German name could be suspected of treason, Raymond was briefly arrested while in the company of a NSB member for "acting suspiciously on public property," according to a police report from May 1940.

The Germans pressed Raymond into military service, first as a laborer for the Luftwaffe unit in charge of anti-aircraft defense in the Dutch province of Friesland, then as a soldier on the eastern front, where for a time he guarded Russian prisoners of war. Later he served as a telegraph operator on the western front, where he was eventually captured by US soldiers. After the Liberation, he was held in a succession of prisoner-of-war camps, first in Germany and then in the Netherlands. In an official statement in his file, he claimed that he had always felt "more Dutch than German" and had never committed any "dehumanizing acts." He also claimed that he was "never a member of the NSB or any German political organization."

Raymond and Roza do not appear to have known each other during the war. They married in 1951, a year after Sonja was born. It was the third and final time Roza got married. Sonja told me that she hated her hard-drinking father. There were two main reasons for that. The first was that Raymond lusted after his own stepdaughters, Bettie and Roos. Sonja told me that he would flirt with them and touch them inappropriately. That revolted her. The other thing that Sonja hated about her father was his friends.

Despite his statement that he had never been a member of the NSB, Raymond for a time had worked for *Het Vaderland* (The Fatherland), a Hague-based newspaper that maintained a pro-German stance during the war, and he had many loutish buddies who had either been members of or were sympathetic to the Dutch Nazi Party. They used to hang out at Sonja's house. After Raymond and Roza divorced in November 1962—she used Raymond's lascivious behavior toward her daughters as a justification in court for ending the marriage—Sonja's mother began a relationship with one of her ex-husband's NSB friends. Sometimes, when Sonja descended from her little attic room to use the toilet, she would catch her mother and that man making love.

The fact that Sonja came from a family with a German father

who had fought for Hitler and a Jewish mother who had slept with the enemy was probably too much for my parents to bear. They simply could not tolerate being related to such people. As much as my mother gave lip service to the idea of forgiveness, she also never forgot who had murdered her friends from the Annex and corrupted her sister Nelly.

But what, I wondered, did any of that tawdry history have to do with Sonja, who had been born five years after the war ended? Why should she be blamed for things her parents had or hadn't done two decades earlier? Wasn't she innocent? And why, furthermore, did my mother keep all her suspicions from me? If she believed that the sin of the father or the mother passed on to the children, that the family's well had somehow been poisoned by Sonja's parents' misdeeds, why couldn't she just say as much? Why did she have to keep me in the dark, frustrated and confused? My mother, by her actions if not by her words, had taught me the meaning of loyalty. But she either didn't understand how I felt toward Sonja or thought that my loyalty was sorely misplaced.

MOVING OUT

A few months after my nineteenth birthday, I had had enough. I was sick of my parents fighting, of the persistent Voskuijl family tension, which I thought couldn't have improved that much since my family had lived in the four-room apartment on Lumeijstraat. Before I had met Sonja, the tension had been manageable. But when my parents turned against the woman I loved and then didn't even have the decency to tell me why, they forced me to make a choice between her and them. And I chose her.

With a heavy heart, I left home and moved in with my grandmother Christina. She was not about to take sides in the conflict, but she understood my position. She took me in, and in the months that followed she began to open up, to talk about the past, and now I realize that she planted the seeds of curiosity that led to my decision, many years later, to tell my family's story.

Christina spoke to my mother regularly, so I asked her to try to find out what was behind my parents' opposition to Sonja. I thought maybe she could succeed where I had failed. But according to my grandmother, all my mother would say was that Sonja was "not the right girl" for me and that it would be "wrong" for her to explain why. She asked my grandmother to "take good care of Jopie," using my childhood nickname, which she loved (and I hated).

My grandmother felt sorry that she couldn't offer me more information. "She isn't telling me the whole story, Joop," she said, and gave me a hug.

Sonja could not move into my grandmother's place with me. Unmarried couples did not live together in those days, and besides there wasn't much space in my grandmother's apartment. So Sonja rented a room in Diny's place so that we could see each other more easily and be free from our parents and their pasts. (During that time, Diny and Sonja became close, and Sonja told Diny about her mother's relationships with NSB men.)

We got married, almost in secret, on September 21, 1970, shortly after my twenty-first birthday, the age when I was legally allowed to marry without parental consent. We didn't have any money, so it was a simple ceremony at city hall, followed by a party at Roza's apartment. None of my family was present. I had decided to tell neither my parents nor my grandmother, because I was afraid, among other things, that my father would show up and spoil the affair.

Sonja's brother-in-law and her boss served as our witnesses. Roza played the piano, and Sonja's sister Roos sang. It was lovely in its small way, but I could not forget, even for a moment, that my family—especially my parents—were not there. So although I was present in body, smiling and dancing with Sonja, my mind was far away.

By that point in time, I was working as a technician in a laboratory that designed parts for industrial companies. Among other things, we built the centrifuges that were used to make enriched uranium. Because I did the product testing on the centrifuges, I had to get an official security clearance from the Dutch government. Through an employee program, I was able to buy a small house in the town of Weesp, not far from Amsterdam. Sonja and I both wanted to have a baby, and early in 1973, we were delighted when Sonja learned she was pregnant.

Naturally, she wanted to share the happy news with my mother, thinking that it might lead to a reconciliation in the family. One day while I was at work, she took it upon herself to call her at home. My mother hadn't heard from us in four years, and she apparently didn't even know that we were married. So when Sonja told her that she would soon have a grandchild, my mother was shocked.

"Was that your intention?" she asked Sonja, implying that the pregnancy might have been an accident, that the child was unwanted.

The cruelty of the question was a breaking point for Sonja. She would never forgive my mother, and as a result, my mother would never meet our daughter Rebecca, who was born on September 1, 1973. Lord knows I tried to patch things up. On seven separate occasions, I went home to my parents' house to resolve our differences. I just wanted us to be together like normal families. I tried to explain my position. But there was barely enough time for my mother to pour me a cup of coffee before my father would say something such as "Don't mention your wife at this table."

I think I could have reconciled with my mother if only my father hadn't been there, dominating the conversation and making civil communication all but impossible. The first time I returned home, after five years, my mother actually apologized for what she had said to Sonja about the baby being an accident. She had been caught off guard, she told me. And to make up for it she sent us a gift, a baby bib, along with a card congratulating us.

That was more than enough for me, but for Sonja it was too late; the damage was done. She thought I was being weak by wanting to forgive my mother. I often felt caught between my parents, who would not let go of their disapproval of Sonja and her family, and my wife, who thought I was stooping every time I tried to smooth things over.

As my father insulted my wife, my mother, always diplomatic to a fault, pretended that nothing was wrong. She just wanted peace, even if it meant sweeping our problems under the rug. Eventually, I realized, nothing was going to change. My parents didn't want to be associated with Roza; they didn't want her or her daughter in our family; and for whatever reason they refused to explain why.

Maybe one had to live through the war to understand why.

In the end I let them go. I felt I had no choice.

Though I loved Sonja very much, our marriage was not strong. She had a difficult childbirth and our relationship changed after our daughter was born, from one characterized by mutual love to one that felt draining, based more on care and obligation. Though I now had my own family and was free from my parents' judgment, I often felt terribly alone.

The train I took every day from Weesp to the laboratory where I worked passed through East Amsterdam, so near to my parents' house that if I sat on the left side of the train in the morning or the right side at night, I could catch a glimpse of the house. I didn't always have the strength to look; sometimes I turned my back. But when I did look, I usually saw my mother hanging out the laundry or sitting with one of my siblings in the garden. It hurt to see them, that close yet somehow, for reasons I still don't fully understand, out of reach.

One day, I was at work at the laboratory when my supervisor stopped by my desk to say that a certain Mevrouw Groen—Mrs. Green—was waiting downstairs to talk to me. I actually knew a woman by the name of Groen, so I didn't think much of it, but when

I went downstairs I was shocked to discover my mother sitting quietly in a chair.

"Why in heaven did you not give your real name?" I asked her, bewildered. "What is wrong with you?"

I could see that she was wounded by my harsh reaction. She was hardly able to say anything in reply and left a few minutes later with tears in her eyes. She couldn't explain why she had given my boss a fake name—I'm not even certain that she knew why she had done it. I watched as she turned down the small street leading from the laboratory and slowly headed toward the bus station. I should have run after her. She very likely had come to try to make up with me. But when she couldn't bring herself to say that I was her son, when it was apparent that our troubled relationship was now yet another thing that she was hiding from, I couldn't conceal my disappointment.

Thinking back to that moment, I am filled with shame and regret, wishing that it had played out differently. My mother would live another nine years, but the day she stopped by my work disguised as Mrs. Green was the last time I ever saw her alive.

CHAPTER 17

The Sweet Peace

Now I am faced with one last unanswerable question: How much of my mother's behavior after the war—her secretiveness, her reluctance to talk about the past, her anxiety around journalists, her discomfort about being associated with Anne Frank, her guilt at taking money from Otto, her depression, her attempted suicide—how much of all that could be explained by a guilty conscience? Had she secretly suspected all along that it was a member of her own family who betrayed the Annex?

My mother never spoke to me about whether her sister Nelly could have been the one who had told the Nazis that Jews were hiding at 263 Prinsengracht. As far as I know, she mentioned the possibility only once in her life, to my aunt Diny. The two women took a long walk together in Amsterdam in the summer of 1960. It was about half a year after my mother's suicide attempt, when she was forty years old and already pregnant with my sister, Anne.

My mother loved my sister from the moment she was born, but while she was pregnant she felt that she didn't have the strength, physically or mentally, to take care of another child. "Why, I feel sick getting a fourth baby," she said.

Diny was twenty-eight years old then. A few years earlier, she had given up her job as a telegraph operator to start a family with her husband, Jan, and she had just given birth to her second daughter, Hendrie, earlier that year. Though Bep was the oldest and Diny the youngest, the two sisters were alike in many respects: they were the best educated of the Voskuijl girls, and both were very devoted to their family.

Diny tried to cheer my mother up. She thought of ways to help: maybe she could babysit or donate her infant daughter's clothes as soon as she grew out of them. She told my mother to take heart. "It won't be as hard as it seems."

It was a beautiful sunny day, and my mother seemed to relax as the pair made their way through the Jordaan neighborhood in the heart of the city. In those days, the famed Bols distillery was still making jenever in its original location on the Rozengracht Canal. Out in front of the distillery there was a terrace where people sat beneath parasols sipping jenever and drinking beer. For my mother, that section of Amsterdam was always beautiful—and always haunted. The Secret Annex was only five minutes away by foot; nearby were the butcher shop and greengrocer where she had hunted for contraband food during the war; a few more blocks away stood the pharmacy on the Leliegracht Canal where she had hidden in the back room on the day of the raid.

My mother was never a big drinker, and she was pregnant, but on that special day with Diny, she felt like having a drink. She ordered a liqueur on ice. She was enjoying a rare moment of serenity with her favorite little sister. Despite their close connection, Diny had never before seen my mother in such an open and vulnerable place, so eager to share, so willing to talk about things that normally she wouldn't dare to mention.

And that was when it happened.

"She told me about her personal life, about her unhappy marriage with Cor and other things," recalled Diny. "And then, without being asked, she told me, 'Rumor has it that Nelly is the betrayer. As a matter of fact, we think that's true, but things should be proven first. Otto says he doesn't want to know any more.'"

Diny was silent for a moment. She could not believe what she was hearing. My mother covered her face with her hands. "Yes, Dien," she said, speaking in the Amsterdam dialect. "*Ons eige zussie,*" which means *our own sister*.

When Diny told me that in 2021, she was recalling a conversation that had occurred more than a half century earlier, yet she keenly remembered how shocked she had been by those words. I asked her repeatedly whether my mother had elaborated on the statement about Nelly—whether she had explained, for instance, where the rumor had come from, what (if any) evidence it was based on, or why my mother and Otto thought it was true. But she could remember nothing more.

If Diny is correct in dating the encounter to the summer of 1960, it means that my mother may have suspected her sister several years before Karl Silberbauer reemerged, claiming that the betrayer had had "the voice of a young woman." It also means that she may have suspected her sister when she tried to take her own life in the winter of 1959.

And if Otto shared my mother's suspicion that it was Nelly, that would explain his disinclination to pursue the identity of the betrayer; perhaps he knew that in doing so, he would be exposing my mother and her family to harsh public scrutiny while tarnishing the reputation of the Annex's devoted helpers.

I have spent many long nights considering these possibilities, these *if*s. Yet that one recollection of Diny's is the only explicit suggestion we have that my mother and the other members of the Opekta Circle considered Nelly a suspect. And though I trust my aunt completely—I have been interviewing her for a decade, and her recollections have been specific and, in every case that I can verify, accurate—I hardly think that we can come to a conclusion based on a single memory.

M.K.

Nelly Voskuijl's name never surfaced in any of the official police investigations into the betrayal of Anne Frank. And in editing the diary for publication, Otto chose to cut out all the passages dealing with Nelly, most likely to protect my mother and her family.

When Otto died in 1980, he donated his daughter's writings to the Dutch state. That was how the diaries came into the possession of the State Institute for War Documentation (known at the time by its Dutch acronym, RIOD).* When its director, Harry Paape, read through Anne's notebooks in the early 1980s, he noticed that the original texts often deviated from the published version and that many of Anne's entries dealing with sexual topics and her anger toward her mother, for instance, had been omitted altogether.

At the time, most readers didn't know that they were reading a bowdlerized version of Anne's original diary. When the news found its way to the press, it spurred outrage. Headlines such as "Otto Frank's Censorship" filled Dutch newspapers. My mother followed the commotion; she cut out various articles and saved them in her scrapbook. One story, from the newspaper *Trouw*, quoted Harry Paape as defending Otto from criticism:

> Otto Frank felt obligated to protect Anne from the outside world.
> He was unable to predict what would happen with the diary. . . . He
> simply wanted to erect a small shrine for one of the daughters he'd
> lost, not suspecting that this daughter would become the monument
> of the persecution of Jews.

---

* In 1999, RIOD changed its name to the Netherlands Institute for War Documentation (NIOD). In 2010, it became the NIOD Institute for War, Holocaust and Genocide Studies.

Given the public scrutiny as well as the enduring interest in Anne Frank's story, Paape soon devised plans to compile an integral "critical edition" of the diaries that would contain all the unexpurgated entries. They would include not only Anne's discussions of sexuality and some harsh lines about her mother and her schoolmates but also never-before-seen material about my family—from Anne's disapproval of my mother's relationship with Bertus to three long entries dealing with Nelly.

In addition to being a scholarly resource that would present the different versions of Anne's diary side by side, the critical edition would also be a bulwark against future attacks on the legitimacy of the diary by Holocaust deniers and conspiracy theorists. No critic of the diary could credibly claim that it was a fake after wading through the book's fortress of footnotes, facsimiles of original diary pages, scholarly reports, and forensic analyses of Anne's handwriting and the paper she used.

Paape enlisted two of his younger colleagues at RIOD, David Barnouw and Gerrold van der Stroom, to help edit the book, which eventually ran to more than seven hundred pages. Over the course of their research, the trio sought out everyone who had been connected to the Secret Annex. They contacted my mother, and on February 25, 1981, they visited her at home. She told them that she had known since the beginning that the published diary had been edited for content; Otto had explained to her that "he left out a lot of private matters pertaining to the family and Miep and me."

Though Otto had left instructions in his will that Anne's physical writings would belong to the Dutch state, his estate still controlled the copyright to the works and any subsequent editions drawn from them, so Paape had to clear the final text with Otto's family. In the fall of 1982, a representative from RIOD visited Otto's second wife, Fritzi, and showed her all the original diary entries that they now intended to publish in full. Fritzi was alarmed when she saw that the

RIOD people planned to hold nothing back, and afterward she wrote my mother to warn her:

> I want to try to convince the institute's director to leave some passages out, for I don't believe these are suitable for publication. Some of these passages are about you as well. Did my husband at the time [before the diary was published in 1947] tell you that he didn't want to publish anything that may harm you? For instance, there's a passage about your sister Nelly in Anne's manuscript which I'm sure you wouldn't like to see published in the book. I've written Mr. Paape that he must absolutely talk to you and ask your permission for disclosing everything Anne has written about you and your family. I assume somebody is going to visit you in order to discuss this. So it's totally up to you—you can say yes or no. I thought it best to write you in advance, so this visit won't come as a surprise.

Unfortunately, my mother never got a chance to make that decision; she passed away in the spring of 1983, before she was able to meet again with representatives from RIOD. Eventually, the book's editors arranged a meeting with Nelly herself. Both parties agreed that the passages about Nelly would be published but that her name would be replaced in every case by the initials M. or M.K. Critically, the sentences that pointed to the fact that M.K. was a member of the Voskuijl family would be removed altogether.* According to my aunt Willy, who attended the meeting with Nelly, the RIOD representa-

---

* David Barnouw and Gerrold van der Stroom made it known in 2010 that should a new version of the critical edition be published, Nelly, who died in 2001, will be named openly and the censored passages will be included in full. "With her passing in 2001, her privacy right has expired," Barnouw said.

tives told her that the agreement settled the matter definitively. "You won't hear from us again," they said.

Just because Nelly wanted her name out of the critical edition does not mean that she might have had a hand in the betrayal, of course. Anne's unflattering characterization of her as an enthusiastic collaborator would have been reason enough for her to vehemently guard her privacy.

A STRAINED RELATIONSHIP

Whether or not my mother suspected Nelly, her relationship with her sister was by no means normal. They saw each other infrequently; she would usually come over once a year for my mother's birthday or some other family function. She always tried to control the conversation, making snide remarks and spouting opinions about every little thing, which rankled my father. It did not take long for him to lose his temper. My mother urgently tried to defuse the situation, as though my father, by picking fights with Nelly, was somehow playing with fire.

"Cor, no!" she'd say, grabbing his arm as soon as he opened his mouth. *"No."*

Nelly would then get up to go to the bathroom, and when she returned she was usually smiling, as if nothing had happened.

Whereas my father's feelings toward Nelly were clear, my mother's feelings were more inscrutable. She tried to be kind and respectful—or should I say diplomatic. I never saw her and Nelly hug or share an intimate or joyful moment, nor did I ever see them argue with each other. When they met, they would exchange a quick, tight-lipped kiss on each cheek and then avoid each other for the rest of the evening, often not exchanging a word until it was time to say goodbye. Sometimes I could tell that my mother was infuriated by Nelly's haughtiness or arrogance. Sometimes I felt she wanted to put her in her place.

I saw the color drain from her face a few times in Nelly's presence. I asked her in those moments why she wouldn't say anything.

"For the sweet peace," she told me, using a Dutch expression.

Nelly may have been adventurous and defiant during the war, but her postwar life was dreary and at times very sad. After returning to the Netherlands from Germany in 1945, she lived for a time in Groningen, where she worked first as an usher in a movie theater and then in a café preparing snacks. She rented a room from the family that owned the café and lived with them until the mid-1950s, when she moved to Rotterdam and got a job as a telegraph operator.

During that time, she would sometimes come home to Lumeij-straat to visit her mother. The house was mostly empty then, and Christina had taken a boarder, a stenographer in his forties who worked at the major Dutch newspaper *NRC*. He was a charming man who played the piano beautifully, and my grandmother, who had dreamed of becoming a singer as a child, often sang duets with him late into the night. Though Christina was a decade older than Carl, a romance unexpectedly developed between them.

Nelly was also interested in Carl; they were closer in age, if perhaps less well matched in terms of temperament. Yet Nelly was persistent. She seduced Carl and eventually forced him to choose between mother and daughter. An aging bachelor who may have wanted to start a family of his own, Carl chose Nelly. They married in 1956 and eventually settled in Koudum, in the north of the Netherlands. But they were not happy together. They never had children, and a few years into the marriage, Carl resumed his love affair with my grandmother. Nelly knew about it, but she and Carl never bothered to get a divorce. Growing up, my siblings and I would whisper about the fact that "Uncle Carl" and Nelly were technically married even though he was clearly my grandmother's companion. No family gathering was complete without Carl playing the piano and my grandmother smiling and singing along.

I don't think my grandmother had any moral qualms about dating her daughter's husband. Maybe she did it because she was still bitter that Nelly had competed with her for Carl's affection, or maybe she never forgave her daughter for the grief she had caused her family, particularly her late husband, Johan, during the war by siding with the occupier. From Christina's perspective, both instances had shown a lack of loyalty, a treacherous tendency to put her own interests above those of her family. Though Nelly's prickly exterior often made it hard to sympathize with her, it was also hard to look at the position of disgrace she occupied in our family and not feel a measure of pity.

After she retired, Nelly spent her free time working as a sexton in a Mennonite church. She enjoyed gardening and doing crossword puzzles. She never really talked about the past, although sometimes she would say things that indicated regret about the choices she had made as a very young woman. "I can't believe I worked for that pig Hitler," she once told Diny.

Nelly always had money troubles and was often on the phone arguing with some business over an unpaid bill. Despite her financial hardships, she donated to the War Graves Foundation, which maintained the grave sites of Dutch soldiers killed in conflict, including that of my uncle Joop Voskuijl, who had been killed in combat during the Indonesian War of Independence on March 19, 1949.

In 1990, when my grandmother Christina was about to turn ninety-one years old, she fell gravely ill. Nelly visited her every day in the hospital, despite the bad blood that had separated them for so long. Along with my aunt Willy, Nelly took care of my *oma*, read aloud to her, and stood by her during all her suffering. Right before her death, Christina called those two daughters to her bedside. On her bony fingers my grandmother wore two rings: her own wedding ring and Johan's. She took the rings off and gave them both to Willy. "There you go, my child," she said. "I thank you for everything."

Nelly told me that she had expected that one of the rings would be given to her, but in the end she didn't get a thing from my grandmother.

My grandmother died on June 19, 1990, and was buried at her own request next to her beloved Carl, who had died in 1979. To her credit, Nelly recognized how much the two people loved each other, and she wanted them to be together. I have a photograph of Nelly from the early 1990s that I cherish in which she is kneeling over Christina and Carl's grave, an old lady in a bonnet placing a pot of flowers in front of a tombstone.

The last time I saw my aunt Nelly was in 1998. I picked her up at home in Koudum to take her to lunch. Before we left, she had to use the bathroom, so I took the opportunity to give myself a tour of her place. There wasn't much to see. Most of the furniture was worn-out; I remember an old TV and a sagging sofa. Yet she had tried to make her home cozy, placing little pots of flowering plants here and there. I noticed a small bookcase filled with paperbacks. One title interested me, a dime novel called *If the Past Becomes the Present*. The book was about a woman who undergoes hypnosis and then becomes obsessed with a past life, so much so that it overwhelms her current one.

I became so interested in the book that I hadn't noticed that Nelly had returned from the bathroom and was now standing right behind me. "Is this one any good?" I asked.

"It is *very* good. Why don't you read it—and if you like it, hold on to it."

The last word I got from Nelly was in 2000. She sent me a post-card, signing it simply "An embrace, Nel." At that point she was in her late seventies and in poor health; she had recently moved into an assisted-living facility. Her sisters Gerda and Willy were her only regular visitors. One day in 2001, she fell down a flight of stairs in her apartment and suffered a catastrophic head injury. Her body was discovered several days later. Hearing the news, I felt such pity and sorrow—this is the kind of death you wish on no one.

Nelly had one last surprise for me. She had left me a small inheritance, about 800 euros, a sizable portion of her savings. I was shocked, and it made me sad to realize that though I had seen her only a handful of times in my adult life, I had been one of the few members of the family who had, on some level, accepted her.

Of course, I did not know then what I do now.

Yet even now—now that all the troubling facts of Nelly's wartime life have been dredged up—I find myself unable—or unwilling—to render a final judgment. There are several reasons why.

First, although I know that my aunt collaborated with the enemy, I cannot know for certain whether she had a hand in the betrayal of the Secret Annex—and how can you judge a person without knowing what, exactly, he or she is guilty of? Second, Nelly was a very young woman trying to carve out a life of her own in an oppressive family environment in the midst of a terrible war. As much as I have tried to put myself into her shoes—and hope that I would have acted differently in her place—I can't know what choices I would have made, what temptations I would have succumbed to, in that time and place.

And finally, if I am being completely honest, I have trouble judging Nelly because I see a part of myself in her. We are both outcasts from the same family, two black sheep who, for different reasons, never found their way back into the fold.

CHAPTER 18

The Empty Notebook

In the first months of 1983, my mother was a regular presence at the Sint Lucas Ziekenhuis, a hospital in Amsterdam, where a team of kidney specialists were preparing her for dialysis. She dreaded the treatment, because her sister Annie also suffered from renal problems, so she knew what to expect. She sent a letter to Fritzi Frank around that time that cataloged her suffering.

"I've been so ill and was given penicillin, which gave me a terrible allergic reaction," she wrote. She was also recovering from a recent surgery to untangle the blood vessels in her wrist, which, she wrote, had gotten "welded together," and she was steeling herself for the discomfort of her first "kidney flushing." "I'm sorry I don't have more cheerful news, but we're going through a tough time at the moment," she wrote. "My only hope is that I will feel a little better."

By that point my mother must have known that she didn't have much time left. In April 1983, when my brother Ton picked her up at home to go to the hospital for another procedure, she told him definitively, "I will not come back here."

That month, my brother Cok and his wife, Leny, visited my mother several times in the hospital. They placed a notepad by her bed and encouraged her to write. "We told her that it was time to put everything that was bothering her down on paper," Leny said years later. "For a lot of people, doing so is healing, but apparently this wasn't the case for her. She never wrote a single word on the notepad."

On the evening of May 5, 1983, Liberation Day, my mother was visited in the hospital by one of her old friends, Hella Walraven. During their conversation, my mother said that she felt her task on Earth had been fulfilled. All four of her children were married and settled, so she could depart this world with peace of mind.

It is hard for me not to think of that statement as a kind of wishful thinking, if not outright denial. The truth is that my mother's final years were some of the hardest of her life, and not only because of her health problems. Her marriage was as tense as ever, providing little in the way of peace and comfort. She had lost her surrogate father, Otto, in 1980; a year later, Victor Kugler had died. That meant the only one left from the Opekta Circle was Miep, and unfortunately Miep and my mother had had some kind of quarrel in the late 1970s from which their friendship never recovered. It's not clear what exactly the fight was about, but she alluded to it in one of her last letters to Otto.

My mother was also undoubtedly anxious about the critical edition of the diaries. She may have feared, based on Fritzi's recent letter, that the team from RIOD would publish everything, revealing Nelly's collaboration with the Nazis and inviting speculation about whether her sister could have been involved in the betrayal. My mother faced a moral dilemma: Should she let the truth finally come out? Or should she stay loyal to her family and keep Nelly's name out of the Diary, just as Otto had done?

Finally, I suspect that my mother felt some measure of guilt, or at least regret, about the state of her relationship with me, her youngest son. I had been her confidant and protector since that day when I was ten years old and found her on the edge of the bathtub with a mouthful of sleeping pills. I had been there for her, but she was not there for my wedding, not there to help me navigate my increasingly difficult marriage, not there for the birth of my child, Rebecca, whom she had never met. I was by no means "settled," despite what she told her friend Hella. I think about all that must have weighed on her as she lay in the hospital bed, all the things she would not write down in that notebook.

On May 6, my father called my three siblings at daybreak and told them to come to the hospital immediately. He wouldn't say why. Anne and Ton were the first to arrive. "When we got off the elevator," Anne told me, "we saw all the people who shared a room with Mom standing outside. In moments like that, you know what's coming, but you don't want to believe it yet. I was told Mom had gotten out of bed, called out that she wasn't feeling well, and then collapsed. They tried to resuscitate her, but to no avail."

Another patient told them that Mom had suddenly fallen forward while she was knitting in her bed. The autopsy showed that the cause of death had not been kidney failure but an aortic aneurysm, a rupture in the main blood vessel connected to her heart, which I'm sure was exacerbated by the great stress she was under.

The Anne Frank House sent out a press release with a message that "Elli" from the Diary had passed away. The museum described her as "one of those Dutch people who were willing to run enormous risks without a single hesitation," writing that she had acted "from a sense of helpfulness she considered to be only self-evident. Also later, she never took credit for it." It was a nice statement, marred only slightly by the fact that they managed to misspell my mother's last name.

Most of the Dutch newspapers gave scant attention to her death. There was one exception, the Amsterdam newspaper *De Telegraaf*, which ran a long obituary titled "She Was Anne Frank's Most Trusted Helper." Despite the harsh words they had exchanged before my mother's death, Miep Gies was quoted saying only good things about her former office mate.

"She was a sweet and gentle personality, a good companion too, someone you could always depend on," she said. In Miep's opinion, "the special thing about [Bep] was that she was so humble. She was heroic without bravura, simply assumed that the hiders in the Annex must be helped. For her, that wasn't a difficult choice to make."

BAD BLOOD

I was not at the hospital the day my mother died. In fact, I did not find out she had passed away until three days later, on Monday, May 9, when I received a phone call at work from my sister-in-law Leny. She asked me if I had heard "the news." She was not exactly surprised to find out that I had been left in the dark. She told me that there had been a conversation at the hospital about whether I should even be invited to the funeral, which was to take place in two days, on May 11.

My grandmother and most of my mother's sisters, including Nelly and Diny, thought I belonged there. "She's his mother," they said. But my father, my eldest brother, Ton, and my sister disagreed. I hadn't been on speaking terms with my parents for more than a decade, and Anne and Ton had always blamed me for the conflict in our family. My other brother, Cok, was caught in the middle; he tried to be kind and friendly to me, but he also didn't want to interfere, probably out of loyalty to Anne and Ton.

My father and my siblings thought that our mother's funeral should not be made into a scene for some kind of reconciliation, much less a family squabble. But my aunts and especially my brothers' wives protested, and in the end my family agreed to allow me to come if I wanted to. The funeral invitations were drafted and dropped into the mail. But mine never arrived. Leny said that she had known something strange was happening, since it was not like me not to respond.

I was stunned into silence by what she told me, trying to process two incredible facts: my mother was gone, and my family did not want me at her funeral. I told Leny that at the very least, I would like to have a chance to say goodbye to her. So Leny offered to sneak me into the funeral chapel before the burial.

"Don't tell your father, Anne, and Ton," she said, ignoring or not remembering the fact that at the time I had no contact with them. "This will be our secret."

She didn't mean much by that, but in a split second I was sent back to another crucial moment in my life, some twenty-four years earlier, when my mother told me after I had found her on the edge of the bathtub with a mouth full of sleeping pills, "Don't tell your father and your brothers. This will be our secret."

That Wednesday, I met Cok and Leny at the cemetery. I knew the neighborhood well; it was Watergraafsmeer, where I grew up, where my mother lived until her death. A few hundred feet away was the soccer pitch where I played as a boy. It was a cold morning, cloudy and drizzling. Cok and Leny looked nervous when they saw me. It felt as though we were trespassing, as though we could all be "caught." Leny took me to the funeral chapel, where I saw my mother's casket. Then she left me alone.

That was one of the heaviest moments of my life, looking down on my mother as she lay there. Almost automatically, I laid my hand over her folded hands and looked at her face. She had a very relaxed expression, one I hadn't often seen while growing up. She looked almost as though she were smiling. I felt a strange sense of relief, being there with her. I thought I stood with her for only a couple of minutes, but Leny said afterward that it was almost a half hour. Apparently, I lost track of time. Just before leaving, I kissed her cold forehead.

As I left the chapel, I felt like a trespasser once again. I started running toward my car. I desperately wanted to avoid seeing my family. Partly that was to respect their wishes—they and, for all I knew, maybe even my own mother didn't want me there. But partly it was out of pride. I didn't want them to see me sneaking around like that.

As I got into my car, I saw Leny and Cok join the influx of mourners. I still remember the sound of their footsteps along the gravel path. Miep and Jan Gies were there. My grandmother Christina walked arm in arm with my aunt Willy. Nelly trailed behind them, alone. At the head of the group, I saw my father, stooped and downcast, supported by Ton and Anne. Looking at their backs as they entered the chapel, I couldn't help but think that they were three cowards, too afraid to face me even in this moment when whatever had separated us should be minimized by our shared loss. I remember thinking how ridiculous it was to be the outcast of the family without even having a clear idea of why I had been cast out in the first place or what I had done wrong. I was weeping soundlessly as I drove away. I felt sick, nauseous. I blamed my father most of all and vowed to myself that I would never forgive him.

ONE LAST CHANCE

Sonja and I divorced in September 1996. As in most failed marriages, we should have probably done it much sooner, but I tried for the sake of our daughter and because of some inbred sense of loyalty to make it work even long after there was nothing keeping us together except guilt and obligation.

Shortly after the divorce papers were finalized, I came home from work one night to find a message on my voice mail. It was from a social worker who had been meeting regularly with my father. She asked if I would be willing to talk to her about my "relationship" with him. I called her back, and she told me that my father was in poor health, that he was in therapy and taking antidepressants, and that he wanted nothing more than to reconcile with me "before it was too late."

Knowing how stubborn and closed-minded my father could be, I was surprised and maybe a little impressed that he would subject himself to therapy. The social worker had only a vague idea of what had transpired between us. I asked her if she knew that my mother had hidden Anne Frank during the war and that my father had always forbidden us from talking about that fact growing up. I asked her if she knew that my father had ostracized me from the family because of the woman I chose to marry, that his opposition to her was so great that he had never even met my daughter, and that he did not want me at my own mother's funeral.

She knew none of this. We spoke on the phone for almost two hours. I tried to explain to her that I would talk to my father only after he apologized. She told me that she understood. Two days later, she called me and said that my father felt bad about "what happened" between us, that he was inviting me to his new home to meet his new wife, a woman by the name of Fie.

I told her that I appreciated the call but I couldn't think of going unless I heard an apology directly from him. A week later I came home and there was another message on my voice mail—"*Met je vader*" (from your father). He said, in his own way, that he was sorry. A mumbled apology on voice mail wasn't exactly what I'd had in mind, but I thought that for my father it was already a big step. So I agreed to visit him.

My father was never comfortable talking about emotional matters. But on that visit he wanted to make clear that my mother had never told him she didn't want me at the funeral. "That was my idea," he said, "together with—"

Then he stopped talking. He wanted to add more to the story but then thought better of it. I noticed that he was less irritable than usual and not drunk. That I credited to Fie, a lovely woman with a strict character who had helped him get sober. She was the one who had encouraged him to speak to the social worker and get treatment for depression. On the day we met, my father gave me a gift, a stopwatch from his days refereeing korfball, a Dutch game similar to basketball. It was one of his most cherished possessions, and I was touched that he wanted me to have it.

It felt good to be back in touch with my father, but I was struck by the fact that fourteen years had passed since my mother's death. Why was he contacting me now? Maybe he felt the end of his life approaching, and he wanted to settle his affairs. But I suspected that it had more to do with the fact that I had just divorced Sonja, the woman he had so long opposed. The news of our breakup had filtered back to him through my siblings, and it was only after she was out of the picture that he reached out to me.

In 1999, I married my present wife, Ingrid, a person who has brought so much serenity into my life and helped me untangle the many knots of my family history. She is intelligent, critical, honest, and trustworthy—and I do not think I would have been able to tell this story without the strong foundation of our marriage.

My father was too sick to attend our wedding, but a year later, we all met for dinner. It was a mostly pleasant night. But at a certain point, my father looked at Ingrid with a strange twinkle in his eye. "You should have come sooner. That is all I can say." Then he smiled and changed the subject.

Sometime before his death in October 2002, my father was interviewed by a representative from the Anne Frank House, giving him one final opportunity to correct the record or reveal a long-hidden truth.

"The secret of my wife," he said, "was that her sister Nelly had a German boyfriend in the war—nothing more."

EPILOGUE

The Things We Leave Behind

If the end of the world would be imminent, I still would plant a tree today.

—*Otto Frank*

Anne wrote down everything. Without her diary, we would not know about my mother's heroism, Johan's steely determination, or Nelly's treachery. She planted the seeds of this story eighty years ago in a canal house in Amsterdam. My mother often said that it was important to remember that many other Dutch people did what the helpers of the Secret Annex did. They just didn't have their good deeds immortalized in a famous diary.

Being connected to that diary was an honor for my mother but also a burden. It detailed her heroism for all the world to see, but she never felt like a hero, and she had to privately cope with all the things that Anne left out of the story, things she couldn't have known: the suffering, the compromises, the shame. That private burden was also not unique to her. It is rare to meet a family in the Netherlands that does not have, buried somewhere, its own wartime secrets, a certain relative's experience that "we just don't talk about."

I am interested in these cases, how they work their way like a blight through the branches of a family tree, spreading shame and silence from one generation to the next. That is the story Jeroen and

I tried to tell in this book, and to do it we needed more than Anne Frank's diary. We had to dig into my memories, to speak with my relatives, to find documents and letters that could answer the questions Anne left us.

One set of documents that I was surprised to discover was missing from the record was my mother's letters. I knew that she had written letters her entire life and that many of them had run to several pages. She was also a fairly meticulous archivist of her own correspondence, especially the letters she had exchanged with Otto and other members of the Opekta Circle. She would catalog all the mail she received from them, along with carbon copies of her replies, in a thick two-ring binder.

When Jeroen and I first set out to research our book, I was astonished to discover that only a handful of the letters relating to the Secret Annex seemed to survive. I inquired of my aunts and siblings, the people who knew what had become of my mother's papers, but they claimed that they had given everything to the Anne Frank House. None of them knew the location of the two-ring binder.

When Jeroen and I counted up the few letters that were available, we found nine letters from my mother to Otto. Most were from the 1950s; a few were from the late 1970s. But from 1960 to 1978—the period after my mother's suicide attempt, when she and Otto may have begun to suspect Nelly of the betrayal—there was not a single surviving letter from my mother to Otto. Yet we know for a fact that they wrote to each other during that period, since we have eight letters from Otto to my mother from those years, seven of which are clearly replies to letters that she sent him.* It is as though somebody

---

* Given their earlier rate of correspondence, it is unlikely that Otto sent Bep only eight letters during that eighteen-year period, meaning that several of his letters to her from this time are probably missing as well.

erased eighteen years of my mother's correspondence. In addition, we could find no correspondence between my mother and Miep Gies, even though I remember my mother frequently reading letters from Miep and writing back to her.

The missing letters were still a mystery in 2010, when I paid a visit to the Anne Frank House. Part of the reason for my visit was to make absolutely certain that there was nothing that remained in its files that it hadn't already turned over to us. My brother Ton (who passed away in 2021) insisted on coming with me. All my siblings had been more or less supportive of my early efforts to tell our mother's story. Ton even gave Jeroen a place to stay near Amsterdam while he was conducting research. He and my sister, Anne, confided things in Jeroen that they would not tell me directly. They both seemed to care very much about getting the details right.

Nevertheless, I was surprised when Ton said he wanted to accompany me to the Anne Frank House. Thus far, he had not been personally involved in our research. I said yes, of course. The meeting yielded no major discoveries, but after we left, Ton asked if I wanted to grab a beer. His offer was out of character; he and I rarely socialized. But I told him I would love to.

We found a quiet place in Dam Square, and Ton ordered us a round of beers. He drank his down quickly, then asked for another and then another. Just as I was thinking how nice it was to make small talk and simply enjoy each other's company, the conversation took a strange turn.

"Well, Joop," he said, "I want to tell you something."

He asked if I knew about the "secret place" where our mother used to store important documents. I don't know why, but I feigned ignorance. "No . . . what secret place?"

He seemed satisfied that I didn't know. He told me that on the highest shelf in the dining room cupboard there was a tall stack of old papers, and right behind it "Mom used to keep important letters, ones she didn't want anyone to see. Well, when she got very sick, she asked me to take that stack of letters . . . and burn them."

I was stunned. "Do you know who the letters were from?"

Ton looked annoyed. "I didn't read them."

I pressed him some more. Then he told me, "I think they were love letters . . . to the neighbor, Mr. Hauben. Do you remember him?"

Of course I remembered him. He was the short, courteous Indonesian man who lived next door; my mother used to listen to concert music with him in the afternoon, and it's true that she sometimes hid the fact from my father so as not to arouse his jealousy. But I couldn't imagine that they had ever been lovers. In fact, I seem to remember that Mr. Hauben's wife was around whenever they were listening to music.

Ton wasn't looking directly at me, and he rolled his eyes as I tried to get him to answer more questions.

"How many letters were there?"

"I don't know, about two centimeters' worth," he said, using his thumb and index finger to show me the size of the stack.

"So you burned about thirty or forty of Mom's love letters? When was this?"

"Right after she went into the hospital. She checked with me a couple of days before she died to make sure I had done it."

Now I could see that he was getting emotional, wiping away tears from his eyes. He seemed to breathe a sigh of relief when I changed the subject and we ordered another round.

I was disturbed by what he told me and angry at him and my other siblings for having handled our mother's correspondence so carelessly after her death. But in their defense, they didn't know that I was planning to write my mother's biography, and at that point in our research, Jeroen hadn't yet discovered the missing diary pages dealing with Nelly's collaboration. So we had no reason to suspect that my mother had a dark truth that she was hiding from the world.

I couldn't see then what Ton was actually telling me. So Jeroen and I dropped the issue, until 2022, when we were at the latest stage of the research for this book. In that period, we reviewed the details of everything my brother had told me, and they didn't add up. Why would a housewife conduct an epistolary romance with a next-door neighbor when she could just whisper over the fence, sparing her an incriminating paper trail? It didn't sound like something our mother would do. And I didn't believe that Ton had known as little about the content of the letters as he claimed to.

Ton had been playing the fool. He wanted me to think that he had innocently followed our mother's wishes, that he believed he was burning old love letters, helping his dying mother cover up a decades-old affair. But he knew that I would eventually discover the truth, that what my mother wanted to burn was not evidence of some antique dalliance but the missing correspondence with the members of the Opekta Circle. He believed that Jeroen and I would leave no stone unturned in our research and wanted to save us the trouble of searching for letters that no longer existed.

One detail would come to haunt me: imagining the look of relief on my mother's face on her deathbed after she asked Ton, "Did you burn those letters?" and he told her that he did.

• • • • • • • • • •

Land is always in short supply in the Netherlands, so burial plots are expensive and typically leased only for a decade or two, after which time the remains are removed. When my mother's burial rights expired, twenty years after her death, in 2003, my sister, Anne, organized the cremation of her remains. The relations between me and my siblings had improved somewhat, so this time I was invited to the ceremony.

I had wanted to make peace with my family for my own sake, for my daughter's, and because I believed that, deep down, it was what my mother had always wanted. But even though we now gathered for special occasions, the bad blood was still there, simmering beneath the surface. And as much as I had hoped that this book project would help me and my siblings heal by tracing our family trauma back to its source, learning the truth—or at least my version of it—did not exactly bring us all together.

In fact, when my sister read an earlier version of this story, she broke off what limited contact she had with me and encouraged Ton to follow suit. She refused to believe that our mother tried to kill herself and attributed my eyewitness account of the event to "false memories." She also thought that it was improper for me to investigate Aunt Nelly's past, that to do so would be to air our family's "dirty laundry."

I regret the distance that still exists between my sister and me, but I am encouraged that the next generation of our family—my daughter, Rebecca; my nieces and nephews, Elly, Robin, Jochem, Hester, and Casper; as well as my grandchildren, the twins Kay-Lee and Ryan—are more willing to talk about this dark history, perhaps because their own childhoods were not overshadowed by it. They give me hope in our future, which is why I have chosen to dedicate this book to them.

The same year we scattered my mother's ashes, I invited Ton, his wife, Marie-José, and their son to my house for dinner. It was during that night that Ton confessed, at the insistence of Marie-José, that he and Anne were the ones who chose not to mail my invitation to the funeral. I was too wounded to say anything in reply, but I was proud of my then-twenty-six-year-old nephew Robin, who expressed fury on my behalf and called his father a coward. That was a difficult moment, but I think it was a step toward reaching some understanding among us all.

Later that night, Ton presented me with "a surprise." It was a photo album that my mother had prepared for me in the final years of her life, which she filled with photographs from my childhood.

There were baby pictures of me in my mother's arms, a photo of my father holding me on my first bicycle, a picture of my mother and me smiling widely as we cleaned dishes next to the stove where I would later have my accident. There was even a picture of me leading Sonja through a ballroom dance.

I cherish each photo in that book, but what I value above all is the album's existence. It proved to me that my mother still loved and cared for me, in spite of everything. She left in the book a note for me to read, a note that she hoped I would get before her death but that I did not see until twenty years later. It was a note written on two sides of a thin sheet of paper, written in the swift script she had learned in secretarial school. It was not poetry, it was not particularly profound, it paled in terms of drama or artistry even when compared to the most tossed-off of Anne Frank's diary entries. And yet to me, it meant more than anything else I've ever read.

My lovely son Joop,

Here is your scrapbook with your pictures from your youth. We feel a lot of sadness over this situation, but we are convinced that you feel the same way, and we think this is terrible. Why did it have to be this way? Why do people have to torment each other so much in this short life? I hope that I am still alive when you get this scrapbook and that everything is fine again.

Goodbye, Joop. Your parents love you, your little sister, too, and your brothers, your grandmother, aunts and uncles, and cousins. Best regards, much love, best wishes also for your wife and child.

The note was signed simply "Your mother."

A NOTE ON SOURCES

Jeroen and I have been trying to share my mother's story with the world for more than a decade. Our earlier efforts led to the Dutch book *Bep Voskuijl: Het zwijgen voorbij* (*Bep Voskuijl: Beyond the Silence*), a more traditional biography that was published in 2015 by Prometheus/Bert Bakker in Amsterdam. An English translation of that book was self-published in 2018.

After our first book came out, Jeroen and I discovered important new facts and witness testimonials that, along with my own personal story, greatly informed the present work. In the following pages, we have tried to provide citations for every fact and quotation taken from published work as well as unpublished letters, documents, and interviews. One major source for this story was my own memory, which, like anyone else's, is imperfect, so I have endeavored where possible to check my recollections against photographs, letters, news reports, and the memories of my family members.

· · · · · · · · · ·

In 2017, I became aware of an investigation by a former FBI agent, Vince Pankoke, who hoped to use modern forensic techniques and "big data" to solve the mystery of who had betrayed the Secret Annex once and for all. Pankoke was working with a "cold case team" made up of thirty professionals, including historians, writers, and experienced investigators, and he claimed that his project had the support of the Anne Frank House and the NIOD Institute for War, Holocaust and Genocide Studies. Given all that, Jeroen and I believed that the cold case team's research would be carried out in an objective manner and that its conclusions could be trusted. We gladly sat for interviews with Vince and shared our findings to help his team achieve their ambitious mission.

Unfortunately, our high hopes for the project were misplaced. *The Betrayal of Anne Frank*, a book summarizing the cold case team's investigation written by Rosemary Sullivan, was excoriated by a chorus of Holocaust experts almost as soon as it was published in 2022. A sixty-nine-page scientific study written by six distinguished Dutch academics refuted the main findings of the book, saying that there was "not any serious evidence" to support the cold case team's accusation that a Jewish notary named Arnold van den Bergh was guilty of the betrayal. The book's Dutch publisher subsequently pulled all copies from the market and issued an apology; a planned publication in Germany was canceled.

Not only have scholars picked apart the cold case team's accusation against van den Bergh, but *The Betrayal of Anne Frank* is filled with many other errors and inaccuracies, several of which pertain to my own family. Out of a sense of loyalty to them, and above all to the historical truth, I have felt compelled to correct those inaccuracies in interviews and online.

NOTES

The books that we cite most often are referred to using the following short titles.

Bas von Benda-Beckmann, *After the Annex: Anne Frank, Auschwitz and Beyond* (London: Unicorn, 2023): *After the Annex*

Anne Frank, *The Diary of Anne Frank: The Revised Critical Edition*, edited by David Barnouw and Gerrold van der Stroom (New York: Doubleday, 2003): *Diary (RCE)*

Anne Frank, *The Diary of a Young Girl: The Definitive Edition*, edited by Otto Frank and Mirjam Pressler (New York: Bantam Books, 1995): *Diary (DE)*

Miep Gies and Alison Leslie Gold, *Anne Frank Remembered: The Story of the Woman Who Helped to Hide the Frank Family* (New York: Simon & Schuster, 2009): *Anne Frank Remembered*

Dienke Hondius, *Terugkeer: Antisemitisme in Nederland rond de bevrijding* (The Hague: SDU, 1990): *Terugkeer*

Carol Ann Lee, *Roses from the Earth: The Biography of Anne Frank* (London: BCA, 1999): *Roses*

————, *The Hidden Life of Otto Frank* (New York: William Morrow, 2003): *The Hidden Life*

Geert Mak, *Amsterdam: A Brief Life of the City* (London: Vintage Books, 2010): *Amsterdam*

Melissa Müller, *Anne Frank: The Biography* (New York: Picador, 2013): *Anne Frank*

Jacob Presser, *Ashes in the Wind: The Destruction of Dutch Jewry* (London: Souvenir Press, 1968): *Ashes*

Mirjam Pressler, *Treasures from the Attic: The Extraordinary Story of Anne Frank's Family* (New York: Doubleday, 2011): *Treasures*

Ernst Schnabel, *The Footsteps of Anne Frank* (London: Pan Books, 1972): *The Footsteps*

NOTES

Eda Shapiro and Rick Kardonne, *Victor Kugler: The Man Who Hid Anne Frank* (Jerusalem: Gefen Publishing House, 2008): *Victor Kugler*

Simon Wiesenthal and Joseph Wechsberg, *The Murderers Among Us: The Simon Wiesenthal Memoirs* (New York: McGraw-Hill, 1967): *The Murderers*

We quote from the following archives, and in these notes, they are referred to using the following abbreviations.

ACA: Amsterdam City Archives
AFH: Anne Frank House, Amsterdam
CBG: CBG Center for Family History, The Hague
CM: Claudia Morawetz, personal collection
DLM: Deutsches Literaturarchiv Marbach, Germany
LL: Landesgericht (district court) Lübeck, Germany
NA: National Archives, The Hague
NIOD: NIOD Institute for War, Holocaust and Genocide Studies, Amsterdam (before January 1, 1999, the State Institute for War Documentation, RIOD)
ÖS: Österreichisches Staatsarchiv, Vienna
USHMM: United States Holocaust Memorial Museum, Washington, DC

Prologue: A Letter from Belgium

xi known in English: The diary was first published in Great Britain in May 1952 by Vallentine Mitchell in an edition of five thousand copies. It was published in the United States in June 1952 by Doubleday, also in an edition of five thousand copies. A second printing in the US of fifteen thousand copies was rushed through, as the first printing sold out only hours after hitting the shelves.

xii *Shoah*: The film, which received numerous nominations and awards at film festivals around the world, was distributed by New Yorker Films and released in Paris in April 1985.

xii the Sobibor death camp: According to the Dutch historian and Sobibor survivor Jules Schelvis (1921–2016), more than 170,000 Jews were deported to the camp from May 1942 until it was disbanded by the Nazis in late 1943, following a successful revolt of the prisoners. 34,313 Jews were deported there from the Netherlands, only 18 of whom made it through the war alive. See Jules Schelvis, *Sobibor: A History of a Nazi Death Camp* (London: Bloomsbury, 2014).

xiii three of the "helpers": Not very much is known about Jo Kleiman's personal experiences during the Secret Annex period, yet he frequently guided journalists and tourists through the Annex in the 1950s and in 1957 was closely

involved in the establishment of the Anne Frank Foundation, whose aim
was the preservation of the Annex (and which later opened the Anne Frank
House in 1960). Kleiman died on January 28, 1959, in Amsterdam.

xiii The usual explanation: This distorted picture was especially fueled by the
many film and stage adaptations of Anne Frank's story, in which Bep usually
played a minor role or simply didn't appear.

xv a rare recording: The interview, conducted by the Canadian composer Oskar
Morawetz (1917–2007) on October 9, 1978, is discussed in greater detail in
chapter 15.

Part I: Anne

1 "Never have they uttered": Diary (DE), January 28, 1944, 178.

Chapter 1: The Bookcase Swings Open

3 the twenty-eight thousand Jews: Jaap Cohen, "How Unique Was the Secret
Annex? People in Hiding in the Occupied Netherlands," Anne Frank House,
https://www.annefrank.org/en/anne-frank/go-in-depth/how-unique-was
-secret-annex-people-hiding-occupied-netherlands/. The NIOD Institute for
War, Holocaust and Genocide Studies presents slightly different numbers,
based on research from 1989: "It is estimated that more than 350,000 people
went into hiding for shorter or longer periods of time during the Occupation. About 25,000 Jews went into hiding, of whom about a third were caught
later." See Hans Blom, *Crisis, bezetting en herstel: Tien studies over Nederland
1930–1950* (Rotterdam/The Hague: Nijgh & Van Ditmar, 1989).

4 Seventy-five percent of Dutch Jews: Presser, *Ashes*, 232.

4 Only five thousand: Ibid.

4 "All my hope is the children": Otto Frank, letter to Alice Frank, May 25,
1945, quoted in Daniel S. Levy, "How Anne Frank's Diary Survived," *Time*,
June 14, 2017.

6 "What Papa's eyes saw": Willy Voskuijl, written statement, August 12, 2009.

6 all four of them were murdered: Personal record cards of Hijman Nabarro
(1896–1943), Elisabeth Uijenkruijer (1895–1942), Jacob Nabarro (1921–1943),
and Selma Nabarro (1927–1942), ACA; "Hijman Nabarro," Joods Monument,
https://www.joodsmonument.nl/en/page/202389/hijman-nabarro; "Hijman Nabarro 1896-1943," Oorlogsgravenstichting, https://www.oorlogsgravenstichting
.nl/personen/108300/hijman-nabarro.

7 His grandfather and two of his aunts: Ibid.

7 "the Jews were all in hiding": Mak, *Amsterdam*, 97.

7 "clean facades and flowerpots": Ibid., 98.

7 carried it out "like clockwork": Uri Dan, "Eichmann's Prison Diary: Holocaust Was a Horror," *New York Post*, March 1, 2000.

8 "Concerning the Jewish Question": Mak, *Amsterdam*, 102.

8 "we would not have been": Ibid.

10 The National Socialists' share: Harold J. Goldberg, *Daily Life in Nazi-Occupied Europe* (Santa Barbara, CA: Greenwood, 2019), 5–6.

12 Otto liked her immediately: Gies and Gold, *Anne Frank Remembered*, 49.

14 "Won't someone offer a seat": Jean Schick Grossman, "Anne Frank: The Story Within Her Story," December 5, 1954 (unpublished manuscript), AFH.

14 the children in his house: Diny Voskuijl, interview by Joop van Wijk-Voskuijl and Jeroen De Bruyn, August 25, 2012.

15 "the man of my dreams": Hiroo Kawamura, "Hunger and Fear in the Secret Annex," *Asahi Shimbun*, April 3, 1965.

Chapter 2: Yellow Stars

17 "a bolt out of the blue": Cok van Wijk, interview by Jeroen De Bruyn, April 6, 2014.

18 In announcing the surrender: "Holland Overrun: Commander Tells Troops Yielding Is Only Way to Save Civilians," *New York Times*, May 15, 1940.

18 "think of our Jewish compatriots": Queen Wilhelmina, radio speech, May 13, 1940. It was the last radio address the queen gave before leaving the Netherlands.

19 "both mad and a coward": Mak, *Amsterdam*, 99.

19 Jacob van Gelderen: Lucas Ligtenberg, *Mij krijgen ze niet levend: De zelfmoorden van mei 1940* (Amsterdam: Balans, 2017); Han van der Horst, *Zwarte Jaren* (Amsterdam: Prometheus, 2020); "Jacob van Gelderen," Joods Monument, https://www.joodsmonument.nl/en/page/227548/jacob-van-gelderen.

19 Otto's relatives in Great Britain: Milly Stanfield, interview by Carl Fussman, in "The Woman Who Would Have Saved Anne Frank," *Newsday*, March 16, 1995.

20 were pleasantly surprised: Mak, *Amsterdam*, 101.

20 "We're not likely": Anne Frank, letter to Alice Frank, undated, quoted in Müller, *Anne Frank*, 149.

20 she would be forced: Lee, *Roses*, 74.

20 389 Jewish men: This figure has only recently been investigated by the Dutch historian Wally de Lang and was published in her book *De razzia's van 22 en*

23 februari 1941 in Amsterdam: Het lot van 389 Joodse mannen (Amsterdam: Atlas Contact, 2021).

20 on February 25, 300,000 Dutch people: Loe de Jong, *Het Koninkrijk der Nederlanden in de Tweede Wereldoorlog* (The Hague: Martinus Nijhoff, 1985), part 4.

21 "Bep told us difficult times": Diny Voskuijl, interview by Jeroen De Bruyn, September 2, 2012.

22 They loved watching: Willy Voskuijl, report of an interview by Dineke Stam and Rian Verhoeven, April 8, 1994, AFH.

22 The Nazis sent: Personal record card of Jonas Bed (1903–1945), ACA; "Jonas Bed," Joods Monument, https://www.joodsmonument.nl/en/page/183938/jonas-bed.

23 "I warned him *not* to do it!": Diny Voskuijl, interview by Joop van Wijk-Voskuijl, August 21, 2021.

25 "He was a quiet person": Gies and Gold, *Anne Frank Remembered*, 51.

25 "all industrial and commercial firms": Schnabel, *The Footsteps*, 51–52.

26 Otto Frank paid the Dutch Nazi (footnote): See Otto Frank, letter to the Bureau Nationale Veiligheid (Netherlands Bureau of National Security), August 21, 1945, quoted in Lee, *The Hidden Life*, 75; Schnabel, *The Footsteps*, 59.

Chapter 3: Full Secrecy

30 "I am not a hero": Gies and Gold, *Anne Frank Remembered*, xi.

32 Bep claimed that Otto Frank (footnote): See Bep Voskuijl, report of an interview by David Barnouw and Gerrold van der Stroom, February 25, 1981, NIOD.

33 "Bep, do you agree": Bep Voskuijl, testimony for the district court of Lübeck, September 29, 1959, in Rheine, Germany, LL.

33 After the war, my mother: See, e.g., Bob Wallagh, "Elly van Wijk kende de geheimen van het Achterhuis" (Elly van Wijk Knew the Secrets of the Secret Annex), *Rosita*, February 27, 1960.

33 She had considered it: In a letter to an American schoolteacher, Jaqueline Shachter, dated March 17, 1965, Bep used this phrase; AFH.

35 "We'll leave": Diary (DE), July 1, 1942, 18.

35 "Just enjoy": Ibid.

36 "We have to do something": Diny Voskuijl, interview by Joop van Wijk-Voskuijl and Jeroen De Bruyn, August 25, 2012.

36 From now on, Jo said: Bob Wallagh, *Verfilmd verleden: De camera's op het dagboek van Anne Frank* (Maastricht: Leiter-Nypels, 1959), 42.

36 "I hope you will be": Diary (DE), June 12, 1942, 1.

36 or, as she put it: Diary (DE), June 20, 1942, 6; June 21, 1942, 11.

37 "we fell exhausted": Diary (DE), July 10, 1942, 26.

37 "the enormous change": Ibid.

37 "some strange pension": Diary (DE), July 11, 1942, 26.

37 "an ideal place to hide in": Ibid.

37 "safer to leave a day too early": Diary (DE), August 14, 1942, 30.

38 there were bounties: Sytze van der Zee, "Een fascinatie voor het verraad en het kwaad" (A Fascination with Betrayal and Evil), De Volkskrant, January 23, 2010.

38 "I wish like anything": Diary (RCE), "Deletions and Additions," July 11, 1942 (B-version), 842.

Chapter 4: Mouths to Feed

39 The Nazis confiscated: Stephanus Louwes (director general of the National Bureau for Food Supply), speech, October 1943, quoted in "1940–1941: De vervanging van vlees" (1940–1941: The Replacement of Meat), Verzetsmuseum Amsterdam, https://www.verzetsmuseum.org/nl/kennisbank /1940-1941-de-vervanging-van-vlees.

39 a fact that Anne: Diary (RCE), May 5, 1944 (A-version), 631.

40 "a pack mule": Diary (DE), July 11, 1943, 107.

40 "Everyone's trading": Diary (DE), May 6, 1944, 285.

40 "We constantly lived": Hiroo Kawamura, "Hunger and Fear in the Secret Annex," Asahi Shimbun, April 3, 1965.

41 "certain theatrical qualities": Miep Gies, quoted in Dienke Hondius, "A New Perspective on Helpers of Jews During the Holocaust: The Case of Miep and Jan Gies," in Anne Frank in Historical Perspective: A Teaching Guide, edited by Alex Grobman (Los Angeles: Martyrs Memorial and Museum of the Holocaust, 1995), 39.

42 Little did she know: "De Annahoeve, herinnering aan een tijd die voorbij is," Vrienden van Watergraafsmeer, https://www.vriendenvanwatergraafsmeer .nl/annahoeve-herinnering-aan-tijd-voorbij-is.

44 "What is happening outside?": Ernst Schnabel, personal notes, DLM.

44 "Number nine is not": Diary (DE), August 9, 1943, 125.

44 That was how Otto: Otto Frank, memoir, quoted in Lee, Roses, 119.

45 "incredibly nice of Bep": Diary (DE), December 30, 1943, 158.

46 "How anyone can be so clever": Diary (DE), December 7, 1942, 74.

46 "He's been most helpful": Diary (DE), August 21, 1942, 32.

46 "Easy to say": Diary (DE), November 3, 1943, 144.

47 She asked Willy: Willy Voskuijl, written statement, August 12, 2009; Willy Voskuijl, report of an interview by Erika Prins and Teresien da Silva, March 9, 2006, AFH.

47 "I felt like a princess": Diny Voskuijl, interview by Joop van Wijk-Voskuijl and Jeroen De Bruyn, August 25, 2012.

48 "Ah, they're at it again": Diny Voskuijl, interview by Joop van Wijk-Voskuijl, August 21, 2021.

Chapter 5: Concealment

49 "Will they still be there?": Jan Roelfs, "In Canada leven herinneringen aan het Achterhuis voort: Victor Kugler riskeerde met anderen zijn leven voor familie Anne Frank" (Memories of the Secret Annex Live on in Canada: Victor Kugler and Others Risked Their Lives for the Family of Anne Frank), *Trouw*, July 29, 1978.

49 "short but solid knock": Diary (DE), August 5, 1943, 122.

50 "I would hide it": Shapiro and Kardonne, *Victor Kugler*, 44.

51 "leading away little groups": Ibid., 30.

51 "I was glad": Ibid.

51 Laura Buntenbach: Müller, *Anne Frank*, 280; "Laura Maria Buntenbach (1895-1952)," FamilySearch, https://ancestors.familysearch.org/en/2ZVP-L35/laura-maria-buntenbach-1895-1952.

51 "My wife was in poor health": Shapiro and Kardonne, *Victor Kugler*, 40–41.

52 "I had to put on a good 'act'": Ibid., 41.

52 "You constantly had to be able": " 'Meneer Kraler' maakte pelgrimstocht naar Broadway: Aangrijpend weerzien met het Achterhuis" ("Mr. Kraler" Made Pilgrim's Journey to Broadway: Emotional Reunion with the Secret Annex), *De Telegraaf*, February 11, 1956.

52 "from pent-up tension": Diary (DE), May 26, 1944, 306.

52 "Kugler never said": Otto Frank, letter to Leni Frank, undated, quoted in Pressler, *Treasures*, 233.

55 "Father didn't care": Diny Voskuijl, interview by Joop van Wijk-Voskuijl, November 18, 2021.

55 "Stien, I have to feed": Ibid.

55 "Things are getting": Diary (RCE), August 14, 1942 (A-version), 249.

55 "Now our Secret Annex": Diary (DE), August 21, 1942, 32.

Chapter 6: Sleepover

57 "don't understand": Diary (DE), March 2, 1944, 201.

58 "I don't understand": Diary (RCE), March 8, 1944 (A-version), 544.

58 "Surely I know best": Ibid.

58 "rather disdainful and cool": Ibid.

59 she had been "surprised": Bep also emphasized this during her interview with Oskar Morawetz; audio recording of the interview on October 9, 1978, CM.

59 "What help did those two offer her?": Diary (RCE), March 2, 1944 (A-version), 201–2.

60 "She sat by my side": Bep Voskuijl, letter to Otto Frank, March 22, 1951, AFH.

60 "Isn't that remarkable": Bob Wallagh, *Verfilmd verleden: De camera's op het dagboek van Anne Frank* (Maastricht: Leiter-Nypels, 1959), 44.

60 "she certainly had a sharp tongue": Ernst Schnabel, personal notes, DLM.

60 "because she was the youngest": Bep Voskuijl, letter to Otto Frank, March 22, 1951, AFH.

61 "one big adventure": Ernst Schnabel, personal notes, DLM.

61 "unwavering confidence": Schnabel, *The Footsteps*, 90.

61 "Ah, the plans we made": Ernst Schnabel, personal notes, DLM.

62 Throughout the war, my mother played: Bep Voskuijl, testimony for the district court of Lübeck, September 29, 1959, in Rheine, Germany, LL; Bep Voskuijl, audio recording of an interview by Oskar Morawetz, October 9, 1978, CM.

63 "Her diary was her greatest secret": Ernst Schnabel, personal notes, DLM. Otto Frank's second wife, Fritzi, said that Anne had written her stories down in a separate notebook, "so to be able to read from it without her audience seeing the diary." Fritzi probably heard that from her husband. See Fritzi Frank, report of an interview by David Barnouw and Gerrold van der Stroom, March 3, 1981, NIOD.

63 "I couldn't believe": Bep Voskuijl, letter to Otto Frank, March 22, 1951, AFH.

64 "You shouldn't tell her so much": Ernst Schnabel, personal notes, DLM.

64 Years later she would remember: Bob Wallagh, "Elly van Wijk kende de geheimen van het Achterhuis" (Elly van Wijk Knew the Secrets of the Secret Annex), *Rosita*, February 27, 1960.

65 the "horrible" news: Diary (RCE), September 21, 1942 (A-version), 257.

65 "so well off": Ibid.

65 "Betty Bloemendaal": Diary (DE), June 15, 1942, 3.

65 A photograph from the early 1940s: "Bertha Louise Bloemendal," Joods

Monument, https://www.joodsmonument.nl/en/page/177363/bertha-louise
-bloemendal.

65 The Bloemendal home: Bob Polak, *Naar buiten, lucht en lachen! Een literaire
    wandeling door het Amsterdam van Anne Frank* (Amsterdam: Bas Lubberhui-
    zen, 2006), 152.

65 If my mother did not see: Bep told Ernst Schnabel in June 1957 that she saw
    raids on Jews in her neighborhood, but it's unclear whether the raid in which
    the Bloemendals were arrested was one of those. See Ernst Schnabel, personal
    notes, DLM.

66 "No one is spared": Diary (DE), November 19, 1942, 69.

66 "packed off to Poland": Diary (RCE), November 19, 1942 (B-version), 257.

66 "I feel wicked": Diary (DE), November 19, 1942, 70.

67 "Every now and then": Diary (DE), November 20, 1942, 70.

67 "are regularly killed": This was the BBC's first broadcast describing the use of
    gas against Jews (July 9, 1942, 6:00 p.m., Home News Bulletin).

67 hints about the death camps: Bep Voskuijl, audio recording of an interview by
    Oskar Morawetz, October 9, 1978, CM.

67 "They knew everything": Quoted in Schnabel, *The Footsteps*, 97.

Chapter 7: One Small Act of Carelessness

69 Anne called it a "disaster": Diary (DE), June 15, 1943, 105.

69 "a carcinoma": Written diagnosis by Johan Voskuijl's doctor, May 12, 1943,
    AFH.

69 "an unforgivable error": Diary (DE), June 15, 1943, 105.

70 "our greatest source of help and support": Ibid.

71 "I wouldn't know": Diary (DE), July 23, 1943, 113.

71 "almost impossible to digest": Willy Voskuijl, written statement, August 12,
    2009.

71 "pale as a sheet": Diny Voskuijl, video interview by Teresien da Silva, Novem-
    ber 14, 2011, AFH.

71 "That's all, Stien": Ibid.

71 "The two of them didn't talk": Ibid.

72 "A nervous fit": Diary (DE), September 29, 1943, 136.

73 "put her foot down": Ibid.

73 "the shopping lists": Ibid.

74 "He spreads the most": Diary (RCE), April 25, 1944 (A-version), 640.

74 "unsympathetic": Bep Voskuijl, interrogation by the Amsterdam Criminal
    Investigation Department, December 13, 1963, NIOD.

74   "A person with any brains": Diary (DE), September 16, 1943, 135.

74   "Is this your wallet, Mr. Kugler?": Quoted in Schnabel, *The Footsteps*, 118. For the sake of clarity, we used Victor Kugler's real name and not his pseudonym from *Het Achterhuis*, Mr. Kraler, which Schnabel used in his book.

75   "Oh, yes, of course!": Ibid.

75   "What must the passersby": Diary (DE), September 16, 1943, 136.

76   "too risky": Diary (RCE), April 25, 1944 (A-version), 640.

76   "Isn't it even riskier": Ibid.

76   "One small act of carelessness": Diary (DE), May 18, 1943, 102.

76   "They think the cancer": Diary (DE), April 25, 1944, 273.

77   "if the secret ": Victor Kugler, letter to Otto Frank, February 4, 1964, AFH.

77   "Mr. Kleiman thought": Ibid.

78   "Twenty-five months": Quoted in Schnabel, *The Footsteps*, 118.

Chapter 8: Invasion Fever

79   "Every day I feel": Diary (DE), May 3, 1944, 282.

79   On the English radio: The address Queen Wilhelmina gave on the night of Tuesday, May 9, 1944, on Radio Oranje was repeated on Thursday afternoon, May 11. Her address of Wednesday afternoon, May 10, was repeated that same evening.

80   "Oh, Kitty": Diary (DE), June 6, 1944, 312.

80   "shy, awkward boy": Diary (DE), August 14, 1942, 30.

80   "dark blue eyes": Diary (DE), January 6, 1944, 162.

80   "a famous writer": Diary (DE), May 11, 1944, 296.

80   "overconfident [and] amusing": Diary (DE), April 28, 1944, 275.

80   a "second Anne": Ibid.

80   "who wants only to love": Ibid.

81   "Anne, be honest!": Ibid., 277.

81   "Oh, now I understand Bep": Ibid., 277.

81   A "nice, steady, athletic young man": Diary (DE), May 25, 1944, 304.

82   "When I'd tell": Bertus Hulsman, interview by Joop van Wijk-Voskuijl and Jeroen De Bruyn, February 20, 2014.

83   "And all those times": Bertus Hulsman, video interview by Dineke Stam, December 4, 2007.

84   "hardly appropriate in this situation": Diary (DE), October 9, 1942, 55.

84   The experience left him: Bertus Hulsman, interview by Joop van Wijk-Voskuijl and Jeroen De Bruyn, February 20, 2014.

86   "about being an old maid": Diary (DE), May 25, 1944, 305.

86 "even worse": Ibid., 304.

86 "how long she will be able": Diary (RCE), May 25, 1944 (A-version), 649.

86 "Bep's engaged!": Diary (DE), May 25, 1944, 304.

86 "put an end to her indecision": Ibid.

86 "Bep doesn't love him": Ibid.

86 "who knows how to appreciate her": Ibid., 305.

87 "What a sorry prospect": Ibid., 305.

Chapter 9: All Was Lost

89 "Quiet!": Schnabel, *The Footsteps*, 101.

89 "Bep," she said: Bep Voskuijl, interrogation by the Amsterdam Criminal Investigation Department, December 13, 1963, NIOD.

90 *"Wo sind die Juden?"*: Ernst Schnabel, personal notes, DLM. Bep, Miep, and Jo Kleiman also recalled that sentence while visiting the Annex with a Dutch journalist in the 1950s, when the Annex was threatened with demolition. "All of a sudden someone knocks on the door," he wrote. "Everyone is petrified. . . . It turns out to be one of the staff members of the nearby clothing firm, which purchased the building 263 Prinsengracht to expand the company. He is ringing his key chain and likes to know how much time this will take. Almost thirteen years have passed since [Kleiman], Miep, and Elly found themselves in the same wretched situation: the 'Grüne Polizei' raided the place and took away the Jewish people. Still today, the slightest knock on the door to the Secret Annex sounds like the pounding of the Germans' heavy boots to them. They can still picture the revolvers pointed at them, and they can still hear that one little diabolical sentence: *'Wo sind die Juden?'* " See Bob van Dam, "Herinneringen aan Anne Frank: Het Achterhuis, plek van veel verdriet en tranen" (Memories of Anne Frank: The Secret Annex, a Place of Sorrow and Tears), *Wereldkroniek*, June 8, 1957.

92 Silberbauer ordered: Sytze van der Zee, *Vogelvrij: De jacht op de Joodse onderduiker* (Amsterdam: De Bezige Bij, 2010), 443.

92 she died of typhus: "Cäcilie Emma Sophie Hüsfeldt," Joods Monument, https://www.joodsmonument.nl/en/page/222603/cäcilie-emma-sophie-hüsfeldt.

93 "History cannot be written": Transcript of Gerrit Bolkestein's speech, broadcast on Radio Oranje on March 28, 1944, NIOD.

93 "She was very quiet": Quoted in Schnabel, *The Footsteps*, 110.

94 "I can't, can't describe": Ibid.

94 "split in two": Diary (DE), August 1, 1944, 335.

94 "an amusing clown": Ibid., 336.

94 "Before I realize it": Ibid., 336.

94 "awfully pale": Hiroo Kawamura, "Hunger and Fear in the Secret Annex," *Asahi Shimbun*, April 3, 1965.

94 "Just keep denying": Bep Voskuijl, interrogation by the Amsterdam Criminal Investigation Department, December 13, 1963, NIOD.

95 "Aren't you ashamed": Miep and Jan Gies, report of interviews by David Barnouw and Gerrold van der Stroom, February 19 and 27, 1985, NIOD.

96 "Just come back": Ernst Schnabel, personal notes, DLM; Bep Voskuijl, audio recording of an interview by Oskar Morawetz, October 9, 1978, CM.

96 "the belly of the beast": Ernst Schnabel, personal notes, DLM.

Part II: Nelly

99 "They are sure": Diary (RCE), May 11, 1944 (A-version), 668.

Chapter 10: The Voice of a Young Woman

101 "joy to see": Presser, *Ashes*, 172.

101 Now frail and graying: Adolf Eichmann was hanged on May 31, 1962. That same year, the Chelmno trials, in which eleven of Hitler's henchmen were prosecuted, started in Bonn. In 1963, the second Auschwitz trial, with twenty indicted suspects in the dock, started in Frankfurt, as well as the Belzec trial of eight former SS members in Munich.

101 "a nobody, a zero": Wiesenthal and Wechsberg, *The Murderers*, 182.

102 "Anne Frank's diary": Simon Wiesenthal in the documentary *I Have Never Forgotten You: The Life and Legacy of Simon Wiesenthal* by Richard Trank, 2007.

102 "decided to live for the dead": Wiesenthal and Wechsberg, *The Murderers*, 175.

105 "more cables and letters": Ibid., 181.

105 he had been merely "following orders": "Arrest and Release of Karl Silberbauer," Anne Frank House, https://www.annefrank.org/en/timeline/92/arrest-and-release-of-karl-silberbauer/.

105 "only done his duty": During that same period, Otto Frank made similar statements in interviews with several newspapers. See, e.g., "SD'er die de familie Frank arresteerde in Wenen opgespoord" (SD Man Who Arrested Frank Family Tracked Down in Vienna), *Het Vrije Volk*, November 20, 1963; "Vader van Anne Frank kende Silberbauers naam" (Anne Frank's Father Knew Silberbauer's Name), *Algemeen Handelsblad*, November 21, 1963.

106 "a shred of humanity": Ernst Schnabel, personal notes, DLM.

106 "The only thing I ask": Simon Wiesenthal, "Epilogue to the Diary of Anne

Frank," in *Anne Frank Unbound: Media, Imagination, Memory*, edited by Hyman A. Enzer and Sandra Solotaroff-Enzer (Bloomington, IN: Indiana University Press, 2002), 68.

106 "The next morning": Victor Kugler, letter to Bep Voskuijl, February 11, 1964, AFH.

107 Huf showed up: Karl Silberbauer, interview by Jules Huf in *Kurier*, November 22, 1963. The interview was reprinted in the Dutch magazine *De Groene Amsterdammer* on May 14, 1986.

108 "had no reason to suspect": Bob van Dijk, "Wie pleegde het verraad van het Achterhuis?" (Who Was the Betrayer of the Secret Annex?), *Panorama*, December 13, 1963.

108 "Unfortunately, I can't": Bep Voskuijl, interrogation by the Amsterdam Criminal Investigation Department, December 13, 1963, NIOD.

109 "I want to make clear": Karl Silberbauer, statement, November 25, 1963, Austrian Ministry of the Interior, ÖS.

110 "Our small group saved": Lifestoriescoza, "50 Minutes with Cor Suijk," video interview by Lisa Chait, January 2010, YouTube, September 1, 2017, https://www.youtube.com/watch?v=fqTliPyCFNc.

110 "no stone unturned": Willy Voskuijl, report of an interview by Erika Prins and Teresien da Silva, March 9, 2006, AFH.

111 "voice of a young woman": Cor Suijk told this to his close colleague at the Anne Frank House, Jan Erik Dubbelman. See Jan Erik Dubbelman, interview by Jeroen De Bruyn, March 22, 2011.

111 "I still have my own theory": Otto Frank, "Anne Frank Would Have Been Fifty This Year," *Life*, March 1979.

111 "[Otto] said all the time": Fritzi Frank, video interview by Wouter van der Sluis, October 1993, AFH.

113 "a true dog": Karl Silberbauer, interview by Jules Huf in *Kurier*, November 22, 1963.

113 And when questioned: Willy Lages, interrogation by the Amsterdam Criminal Investigation Department, December 6, 1963, NIOD.

Chapter 11: Gray Mouse

117 Mirjam Pressler's 1992 biography: This book was originally published in Germany as *Ich sehne mich so: Die Lebensgeschichte der Anne Frank* (Weinheim: Beltz & Gelberg, 1992). It was published in English as *The Story of Anne Frank* (London: Macmillan, 1999).

119 That was, sadly: From September 1944, people were regularly executed in

public in Amsterdam. For instance, on March 12, 1945, the German occupier executed thirty political prisoners on Weteringplantsoen in the city center in retaliation for the assassination of a Sicherheitsdienst official.

Chapter 12: Exile and Return

124 Diny vividly remembers: Diny Voskuijl, video interview by Teresien da Silva, November 14, 2011, AFH.

125 Sixteen- and seventeen-year-olds: "Wein, Weib und Gesang" (Wine, Women, and Song), *Het Parool*, November 2, 1944.

125 as many as 145,000 Dutch women: See Monika Diederichs, *Wie geschoren wordt moet stil zitten: De omgang van Nederlandse meisjes met Duitse militairen* (Soesterberg: Aspekt, 2006).

126 a "home away from home": "Erika—einmal anders: Ein gastfreies Haus für unsere Soldaten" (Erika—Something New: A Welcoming Place for Our Soldiers), *Deutsche Zeitung in den Niederlanden*, December 22, 1940.

126 "excellent food": Advertisement, *Deutsche Zeitung in den Niederlanden*, January 4, 1941.

126 "for the Dutch State": "Seyss-Inquart spreekt te Amsterdam: Massale bijeenkomst morgenavond op het IJsclubterrein" (Seyss-Inquart Gives Speech in Amsterdam: Tomorrow Night Mass Meeting at Ice Club Property), *Algemeen Handelsblad*, June 26, 1941.

126 The police report noted: Amsterdam police report, November 1, 1941, ACA.

127 "But she did it anyway": Diny Voskuijl, video interview by Teresien da Silva, November 14, 2011, AFH.

127 "There was this big crack": Ibid.

127 a "Greater German" visa: Nelly Voskuijl, German visa application, December 18, 1942, ACA.

128 "Nelly hardly spoke": Diny Voskuijl, video interview by Teresien da Silva, November 14, 2011, AFH.

128 "This made her return": Ibid.

128 she worked as the secretary: The account of Nelly's work for the Germans is based on information from Anne Frank's diary and interviews with Diny Voskuijl and Bertus Hulsman. There are no employment records on Nelly Voskuijl (or any other documents regarding her collaboration) in the National Archives in The Hague, the Bundesarchiv in Berlin, or the online Arolsen Archives.

129 "Nelly Voskuyl is in L'aône": Diary (RCE), May 6, 1944 (A-version), 655. As noted earlier, in the critical edition of the diaries by NIOD, Nelly's name was

replaced by initials, and several sentences were left out. As a result, some of the unexpurgated quotes from the diary pertaining to Nelly come from the NIOD typescript of the full-length diary passages.

129 "did nothing over there": Diary (RCE), May 11, 1944 (A-version), 668.

129 "She rang one": Diary (RCE), May 6, 1944 (A-version), 655.

130 "tin hat and gas mask": Diary (RCE), May 11, 1944 (A-version), 668.

130 "the old trouble again": Diary (RCE), May 19, 1944 (A-version), 674. We have again added some additional parts from the NIOD typescript.

130 "stays in bed": Ibid.

130 another interview: Bertus Hulsman, video interview by Dineke Stam, December 4, 2007.

132 "Inwardly Nelly was very mad": Diny Voskuijl, letter to Joop van Wijk-Voskuijl, October 2012.

132 "Why don't you go to your Jews!": Like Bertus, Diny didn't remember the precise timing of this quote. Nelly could have said it on multiple occasions during the Occupation. Yet given Diny's statement that Nelly was irritated by the secret confidence that had developed between Johan and Bep, we can assume that the comment occurred *after* Johan took his job at Opekta in 1941— when there was already persecution against the Jews—and very likely after the Franks went into hiding in 1942. Before that point, there would have been no reason for Bep and Johan to be whispering secretly about their work.

133 "Please, Father, not my head!": Diny Voskuijl, written statement, June 9, 2022. Because of a miscommunication, Diny did not convey to us in interviews for the first edition of this book that the violent incident in which Johan attacked Nelly occurred on August 5, 1944—only one day after the raid on the Secret Annex. She clarified this issue during the fact-checking of the present edition.

Part III: Bep

135 "Please know that I will do": Bep Voskuijl, letter to Otto Frank, December 31, 1958, AFH.

Chapter 13: Scraps

138 "We were both shocked": Bertus Hulsman, interview by Joop van Wijk-Voskuijl and Jeroen De Bruyn, February 20, 2014.

138 "I scarcely dared": Quoted in Schnabel, *The Footsteps*, 157.

138 "When, all those years": Bertus Hulsman, interview by Joop van Wijk-Voskuijl and Jeroen De Bruyn, February 20, 2014.

139   What actually happened: The most important of these sources are: Ernst Schnabel, personal notes, DLM; Bep Voskuijl, testimony for the district court of Lübeck, September 29, 1959, in Rheine, Germany, LL; Bep Voskuijl, audio recording of an interview by Oskar Morawetz, October 9, 1978, CM; Bob van Dijk, "Wie pleegde het verraad van het Achterhuis?" (Who Was the Betrayer of the Secret Annex?), *Panorama*, December 13, 1963; Diny Voskuijl, interviews by Joop van Wijk-Voskuijl and Jeroen De Bruyn; recollections of Joop van Wijk-Voskuijl, based on what his mother told him.

140   "It's hard not to be": Quoted in Laureen Nussbaum, "Anne Frank, schrijfster" (Anne Frank, Writer), *De Groene Amsterdammer*, August 23, 1995.

140   As Miep later recalled: Miep and Jan Gies, report of interviews by David Barnouw and Gerrold van der Stroom, February 19 and 27, 1985, NIOD.

141   my mother noticed: Bep Voskuijl, testimony for the district court of Lübeck, September 29, 1959, in Rheine, Germany, LL.

141   she could barely conceal her fury: Schnabel, *The Footsteps*, 157.

142   the Reiches: Personal record cards of Ernst Robert Reiche (1902) and Flora Elsa Weichold (1903); registration document from the Register of Foreign Nationals, June 3, 1922, ACA. The Reiche family was officially deregistered from the municipality of Amsterdam in March 1946.

144   According to the historian: Mak, *Amsterdam*, 122.

145   "We were using filler": Gies and Gold, *Anne Frank Remembered*, 238–39.

145   "formality, bureaucracy, and coldness": Hondius, *Terugkeer*, 87.

146   In the summer of 1945: "Een Joodse kwestie" (A Jewish Affair), *De Patriot*, June 2, 1945.

146   "Not another Jew!": Hondius, *Terugkeer*, 100.

147   "Gentlemen": Bep Voskuijl, letter to the Leidsche Onderwijsinstellingen, June 11, 1945, AFH.

147   "As soon as we receive": Leidsche Onderwijsinstellingen, letter to Bep Voskuijl, June 15, 1945, AFH.

148   he still felt: Bertus Hulsman, interview by Joop van Wijk-Voskuijl and Jeroen De Bruyn, February 20, 2014.

149   "She really liked Kugler": Diny Voskuijl, interview by Joop van Wijk-Voskuijl and Jeroen De Bruyn, August 25, 2012.

Chapter 14: Uncle Otto

151   "How can I begin": Otto Frank, letter to his family in Switzerland, May 15, 1945, quoted in Pressler, *Treasures*, 235.

151   Only 127 of the 1,019 Jews: von Benda-Beckmann, *After the Annex*; Presser, *Ashes*.

152 She told him of Edith's: Rosa de Winter-Levy, *Aan de gaskamer ontsnapt!* (Doetinchem: C. Misset, 1945), 29.

152 "Only the thought": Otto Frank, letter to Alice Frank, March 28, 1945, quoted in Pressler, *Treasures*, 218.

153 Jo had survived: On September 18, 1944, Jo Kleiman was released from the SS prison camp of Amersfoort in the Dutch province of Utrecht at the insistence of the Red Cross. He was in poor health, and the Germans considered him unsuitable to work as a forced laborer.

153 My mother remembered: Bep Voskuijl, audio recording of an interview by Oskar Morawetz, October 9, 1978, CM.

153 "I really hung": Diny Voskuijl, interview by Jeroen De Bruyn, September 2, 2012.

153 "Recalling memories": Ibid.

154 "I just can't think": Otto Frank, letter to Leni Frank, June 21, 1945, quoted in Lee, *The Hidden Life*, 182.

154 Margot was the first: For decades, it was believed that Anne and Margot had died in late March 1945, as documents from the Red Cross show. However, in 2023, the Anne Frank House published a book in which it claimed that their deaths had most probably occurred in early February 1945. See von Benda-Beckmann, *After the Annex*.

154 "No one has to know": Otto Frank, letter to Herbert Frank, July 24, 1945, quoted in Lee, *The Hidden Life*, 192.

155 "My friends, who had been": Otto Frank, memoir, quoted in Lee, *The Hidden Life*, 192.

155 "sweet card": Alice Frank, letter to Otto Frank, August 4, 1945, quoted in Pressler, *Treasures*, 233.

155 "I still don't have": Otto Frank, letter to Alice Frank, August 22, 1945, quoted in Lee, *The Hidden Life*, 194.

156 "divert myself": Otto Frank, letter to Leni Frank, June 21, 1945, quoted in Lee, *The Hidden Life*, 182.

156 "to build a new existence": Otto Frank, memoir, quoted in Lee, *The Hidden Life*, 195.

156 "How can I begin": Otto Frank, letter to his family in Switzerland, May 15, 1945, quoted in Pressler, *Treasures*, 235.

156 "Here I'm": Otto Frank, letter to Walter and Julius Holländer, August 20, 1945, quoted in Lee, *Roses*, 213–14.

157 "unparalleled sacrifice": Otto Frank, letter to his family in Switzerland, May 15, 1945, quoted in Pressler, *Treasures*, 235.

157 "a man who knows": Diary (DE), May 25, 1944, 305.

157 "Look, Cor": Rie van Wijk, interview by Joop van Wijk-Voskuijl, November 11, 2009.

158 "All the surrounding neighbors": Quoted in Jean Schick Grossman, "Anne Frank: The Story Within Her Story," December 5, 1954 (unpublished manuscript), AFH.

160 "Usually when I asked": Diny Voskuijl, interview by Joop van Wijk-Voskuijl and Jeroen De Bruyn, August 25, 2012.

168 "Dear Mr. Frank": Bep Voskuijl, letter to Otto Frank, September 4, 1957, AFH.

168 "I just can't stop": Bep Voskuijl, letter to Otto Frank, June 25, 1960, AFH.

168 "I immediately deposited": Ibid.

170 "It was Anne's money": Lee, *The Hidden Life*, 306.

Chapter 15: Denial

171 "a grave mistake on the part of the police" (footnote): David Barnouw and Gerrold van der Stroom (NIOD), interview by Jeroen De Bruyn, July 30, 2010.

172 "When sending you *Het Achterhuis* now": Otto Frank, letter to Christina Sodenkamp, June 1947, AFH.

172 "She was overcome": Diny Voskuijl, interview by Joop van Wijk-Voskuijl and Jeroen De Bruyn, August 25, 2012.

173 She also made scrapbooks: Bep would later donate the scrapbooks to the Anne Frank House, where they are kept in the archives of the Collections Department.

173 "Anne's story was always": Cok van Wijk, interview by Jeroen De Bruyn, April 6, 2014.

173 she had explained that Bep: Bep Voskuijl, letter to Otto Frank, December 31, 1958, AFH.

173 Two days later, she wrote: Ibid.

174 she was put "at ease" (footnote): Bep Voskuijl, letter to Otto Frank, April 19, 1959, AFH.

174 "a loss for words": Bep Voskuijl, letter to Otto Frank, December 31, 1958, AFH.

174 "I hope you don't": Bep Voskuijl, letter to Otto Frank, September 4, 1957, AFH.

174 "I do hope": Bep Voskuijl, letter to Otto Frank, March 22, 1951, AFH.

175 In 1958, two residents: "Nazis Drop Forgery Claims Against Anne Frank's Diary," *The Sentinel*, November 9, 1961.

175 "You can count on me": Bep Voskuijl, letter to the district court of Lübeck, August 9, 1959, AFH.

175 "beyond doubt": "Nazis Drop Forgery Claims Against Anne Frank's Diary," *The Sentinel,* November 9, 1961.

175 "I'm shocked": Lothar Schmidt, letter to Otto Frank, June 12, 1959, quoted in the documentary *Otto Frank: Father of Anne* by David de Jongh, 2010.

176 "totally incapable": Robert Faurisson, *Is the Diary of Anne Frank Genuine?* (Torrance, CA: Institute for Historical Review, 1985), 178. The content of this book is based on a report Faurisson wrote in French in 1978 ("Le journal d'Anne Frank: est-il authentique?"), which he used in a legal battle Otto Frank fought in Frankfurt between 1976 and 1978 against the German neo-Nazi Heinz Roth.

176 "wasn't interested": Bep Voskuijl, letter to Otto Frank, August 29, 1978, AFH.

176 "How dare they question": Jos van Noord, "Geen twijfel aan echtheid dagboek van Anne Frank: Westduits onderzoek verkeerd uitgelegd" (No Doubt of Authenticity of Anne Frank's Diary: West German Investigation Explained Incorrectly), *De Telegraaf,* October 7, 1980.

177 "No one has ever asked us": Jan Roelfs, "In Canada leven herinneringen aan het Achterhuis voort: Victor Kugler riskeerde met anderen zijn leven voor familie Anne Frank" (Memories of the Secret Annex Live on in Canada: Victor Kugler and Others Risked Their Lives for Anne Frank's Family), *Trouw,* July 29, 1978.

177 although he drew the line: Loes and Victor Kugler, letter to Bep Voskuijl, April 22, 1975, AFH.

177 "Our time at the office": Bep Voskuijl, letter to Victor Kugler, June 1, 1959, AFH.

178 "refrain from giving interviews": Otto Frank, letter to Loes and Victor Kugler, September 23, 1978, AFH.

178 "Victor and Lucy Kugler": Shapiro and Kardonne, *Victor Kugler*, 100.

178 "last piece of the puzzle": Claudia Morawetz, email to Jeroen De Bruyn, September 10, 2009.

179 Parts of the interview: Bep Voskuijl, audio recording of an interview by Oskar Morawetz, October 9, 1978, CM.

179 a documentary: The documentary was called *The Man Who Hid Anne Frank,* as it focused largely on Victor Kugler's role as a helper. The film was broadcast in Canada by CBC Television on December 17, 1980.

179 "She wasn't a big talker": Holly Rasky, interview by Jeroen De Bruyn, August 27, 2012.

Chapter 16: A Girl Named Sonja

190 Roza's personal record card: Personal record card of Roza van Weezel (1914–1996), ACA. Roza was baptized on April 2, 1944, "in the Dutch Reformed Church in Watergraafsmeer, after making her profession of faith."

190 Jacqueline, her father, and her sister: See Jacqueline van Maarsen, *My Name Is Anne, She Said, Anne Frank: The Memoirs of Anne Frank's Best Friend* (London: Arcadia, 2007).

190 Her sister Jeanette: Jeanette van Weezel, video interview by the Survivors of the Shoah Visual History Foundation (today called the USC Shoah Foundation), December 16, 1995, USHMM. Jeanette van Weezel and her Romanian-born husband, Gustav Havas, along with their two children, immigrated to the United States in 1954.

190 "acting suspiciously": Amsterdam police report, May 13, 1940, ACA.

191 In an official statement: Raymond Fremdt, report of an interrogation conducted in the penitentiary institution of Vught, June 27, 1946, file on Raymond Fremdt from the Central Archive of Special Jurisdiction, NA.

Chapter 17: The Sweet Peace

197 "Why, I feel sick": Diny Voskuijl, interview by Joop van Wijk-Voskuijl and Jeroen De Bruyn, August 25, 2012.

198 "It won't be as hard": Ibid.

198 "She told me about": Diny Voskuijl, interview by Joop van Wijk-Voskuijl, March 9, 2021.

200 "Otto Frank's Censorship": Richter Roegholt, "De censuur van Otto Frank," *Het Parool*, February 3, 1981.

200 "Otto Frank felt obligated": Fred Lammers, "Otto Frank liet grote gedeelten uit Annes dagboek weg" (Otto Frank Left Out a Large Part of Anne's Diary), *Trouw*, January 30, 1981.

201 "he left out a lot": Bep Voskuijl, report of an interview by David Barnouw and Gerrold van der Stroom, February 25, 1981, NIOD.

202 "I want to try": Fritzi Frank, letter to Bep Voskuijl, November 19, 1982, AFH.

202 "With her passing in 2001" (footnote): David Barnouw and Gerrold van der Stroom (NIOD), interview by Jeroen De Bruyn, July 30, 2010.

204 After returning to the Netherlands: In 2013, Melissa Müller published an updated edition of her 1998 biography of Anne Frank. In the book, she claimed

that Nelly Voskuijl had been taken into custody on October 26, 1945, and "presumably incarcerated in Groningen for several years." Furthermore, she wrote that Nelly had been "charged with collaboration with the Germans" and "couldn't continue her life until 1953." However, none of this can be proven. There is no file on Nelly in the Central Archive of Special Jurisdiction (kept in the National Archives in The Hague), and no file about Nelly's collaboration can be found in archives in Groningen, either. According to Nelly's personal record card in the Amsterdam City Archives, October 26, 1945, was the administrative date she moved to 14 Grote Rozenstraat in Groningen. Moreover, Diny Voskuijl frequently visited Nelly in Groningen after the war and firmly denies that her sister was ever incarcerated. In her biography, Müller didn't give a source for her claims regarding Nelly.

205 "I can't believe": Rhijja Jansen, "'Dat Nelly fout was, daar werd nooit over gesproken': Diny Voskuijl over goed en fout binnen één gezin" ("The Fact That Nelly Was on the Wrong Side During the War Was Never Discussed": Diny Voskuijl About the Good and Bad Within One Family), *De Volkskrant*, April 26, 2018.

205 Despite her financial hardships: File on Johannes Hendrik Voskuijl from the War Graves Foundation archives, NA. Like many young Dutch men, Voskuijl had been recruited from the Dutch military to take part in what the Dutch government then called the Politionele Acties (Police Actions), intended to restore law and order in the Dutch East Indies. He was sent to the colony in July 1948. According to the files, Voskuijl was hit by enemy fire while driving an army truck near the town of Ajibarang, Central Java, and died on the way to the nearest hospital. He was twenty-one years old. His body was buried in the military cemetery in Pandu, Western Java.

206 Her body was discovered: Nelly Voskuijl's date of death was listed as April 15, 2001; extract from the Global Municipal Database, CBG.

Chapter 18: The Empty Notebook

209 "I've been so ill": Bep Voskuijl, letter to Fritzi Frank, April 6, 1983.

209 "We told her": Leny van Wijk, interview by Jeroen De Bruyn, April 6, 2014.

210 All four of her children: Anne van Wijk, email to Joop van Wijk-Voskuijl, August 9, 2009.

210 She had lost her surrogate father: Otto Frank died on August 19, 1980, in Birsfelden, Switzerland. Victor Kugler died on December 14, 1981, in To-

ronto, and his wife, Loes, died on June 8, 1991. Jan Gies died on January 26, 1993, in Amsterdam. Miep Gies lived to be a hundred years old; she died on January 11, 2010, in Hoorn, the Netherlands.

211 "When we got off": Anne van Wijk, email to Joop van Wijk-Voskuijl, September 21, 2010.

211 The museum described her: Press release, Anne Frank House, May 9, 1983, AFH.

211 "She was a sweet": Jos van Noord, "Ze was de meest vertrouwde helpster van Anne Frank: Vandaag begrafenis van Elli Vossen uit *Het Achterhuis*" (She Was Anne Frank's Most Trusted Helper: Today Funeral of Elli Vossen from *Het Achterhuis*), *De Telegraaf*, May 11, 1983.

216 "The secret of my wife": Cor van Wijk, notes of an interview by the Anne Frank House, September 28, 1994, AFH.

Epilogue: The Things We Leave Behind

217 "If the end": Otto Frank, quoted in Cara Wilson-Granat, *Tree of Hope: Anne Frank's Father Shares His Wisdom with an American Teen and the World* (Charleston, SC: Palmetto Publishing, 2021), 117.

A Note on Sources

226 A sixty-nine-page scientific study: Dr. Bart Wallet et al., "The Betrayal of Anne Frank: A Refutation," SPUI25, March 2022, https://spui25.nl/programma/the-betrayal-of-anne-frank-a-refutation.

INDEX

ACKNOWLEDGMENTS

This book would not exist without the generosity and assistance of many people we met along the way. First of all, we would like to thank our editor, LaSharah Bunting. Her unwavering enthusiasm and dedication made her a delight to work with, and her ideas and thoughtful edits improved our manuscript immeasurably. We are also grateful to her wonderful colleagues at Simon & Schuster, including Maria Mendez, Lynn Anderson, Chonise Bass, Brianna Scharfenberg, Alyssa diPierro, and Priscilla Painton.

Our agents, Peter and Amy Bernstein, recognized the potential in this story and put us on the road to publishing it. Their advice, on both business and editorial matters, was invaluable. We are also indebted to Efraim Zuroff, the director of the Simon Wiesenthal Center in Jerusalem, who introduced us to Peter and Amy and believed in this project from the start.

With her concern for our project, her improvements to the manuscript, and her assistance in ways too numerous to mention, Ingrid van Wijk-Wolff was a tremendous support during the many years we spent on this book. Eric De Bruyn and Petra Larosse were unfailingly helpful and a great source of security and warmth. Our heartfelt thanks go out to them.

We are indebted to Barbara Eldridge, Christoph Knoch, and the late Buddy Elias of the Anne Frank Fonds in Basel, Switzerland, for their encouragement and for granting us the Margot Frank Stipendium, which helped us a great deal in carrying out our research.

261

ACKNOWLEDGMENTS

We thank the staff of the NIOD Institute for War, Holocaust and Genocide studies in Amsterdam for guiding us through its archives, and David Barnouw and Gerrold van der Stroom in particular for sharing details from their encounters with Bep, Nelly, and Willy Voskuijl in the early 1980s. Marie-Christine Engels, Alan Moss, and Robbert Boukema of the National Archives in The Hague dug deep into their collections for us, looking for any file that could possibly be of value. Despite the volume of requests we made (often on deadline), they never lost their patience.

We are grateful for the help and advice of the following people: Wouter Bax (newspaper *Trouw*), Miriam Boonen (Instituut Schoevers), Miriam Häfele (Deutsches Literaturarchiv Marbach), Marjon Hardonk (newspaper *De Volkskrant*), Jacques Hartman (CBG Center for Family History), Kunihiro Hayashida (newspaper *Asahi Shimbun*), Diane Keyser (Forum der Joodse Organisaties, Antwerp), Jaap Klein (newspaper *Het Parool*), Peter Kroesen (Amsterdam City Archives), Bert Kuipers (municipality of Groningen), Megan Lewis (United States Holocaust Memorial Museum), Maureen McNeil (Anne Frank Center, New York City), Els van der Meer (Camp Vught National Memorial), Mr. Willem van der Meer (legal advisor), Keiko Miura (Anne's Rose Church, Japan), Elisabeth Overgaauw (War and Resistance Center Groningen), Frank Rettig (Bundesarchiv), Margreet Visch-Camphuis (Groningen Archives), and Dr. Bart Wallet (professor of Jewish Studies at the University of Amsterdam). We are particularly thankful to Jan Erik Dubbelman, the emeritus director of the International Education Projects at the Anne Frank House, for giving us an important new lead and for his kind support.

We also offer our heartfelt gratitude to those who shared their memories of Bep: Jacqueline van Maarsen (the Netherlands), Claudia Morawetz (Canada), Father John Neiman (United States), Frank Perk (the Netherlands), Arlene and Holly Rasky (Canada), Takeo Sato (Japan), and Cok, Leny, Anne, Ton, and Rie van Wijk.

The following group of people supported us in various ways. In the Netherlands: Jon Elbert, Simon Hammelburg, David de Jongh, Loes Liemburg, and Herman Vuijsje; in Belgium: Benedite Baerts, Diane Broeckhoven, Stefanie De Bruyn, Nina Moerkens, Marte Nevelsteen, Hannelore Riemenschneider, Silke Riemenschneider, and Anneke Van de Voorde; in Canada: Rick Kardonne, Barbara Legault, and Rita Visser; in the United States: Ralph Melnick and Cara Wilson-Granat. To all of them we owe a debt of gratitude.

Diny Voskuijl and Bertus Hulsman were a tremendous help by sharing their vivid and often painful memories. Despite their venerable ages, they were always on hand to answer our many questions, helping us fill in gaps in our story and creating new connections. For their pluck, loyalty, and friendship, we are truly grateful.

And finally, we are greatly indebted to our consulting editor, Stephen Heyman, who mentored us throughout the entire writing process. With his keen eye, wonderful ideas, and empathy, he was indispensable to this project in many ways. For his devotion and all the time he freed up to work with us during the past years—both virtually and in person—we would like to express our warmest thanks.

ABOUT THE AUTHORS

Joop van Wijk-Voskuijl is the third of Bep Voskuijl's four children. He was born in 1949 in Amsterdam. After a successful career as a video producer (creating corporate movies for major Dutch companies) and marketing manager (for national newspapers such as *NRC Handelsblad* and *Algemeen Dagblad*), Joop retired in 2010 to pursue research and writing with the goal of telling his mother's story. He also volunteers as a guest lecturer, teaching Dutch schoolchildren and other groups about Anne Frank, the Holocaust, and the resistance during World War II.

Jeroen De Bruyn was born in 1993 in Antwerp. At age fifteen—the same age as Anne when she died of typhus in the Bergen-Belsen concentration camp—Jeroen began doing original research on the Secret Annex. He got to know the Anne Frank House firsthand during an internship there in 2011. He went on to study journalism, subsequently contributing to prominent Flemish newsmagazines such as *Knack* and *Joods Actueel*, and working as a senior editor for the major Belgian newspaper *Gazet van Antwerpen*.